PREVENTION AND CONTROL
OF JUVENILE DELINQUENCY

PREVENTION AND CONTROL OF JUVENILE DELINQUENCY

SECOND EDITION

RICHARD J. LUNDMAN
The Ohio State University

New York   Oxford
OXFORD UNIVERSITY PRESS
1993

Oxford University Press

Oxford   New York   Toronto
Delhi   Bombay   Calcutta   Madras   Karachi
Kuala Lumpur   Singapore   Hong Kong   Tokyo
Nairobi   Dar es Salaam   Cape Town
Melbourne   Auckland   Madrid
and associated companies in
Berlin   Ibadan

Published by Oxford University Press, Inc.,
200 Madison Avenue, New York, New York 10016

Oxford is a registered trademark of Oxford University Press

Library of Congress Cataloging-in-Publication Data
Lundman, Richard J., 1944–
Prevention and control of juvenile delinquency
Richard J. Lundman. — 2nd ed.
p. cm.   Includes bibliographical references (p.   ) and index.
ISBN 0-19-506407-0
1. Juvenile delinquency—United States
2. Juvenile delinquency—United States—Prevention
3. Juvenile justice, Administration of—United States.
I. Title.
HV9104.L86   1993   364.3'6'0973—dc20
92-9081

9 8 7 6 5 4 3

Printed in the United States of America

For my parents,
Oscar Y. and Mabel J. Lundman,
and my children,
Julie M. and Robert J. Lundman

PREFACE

This book is about the prevention and control of juvenile delinquency. Chapter 1 identifies types of delinquent acts, establishes the frequency and seriousness of delinquent behavior, and provides an overview of major delinquency prevention and control intervention points. Part One then examines the individual-treatment and area-project approaches to the prevention of delinquency. Part Two is devoted to efforts to control delinquency by diverting juveniles away from the juvenile justice system. Part Three also is devoted to control efforts and examines probation and parole, attempts to scare juveniles "straight," community-based treatment including intensive supervision programs, and the use of correctional facilities to incapacitate and deter juvenile offenders. Part Four concludes the book with specific recommendations for future prevention and control efforts.

Goals and Distinguishing Features

This book has four goals, and each distinguishes this text from others devoted to these same topics. The first goal is to provide a complete description and careful analysis of major delinquency prevention and control strategies and efforts. Some books devote exclusive attention to a single project, thereby forcing readers to assemble many different materials for a comprehensive understanding of prevention and control efforts. Others superficially cover a large number of projects and require frequent use of original materials for complete information. This book is a single source of complete description and careful analysis of major prevention and control efforts.

The second goal is to focus primary attention on projects that have shaped the thoughts and actions of persons concerned with youth crime. Other texts frequently give undue attention to obscure or poorly designed and measured projects. This book examines the Cambridge-Somerville Youth Study, Youth Consultation Service (*Girls at Vocational High*), the Chicago Area Project, the Midcity Project, Sacramento County Diversion Project, Adolescent Diversion Project, California's Community Treatment Project, Juvenile Awareness Project ("Scared Straight"), the Provo and Silverlake experiments, Jerome Miller's "experiment" in Massachusetts, and Unified Delinquency Intervention Services (*Beyond Probation*). In addition, cohort studies (Professor Wolfgang's 1945 and 1958 birth cohorts) are used to assess the logic of incapacitation crime control hypothesis. Last, national evaluations of prevention, diversion, and restitution are used to probe the generalizability of observations and conclusions.

The third goal is to sensitize readers to the conditions that must be present to determine whether a project has accomplished its announced goals. Most standard texts devote little or no attention to important evaluative tools, such as experimental designs, objective measures of results, and replication. This book defines and illustrates these and other evaluative tools and demonstrates their role in determining whether a project actually prevented or controlled delinquency.

The final goal is to show how complete description and careful analysis of major projects serve as a foundation for the future. Most other texts fail to link what has been attempted in the past with what should be done in the future. This book uses the lessons of the past to advance firm recommendations for future prevention and control efforts.

Intended Audiences

This book is designed for use in a variety of disciplines and programs. It is intended for use in sociology, criminology, and criminal justice courses on juvenile delinquency, prevention and control of delinquency, corrections, and penology. It is also

PREFACE

This book is about the prevention and control of juvenile delinquency. Chapter 1 identifies types of delinquent acts, establishes the frequency and seriousness of delinquent behavior, and provides an overview of major delinquency prevention and control intervention points. Part One then examines the individual-treatment and area-project approaches to the prevention of delinquency. Part Two is devoted to efforts to control delinquency by diverting juveniles away from the juvenile justice system. Part Three also is devoted to control efforts and examines probation and parole, attempts to scare juveniles "straight," community-based treatment including intensive supervision programs, and the use of correctional facilities to incapacitate and deter juvenile offenders. Part Four concludes the book with specific recommendations for future prevention and control efforts.

GOALS AND DISTINGUISHING FEATURES

This book has four goals, and each distinguishes this text from others devoted to these same topics. The first goal is to provide a complete description and careful analysis of major delinquency prevention and control strategies and efforts. Some books devote exclusive attention to a single project, thereby forcing readers to assemble many different materials for a comprehensive understanding of prevention and control efforts. Others superficially cover a large number of projects and require frequent use of original materials for complete information. This book is a single source of complete description and careful analysis of major prevention and control efforts.

The second goal is to focus primary attention on projects that have shaped the thoughts and actions of persons concerned with youth crime. Other texts frequently give undue attention to obscure or poorly designed and measured projects. This book examines the Cambridge-Somerville Youth Study, Youth Consultation Service (*Girls at Vocational High*), the Chicago Area Project, the Midcity Project, Sacramento County Diversion Project, Adolescent Diversion Project, California's Community Treatment Project, Juvenile Awareness Project ("Scared Straight"), the Provo and Silverlake experiments, Jerome Miller's "experiment" in Massachusetts, and Unified Delinquency Intervention Services (*Beyond Probation*). In addition, cohort studies (Professor Wolfgang's 1945 and 1958 birth cohorts) are used to assess the logic of incapacitation crime control hypothesis. Last, national evaluations of prevention, diversion, and restitution are used to probe the generalizability of observations and conclusions.

The third goal is to sensitize readers to the conditions that must be present to determine whether a project has accomplished its announced goals. Most standard texts devote little or no attention to important evaluative tools, such as experimental designs, objective measures of results, and replication. This book defines and illustrates these and other evaluative tools and demonstrates their role in determining whether a project actually prevented or controlled delinquency.

The final goal is to show how complete description and careful analysis of major projects serve as a foundation for the future. Most other texts fail to link what has been attempted in the past with what should be done in the future. This book uses the lessons of the past to advance firm recommendations for future prevention and control efforts.

INTENDED AUDIENCES

This book is designed for use in a variety of disciplines and programs. It is intended for use in sociology, criminology, and criminal justice courses on juvenile delinquency, prevention and control of delinquency, corrections, and penology. It is also designed for use in social work programs, especially as casework, groupwork, and community organization skills are applied to the problem of juvenile delinquency. Furthermore, students of public administration and those already employed as policy makers and program administrators will find the book useful because of the attention given the many problems surrounding design, implementation, and evaluation of prevention and control projects.

Because this book has several audiences, special care is taken to introduce and illustrate important concepts and tools. Chapter introductions lay the groundwork for the projects examined. Boxed materials provide instruction on how to read a table, explain important evaluative tools, including experimental designs and replication, and define data collection techniques, such as life histories and cohort studies. Presentation of project results is limited to percentage figures.

Acknowledgments

Many people helped me write this book. Several thousand students in a variety of my classes listened patiently as my ideas took shape. Colleagues as well as administrators of juvenile correctional facilities and programs read and criticized particular chapters, provided guidance and assistance, and answered my phone calls and letters, especially LaMar T. Empey, Floyd Feeney, James O. Finckenauer, Patrick Gurney, Joan McCord, Pat O'Halloran, James F. Short, Jr., and James C. Yarborough. Kenneth W. Eckhardt, Hugh Barlow, and an anonymous reviewer for Oxford read the first edition and provided strong guidance. I again want to single out Professor Barlow, for he helped make this a far better book. All of the many people at Oxford have been extraordinarily kind and helpful for a very long time. I thank all of you for your help.

Columbus, Ohio   R.J.L.
April 1992

CONTENTS

PREVENTION AND CONTROL
OF JUVENILE DELINQUENCY

1

JUVENILE DELINQUENCY

This book is about the prevention and control of juvenile delin-quency. It identifies types of delinquent acts and establishes the frequency and seriousness of delinquent behavior. It describes and analyzes major prevention and control projects, starting with attempts to identify and treat juveniles perceived as headed for trouble with the law and ending with the use of correctional facilities to incapacitate and deter chronic offenders. It concludes with specific recommendations for the prevention and control of juvenile delinquency.

TYPES OF DELINQUENT ACTS

There are two types of delinquent acts.[1] Young people 17 years of age and under[2] are subject to legal intervention for acts that would be criminal if committed by adults. Juveniles who vandal-ize buildings, shoplift, or use illegal drugs risk arrest by the police, detention in a facility reserved exclusively for youthful offenders, adjudication as delinquent by a juvenile court, and commitment to a correctional facility accepting only adolescent offenders. Delinquent juveniles are subject to the same laws and some of the same law enforcement responses as criminal adults.

Juveniles also are subject to legal intervention if they commit acts called status offenses. For example, adolescents who run away, skip school, defy their parents, or stay out too late are subject to arrest and formal juvenile justice system processing.

Status offenses apply only to juveniles and are not considered criminal if committed by adults.[3]

FREQUENCY AND SERIOUSNESS
OF DELINQUENT BEHAVIOR

To gather information about juvenile delinquency from the news media is to come away with the impression that youth crime is violent crime. Consider several examples. In Texas a 10-year-old boy is found guilty of brutally beating a 101-year-old woman to death.[4] In New York a 14-year-old shoots two other teenagers with a semiautomatic pistol following a dispute over a girl.[5] A 9-year-old Pennsylvania boy is not allowed to ride snowmobiles without his parents while a 6-year-old neighbor girl can.[6] He becomes angry, gets a rifle, and murders the little girl as she rides by on a snowmobile. In California, a 10-year-old boy is arrested and charged with raping four playmates in the apartment complex where he lives with his parents.[7]

Incidents such as these understandably concern many people. Criminal justice experts assert that contemporary juveniles are more willing to kill and commit other serious crimes than members of earlier generations of youth.[8] Television journalists narrate stories on "Killer Kids" while newspapers present stories on "Juveniles Who Kill" and magazines devote space to "Kids Who Kill."[9] Others draw more far drastic conclusions from acts such as these. Here are the chilling words of print journalist Pete Hamill, written in the early 1980s: "The young mutants continue their grisly parade down the avenues of America. I've seen them in police stations. . . . They stand accused of atrocity—the murder of old people, the destruction of children—but their faces are blank, their responses devoid of remorse. . . . On the surface they appear to be ordinary young people. Then you look at their eyes and you know they are already wormy with death."[10]

The reasons for such concern are obvious. Murder and rape are alarming whenever they occur, more so when the people doing the killing and the raping are children. The images associated with these acts also attract attention, especially the idea of a group of "young mutants" for whom murder and rape are routine behaviors. But it is very important to put acts and images in perspective by establishing the frequency and seriousness of delinquent behavior.

The sections that follow use two important sources—the *Uniform Crime Reports* (an annual publication of the Federal Bureau of Investigation) and the self-report study—to shed light on delinquency.

UNIFORM CRIME REPORTS

Every year since 1930, the FBI has used information provided by local police departments to estimate the frequency of a limited number of serious or "index" crimes. Currently there are two general types of index crimes, with four specific offenses in each category:

INDEX CRIMES AGAINST PERSONS

1. *Murder and nonnegligent manslaughter*: Willful . . . killing of one human being by another.
2. *Forcible rape*: Carnal knowledge of a female forcibly and against her will. Assaults or attempts to commit rape by force or threat of force are also included.
3. *Robbery*: Taking or attempting to take anything of value from the care, custody, or control of a person or persons by force or threat of force or violence and/or by putting the victim in fear.
4. *Aggravated assault*: An unlawful attack by one person upon another for the purpose of inflicting severe . . . bodily injury . . . usually accompanied by the use of a weapon or by means likely to produce death or great bodily harm.

INDEX CRIMES AGAINST PROPERTY

5. *Burglary*: The unlawful entry of a structure to commit a felony or theft. . . . use of force to gain entry is not required.
6. *Larceny-theft*: The unlawful taking, carrying, leading, or riding away of property from the possession or construc-

tive possession of another . . . such as shoplifting . . .
bicycle thefts . . . in which no use of force, violence, or
fraud occurs.

7. *Motor vehicle theft*: Theft or attempted theft of a motor
   vehicle.

8. *Arson*: Willful or malicious burning or attempt to burn
   . . . [the] personal property of another.[11]

Using the most recent data available (see Box 1.1), arrests of
juveniles for index crimes in 1990 are presented in Table 1.1. In
reading this table (see Box 1.2), three observations are important. First, there were 655,377 arrests of juveniles for index offenses in 1990. Second, arrests of juveniles for index crimes
against persons were far less frequent than arrests for index

---

Box 1.1 The Most Recent Data Available

By the time you read a book, some of the information is old. If
you are reading this book upon publication in 1993, then the data
on index arrests I am asking you to consider are already three
years old. If you are reading this in 1999, the data are nine years old.

The reference section of your library has two sources you can
use to quickly update information on juvenile delinquency. The
first is the *Uniform Crime Reports* published in the summer of
each year for the previous year. The formal full title of this
publication is noted in the source information at the bottom of
this box. To find information on juvenile delinquency, use the
reports' comprehensive contents pages. Find the section on "Persons Arrested" and then the tables that detail "distribution by
age." You can also use the *Sourcebook of Criminal Justice Statistics*. This too is an annual publication. You should look under
"juvenile delinquency" in the index at the back of this source.

Source: FBI, *Crime in the United States: Uniform Crime Reports, 1990*
(Washington, D.C.: U.S. Government Printing Office, 1991); Kathleen
Maguire and Timothy J. Flanagan (eds.), *Sourcebook of Criminal Justice
Statistics—1990* (Washington, D.C.: U.S. Government Printing Office,
1991).

Box 1.2 How to Read a Table

The first step in reading a table is to examine the title. The title tells you what the table is about and how the information in it is arranged. Table 1.1, for instance, is about arrests of juveniles for index crimes in 1990. The information in the table is arranged by type of crime, number of juvenile arrests, and percent of juvenile index arrests.

The next step is to review the information in the table. You might wish to isolate what you believe are the important observations to be made from the table. You should then locate any qualifying notes about these observations. For example, the first observation you might make based on Table 1.1 is that there were 655,377 arrests of juveniles for index offenses in 1990. A qualifying note about this observation is marked by a letter "b" in the body of Table 1.1.

The final step is to examine a table for other points that you think are important. This will permit you to draw your own conclusions about the information in the table. For example, although it is true that only 14 percent of the index arrests of juveniles in 1990 were for crimes against persons, there were 91,317 arrests of juveniles for these violent offenses. You might want to use this figure to advance your own observation about the frequency of violent juvenile crime.

---

crimes against property. Arrests of juveniles for crimes against persons accounted for only 14 percent of all index arrests, with arrests for homicide making up less than 1 percent of the total. Third, more than half (57 percent) of the arrests of juveniles for index offenses in 1990 were for larceny-theft.

The *Uniform Crime Reports* also profiles arrests of juveniles for nonindex offenses (see Table 1.2). In 1990 slightly over 1 million arrests of juveniles occurred for such acts as vandalism, drug abuse, buying or attempting to buy hard liquor, beer, or wine, and for status offenses such as curfew violation and running away. Arrests for these nonindex offenses increased the total number of juvenile arrests in 1990 to nearly 1.8 million.

Table 1.1   Arrests of Juveniles for Index Crimes in 1990:
Type of Crime, Number of Juvenile Arrests, and Percent of
Juvenile Index Arrests

Type of Crime	Number of Juvenile Arrests	Percent of Juvenile Index Arrests
Murder	2,555	a
Forcible rape	4,628	1
Robbery	32,967	5
Aggravated assault	51,167	8
Burglary	112,437	17
Larceny-theft	372,133	57
Motor vehicle theft	72,930	11
Arson	6,560	1
Totals	655,377[b]	100

[a]Less than 1 percent.
[b]Total number of juvenile arrests for index offenses in 1990.
Source: FBI, *Crime in the United States: Uniform Crime Reports, 1990*
(Washington, D.C.: U.S. Government Printing Office, 1991), p. 184.

Patterns in Juvenile Arrests. Table 1.3 provides information on
patterns of juvenile arrests between 1960 and 1990 and gives
readers an opportunity to determine whether youth crime is
characteristized by change or stability as measured by officially
reported arrests during this period.

Juvenile arrest statistics are characterized by change. Total
arrests and total juvenile arrests both increased between 1960 and
1990. As a percentage of total arrests, juvenile arrests climbed
steadily from 1960 (when they accounted for 14.3 percent of total
arrests) through 1974 (when they made up 27.2 percent of total
arrests), only to drop off again to 15.7 percent in 1990. When
looked at in terms of arrests per 100,000 people 17-years-old and
under, it is clear that the arrest rate changed as well. In 1960, an
average of 816.6 of every 100,000 adolescents were arrested, while
in 1975, 3,094.5 of every 100,000 young people were taken off the
streets by the police. The pattern since 1980 has been one of
uneven decline. Even in 1990, however, the arrest rate for juveniles was still well above that of the early 1960s.

Stability characterizes the arrest composition index. Between
1960 and 1990, roughly six of ten arrests of juveniles were for
nonindex crimes such as liquor law violations and running
away. Approximately one-third of all juvenile arrests between
1960 and 1990 were for index crimes against property, with lar-

Table 1.2   Arrests of Juveniles for Nonindex Crimes in 1990: Type of Crime, Number of Juvenile Arrests, and Percent of Juvenile Nonindex Arrests

Type of Crime	Number of Juvenile Arrests	Percent of Juvenile Nonindex Arrests
Other assaults	119,058	11
Forgery/counterfeiting	6,760	1
Fraud	9,468	1
Embezzlement	864	a
Stolen property	34,087	3
Vandalism	103,754	9
Weapons	31,991	3
Prostitution/vice	1,281	a
Sex offenses	13,507	1
Drug abuse	64,740	6
Gambling	798	a
Family/children	2,611	a
Drunken driving	15,772	1
Liquor laws	122,047	11
Public drunkenness	19,344	2
Disorderly conduct	95,999	9
Vagrancy	2,531	a
Suspicion	3,095	a
Curfew/loitering	64,568	6
Runaway	138,155	13
All other	248,735	23
Totals	1,099,165	100

[a]Less than 1 percent.

Source: FBI, *Crime in the United States: Uniform Crime Reports, 1990* (Washington, D.C.: U.S. Government Printing Office, 1991), p. 184.

ceny-theft the most common across the entire time period. Arrests for index crimes against persons increased from 2.8 percent of juvenile arrests in 1960 to 5.2 percent of juvenile arrests in 1990. Even with the increase, adolescents who murder and rape, rob and assault, are clearly in a minority among arrested juveniles.

SELF-REPORT STUDIES

A second method of establishing the frequency and seriousness of delinquent behavior is the self-report study.[12] In self-report studies juveniles are asked about their own involvement in delinquency. Although information collection techniques range from the use of anonymous questionnaires to conducting face-to-face

Table 1.3 Arrests and Arrest Composition Index, 1960–1990

		Arrests			Arrest Composition Index (Juvenile Arrests Only)		
	Total (thousands)[a]	Total Less/Equal to 17	Percent Less/Equal to 17	Per 100,000 Less/Equal to 17	Percent Nonindex	Percent Index Property	Percent Index Person
1960[b]	3,679	527	14.3	816.6	60.8[c]	36.4	2.8
1961	3,852	567	14.7	861.3	59.8	37.2	3.0
1962	4,117	653	15.9	973.3	59.6	37.4	3.0
1963	4,511	789	17.5	1,152.8	59.2	38.0	2.8
1964	4,685	961	20.5	1,379.3	60.7	36.7	2.6
1965	5,031	1,074	21.3	1,540.9	62.2	35.0	2.8
1966	5,016	1,149	22.9	1,644.3	62.5	34.5	3.0
1967	5,518	1,340	24.3	1,915.7	63.6	33.4	3.0
1968	5,617	1,457	25.9	2,084.8	64.9	32.0	3.0
1969	5,862	1,500	25.6	2,150.1	64.7	32.1	3.2
1970	6,570	1,661	25.3	2,380.4	64.7	32.0	3.3
1971	6,967	1,797	25.8	2,574.1	64.8	31.7	3.5
1972	7,013	1,794	25.6	2,584.2	64.9	31.4	3.8
1973	6,500	1,717	26.4	2,497.4	64.3	31.9	3.8
1974	6,179	1,683	27.2	2,475.6	60.5	35.5	4.0
1975	8,014	2,078	25.9	3,094.5	60.6	35.3	4.1
1976	7,912	1,973	24.9	2,978.4	62.4	33.8	3.8
1977	9,029	2,170	24.0	3,315.1	62.3	34.0	3.8
1978	9,775	2,279	23.3	3,518.9	61.4	34.4	4.2
1979	9,506	2,143	22.5	3,343.5	60.9	35.0	4.1
1980	9,703	2,026	20.9	3,182.1	61.0	34.7	4.3
1981	10,294	2,036	19.8	3,223.1	62.2	33.6	4.2
1982	10,062	1,805	17.9	2,866.8	63.1	32.7	4.2
1983	10,287	1,726	16.8	2,748.9	62.1	33.6	4.3
1984	8,922	1,538	17.2	2,449.6	62.9	32.9	4.2

1985	10,290	1,763	17.1	2,798.6	62.8	38.0	4.1
1986	10,392	1,748	16.8	2,760.8	63.3	32.6	4.1
1987	10,796	1,781	16.5	2,802.1	63.0	32.9	4.1
1988	10,150	1,635	16.1	2,560.6	63.4	32.4	4.2
1989	11,261	1,745	15.5	2,723.1	63.4	31.8	4.8
1990	11,150	1,755	15.7	2,740.6	62.6	32.1	5.2

[a]Simply add three zeros to get actual number. Thus, 3,679 = 3,679,000. This aplies only to the total arrests and total arrests less/equal to 17. All of the other numbers in this table are actual numbers.

[b]In the early years (especially 1960 to 1970), age information for all arrests is not available because of incomplete reporting by the local police departments that supply the FBI with the information used to compile the *Uniform Crime Reports*. In addition, total arrests and juvenile arrests are underestimates because of differential cooperation by local police departments in reporting arrests. In 1960, police departments responsible for 81.7 million of an estimated 179.3 million people nationwide provided the FBI with data. By 1970, comparable figures were 151.6 million of 205.1 million and by 1990, 193.5 million of 251.1 million people nationwide.

[c]Read the arrest composition index percentages across. Of the 526,905 arrests of juveniles in 1960, 60.8 percent were for nonindex crimes, 36.4 percent for index crimes against property, and 2.8 percent for index crimes against persons. Some of the totals do not add to 100 because of rounding.

Source: Arrest and arrest composition data are from FBI, *Crime in the United States: Uniform Crime Reports, 1960–1990* (Washington, D.C.: U.S. Government Printing Office, 1961–91). Population estimates used to calculate arrests per 100,000 people less than or equal to 17 years of age for 1960 through 1970 are from U.S. Bureau of the Census, Current Population Reports Series, P-25, no. 519, *Estimates of the Population of the United States by Age, Sex, and Race: April 1, 1960, to July 1, 1973* (Washington, D.C.: U.S. Government Printing Office, 1974), pp. 16–26. The 1971 through 1981 population estimates are from U.S. Bureau of the Census, Current Population Reports, Population Estimates and Projections, P-25, no. 917, *Preliminary Estimates of the Population of the United States by Age, Sex, and Race: 1970 to 1981* (Washington, D.C.: U.S. Government Printing Office, 1982), pp. 8–25. The 1982 through 1988 population estimates are from U.S. Bureau of the Census, Current Population Reports, Population Estimates and Projections, P-25, no. 1045, *United States Population Estimates by Age, Sex, Race, and Hispanic Origin: 1980–1988* (Washington, D.C.: U.S. Government Printing Office, 1990), pp. 41–51. Population estimate for 1989 is from U.S. Bureau of the Census, Current Population Reports Series, 0-25, no. 1057, *U.S. Population Estimates by Age, Sex, Race, and Hispanic Origin: 1989* (Washington, D.C.: U.S. Government Printing Office, 1990), p. 7. Population estimate for 1990 is from U.S. Department of Commerce, *Statistical Abstract of the United States, 1990* (Washington, D.C.: U.S. Government Printing Office, 1990), p. 16.

interviews, the intent is to learn whether and how often juveniles
have committed delinquent acts.

Because the data for self-report studies come directly from
juveniles, these surveys are not subject to some of the obvious
limitations of estimates of delinquency based upon officially
reported arrests. The *Uniform Crime Reports* does not include
adolescents who commit delinquent acts but escape police detec-
tion. This is a sizable group because each year only about 20
percent of all index crimes result in arrests.[13] The *Uniform Crime
Reports* also does not count adolescents caught by the police but
released without being arrested. This too is a sizable group because police release approximately 80 percent of the juvenile
offenders who come their way.[14]

The usefulness of self-report data can be illustrated by reviewing the results of a classic study. In the early 1950s, Professors
James F. Short, Jr., and F. Ivan Nye gave anonymous questionnaires to male high school students in two midwestern communities and one western community, and to adolescents in a juvenile
correctional facility in the state of Washington. The questionnaires asked the juveniles whether they had committed particular
delinquent acts and if they had, whether they had committed
those acts more than "once or twice."

Table 1.4 contains some of the index and nonindex offenses
self-reported by the respondents. Four observations are important. First, delinquency is not restricted to juveniles doing time
in a training school. Nearly all of the students in the midwestern
communities and the western city self-reported acts for which
they could have been arrested, referred to court, and perhaps
institutionalized. Second, there are clear differences between the
delinquent acts committed by the training school and the high
school students. Incarcerated juveniles admitted committing
more frequent and more serious delinquent acts than the high
school students. Third, both the high school and training school
adolescents self-reported nonindex crime much more often than
index crime. Fourth, when index offenses were self-reported,
crimes against property were more common than crimes against
persons.

Patterns in Self-Report Data.   Table 1.5 provides information
on self-reported delinquency by high school seniors between 1975

Table 1.4 Self-Reported Delinquent Behavior Among Male Adolescents in Three Samples

General Type of Offense: Index or Nonindex[a]	Percent Reporting Act at Least Once			Percent Reporting Act More Than Once or Twice		
	Midwestern Students	Western Students	Training School Students	Midwestern Students	Western Students	Training School Students
Index offenses						
Robbery	6.3	NA[b]	67.7	2.4	NA[b]	35.5
Larceny-theft[c]	17.1	15.8	91.0	3.8	3.8	61.4
Motor vehicle theft	11.2	14.8	75.2	4.5	4.0	53.4
Nonindex offenses						
Simple assault[d]	24.3	22.5	67.4	6.7	5.2	47.4
Drug Abuse	1.4	2.2	28.1	0.7	1.6	12.6
Liquor laws	67.7	57.2	89.7	35.8	29.5	79.4
Runaway	12.9	13.0	68.1	2.8	2.4	37.7

[a]These are approximations of *Uniform Crime Reports* index and nonindex offenses based on the content of the questions asked the juveniles in the three samples.
[b]Not asked (NA)
[c]"Taken things of medium value ($5–$50)."
[d]"Taken part in 'gang fights.'"

Source: James F. Short, Jr., and F. Ivan Nye, "Extent of Unrecorded Delinquency, Some Tentative Conclusions," *Journal of Criminal Law, Criminology and Police Science* 49 (November–December 1958): 297. Copyright © 1958 by The Northwestern University School of Law. Adapted and reprinted by permission.

Table 1.5   Self-Reported Delinquency in Last 12 Months by High School Seniors: 1975–1990

Year	Percent Self-Reporting Index Crimes[a]		Percent Self-Reporting Nonindex Crimes[a]	
	Armed Robbery[b]	Larceny-theft[c]	Incorrigibility[d]	Vandalism[e]
1975	2.7	5.6	87.9	12.8
1976	2.5	6.1	86.9	11.9
1977	2.8	4.8	86.0	12.4
1978	2.8	5.6	87.1	12.3
1979	2.7	6.9	86.9	14.2
1980	2.9	6.6	86.2	13.2
1981	2.4	7.1	86.3	13.3
1982	2.3	6.9	87.5	12.4
1983	3.0	6.4	88.7	14.1
1984	3.2	6.7	87.5	14.1
1985	3.5	7.0	88.9	13.8
1986	3.4	6.6	88.9	13.2
1987	3.3	8.5	91.2	15.1
1988	2.8	8.5	90.3	14.2
1989	3.7	8.1	90.4	13.2
1990	3.5	10.1	90.7	13.4

[a]These are approximations of *Uniform Crime Reports* index and nonindex offenses based on the content of the questions asked the high school seniors.
[b]"Used a knife or gun or some other thing (like a club) to get something from a person."
[c]"Taken something not belonging to you worth over $50."
[d]"Argued or had a fight with either of your parents."
[e]"Damaged school property on purpose."

Source: Lloyd D. Johnston, Jerald G. Bachman, and Patrick M. O'Malley, *Monitoring the Future* (annual volumes, 1975–1990). (Ann Arbor, Mich.: Institute for Social Research, University of Michigan). Adapted and reprinted by permission of the Institute for Social Research.

and 1990. The patterns traced by these data are reassuringly familiar. High school seniors self-report nonindex crimes such as incorrigibility far more often than index crimes such as armed robbery. When it comes to index offenses, crimes against property such as larceny-theft are self-reported more often than crimes against persons. Interestingly, there is the same evidence of increase across time in the self-report data that was apparent in the *Uniform Crime Reports.*

DELINQUENCY IN PERSPECTIVE

Here, then, is what the *Uniform Crime Reports* and self-report studies teach us about the frequency and seriousness of youth crime. *Delinquency is frequent.* In 1990, almost 1.8 million juveniles were arrested by police. *Delinquency is increasing.* Between 1960 and 1980, arrests per 100,000 juveniles increased significantly, although the pattern since the early 1980s has been one of uneven decline. *Most delinquent acts are not serious.* Juveniles self-report nonindex crimes much more often than index crimes. Putting delinquency in perspective means that violent offenders—adolescents who kill over snowmobile rides—are few and far between. If there are mutants among our young, their numbers are small.

PREVENTION AND CONTROL OF JUVENILE DELINQUENCY

The juvenile justice system consists of public and private agencies[15] that employ individuals to make fateful decisions about the large number of juveniles accused of delinquent acts each year (see Figure 1.1). Most adolescents come to the attention of the juvenile justice system when they are arrested by police and taken to the juvenile bureau for questioning. Officers in the juvenile bureau release about one-third of those arrested,[16] especially those accused of minor offenses who were polite in their conversations with officers. The majority not released—serious and frequent offenders and some of those who were impolite—are referred to juvenile court intake.[17]

In most large juvenile court systems, probation officers make intake decisions.[18] Probation officers assigned to intake can release the juvenile, refer to another agency for assistance, or require the juvenile to meet informally with a probation officer as a condition for not filing a petition with the juvenile court. Intake officers also can petition a case to court.

Once a petition has been filed with the court, a decision must be made whether the juvenile will be detained or released to await an adjudication hearing. If a juvenile is adjudicated delinquent, the judge disposes of the case by sentencing the offender to probation, another form of community treatment, or to a state or private correctional institution followed by parole back to the community.

Most prevention and control intervention points have traditionally been associated with particular juvenile justice system

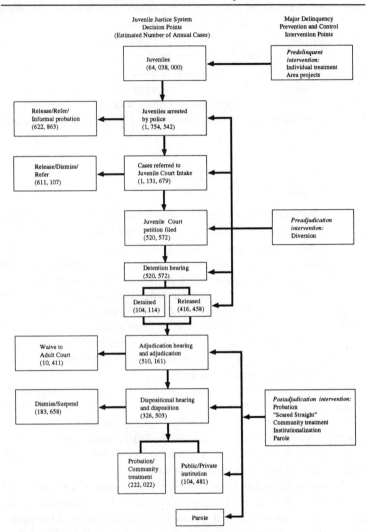

Sources: Estimated arrests and police dispositions are from FBI, *Crime in the United States: Uniform Crime Reports, 1990* (Washington, D.C.: U.S. Government Printing Office, 1991), pp. 33, 235. Estimates of case processing are from Howard N. Snyder, Terrence A. Finnegan, Ellen H. Nimick, Melissa H. Sickmund, Dennis P. Sullivan, and Nancy J. Tierney, *Juvenile Court Statistics, 1987* (Pittsburgh, Pa.: National Center for Juvenile Justice, 1990), pp. 12-14. It is important to recognize that these are *estimates* of the annual number of arrests and cases processed, not actual counts.

decisions (see Figure 1.1). Although it is true that the same intervention technique is sometimes applied at various stages of the juvenile justice system, it is possible to isolate three major prevention and control intervention points: (1) predelinquent intervention; (2) preadjudication intervention; and (3) postadjudication intervention.

PREDELINQUENT INTERVENTION

The goal of predelinquent intervention is to stop delinquency before it begins. A common procedure is to identify and treat individual juveniles believed headed for trouble with the law. A second and somewhat less common intervention is the area project. Here the goal is to identify high-delinquency neighborhoods and then alter some of the social forces thought supportive of delinquency.

Individual Treatment. Supporters of the individual-treatment approach to the prevention of juvenile delinquency[19] believe that youth crime is an individual problem requiring an individually oriented solution. They argue that juveniles become delinquent because their personalities are flawed in ways that encourage or fail to restrain involvement in delinquency. Among the likely causes of such personality problems are parents unable or unwilling to provide their children with proper guidance and assistance.

Two steps are therefore thought to be central to the successful prevention of delinquency. The first is early identification of juveniles headed for trouble with the law. The second is individually tailored treatment to repair or bolster flawed personalities. Treatment usually involves placing juveniles in regular contact with social workers, counselors, or other trained therapists. On occasion these specially trained adults combine therapy with economic, educational, medical, and other forms of individualized assistance.

Area Projects. Supporters of the area-project approach to the prevention of juvenile delinquency[20] believe that youth crime is a community problem requiring a community-oriented solution. They argue that traditions and beliefs supportive of delinquency are passed from older to younger juveniles in high-delinquency neighborhoods. Youthful involvement in crime is an inevitable and natural result of associations with others whose words and deeds signal support for delinquent behavior.

Advocates of this approach therefore argue that it makes little sense to focus primary attention on individual juveniles. They are the symptoms rather than the cause. Instead, preventive attention must be directed at high-delinquency neighborhoods generally and delinquent traditions and beliefs in particular.

PREADJUDICATION INTERVENTION

The goal in preadjudication intervention is to control delinquency by providing arrested juveniles with short-term treatment services without referring them to court. In the past these services consisted of "informal probation."[21] This was an agreement between a juvenile and a probation officer stating that the alleged offender would meet periodically with the officer and stay out of trouble with the law in exchange for not having a petition filed with the juvenile court. Over the past 20 years, however, this informal practice has been replaced by formal diversion programs.

Diversion Programs. Supporters of diversion[22] believe that persistent delinquency is the result of treating first-time offenders as if they were about to become persistently delinquent. They argue that detention, adjudication, and institutionalization provide juveniles with a delinquent self-image and stigmatize them in the eyes of significant others. Juvenile justice system processing therefore does more harm than good.

The best treatment for many alleged offenders, diversion supporters argue, is little or no treatment. This is especially the case when the juvenile is young and charged with nothing more serious than a status or minor property offense. For these types of youthful offenders and perhaps others, diversion away from the juvenile justice system is thought to be the most effective method of controlling delinquency.

POSTADJUDICATION INTERVENTION

The goal of postadjudication intervention is to control delinquency by placing convicted offenders under the formal control

of the state for purposes of rehabilitation, incapacitation, or deterrence. Once a juvenile has been adjudicated delinquent, juvenile court judges have two basic sentencing options. The first is to sentence an offender to probation or another form of community-based treatment. The second is to commit the offender to a state or private correctional institution and follow this with parole.

Probation.   Probation[23] currently is the most frequently employed sentencing option. Each year approximately 70 percent of the adolescents adjudicated delinquent by the juvenile justice system courts are sentenced to probation.[24] As a result, most probation officers have large caseloads and precious little time to do more than meet infrequently with their youthful clients. They rarely have time to provide extensive assistance or strictly enforce the conditions of probation.

"Scared Straight."   Starting in the mid-1970s, some offenders sentenced to probation, along with other juveniles, were taken to state prisons for intensive confrontation sessions with adult inmates serving long-term or life sentences. Using their own experiences as examples, inmates told juveniles of the harsh realities of imprisonment. The purpose of these sessions was to scare juveniles straight[25] by showing them what could happen if they persisted in their delinquent ways.

Community Treatment.   Community-based treatment[26] programs for probationers stand midway between the loose supervision of routine probation and the secure custody characteristic of most correctional facilities for juvenile offenders. Community-based programs typically provide more extensive assistance and stricter enforcement of the conditions of probation. At the same time, community-based programs usually reduce the isolation and mistreatment characteristic of life in correctional facilities for juvenile offenders.

Institutionalization.   The traditional reason for sentencing juveniles to public and private correctional facilities[27] has been rehabilitation. Correctional facilities routinely offer academic and vocational instruction in the hope that better-educated and

vocationally skilled inmates will be less delinquent upon release. Most institutions also supplement these routine efforts with special programs, such as alcohol and other drug counseling.

In recent years, other reasons for sentencing offenders to correctional facilities have gained legitimacy. Incapacitation theorists[28] assert that sentencing repeat offenders to long terms in state correctional facilities will significantly reduce juvenile crime. Deterrence theorists[29] argue that incarceration alerts offenders and other juveniles to the painful consequences of continued involvement in delinquency. This awareness of the pains of imprisonment, they contend, pushes adolescents in the direction of law-abiding behavior out of fear of being punished by the state.

Parole.   Parole[30] is a conditional release from a correctional facility. Unlike probationers who serve all of their sentence in the community, parolees do part of their time in an institution. They are then released to the community, where they serve the remainder of their sentence. Parole officers enforce the conditions of parole and attempt to keep their parolees out of further trouble with the law.

STRUCTURE OF THE BOOK

The remainder of the book is divided into four parts. Part One examines predelinquent intervention. Part Two probes preadjudication diversion programs. Part Three analyzes postadjudication intervention. Part Four concludes with firm recommendations for the prevention and control of juvenile delinquency.

Each chapter has a distinctive structure as well. All begin by establishing the logic behind a particular approach to the prevention or control of juvenile delinquency. Chapters then direct attention to major prevention or control efforts. The projects examined are among the best known and therefore have shaped the thoughts and actions of experts in the field of youth crime. Chapters next probe the generalizability of the results of major projects by examining similar prevention or control efforts. All conclude with an analysis of the effectiveness of particular approaches to the prevention and control of juvenile delinquency.

NOTES

1. A classic analysis of the origins of laws defining delinquent behavior is Anthony Platt, *The Child Savers: The Invention of Delinquency*, 2nd ed. (Chicago: The University of Chicago Press, 1977).

2. Bureau of Justice Statistics, *"What Is Crime?"* in William E. Thompson and Jack E. Bynum (eds.), *Juvenile Delinquency: Classic and Contemporary Readings* (Boston: Allyn and Bacon, 1991), p. 35. There is some variation by state. In most states (39) and the District of Columbia, 17 is the maximum age for juvenile court jurisdiction. In one state (Wyoming) the maximum age is 18, in seven states (Georgia, Illinois, Louisiana, Massachusetts, Missouri, South Carolina, and Texas) the maximum age is 16, and in three states (Connecticut, New York, and North Carolina) the maximum age is 15.

3. Howard N. Snyder, Terrence A. Finnegan, Ellen H. Nimick, Melissa H. Sickmund, Dennis P. Sullivan, and Nancy J. Tierney, *Juvenile Court Statistics 1987* (Pittsburgh, Pa.: National Center for Juvenile Justice, 1990), pp. 31–48. This publication is updated and issued annually and can be found in the reference section of most major public and university libraries.

4. Peter Applebome, "Juvenile Crime: The Offenders Are Younger and the Offenses More Serious," *The New York Times*, February 3, 1987, p. 16; Don Colburn, "Should We Execute Juvenile Killers?" *The Washington Post National Weekly Edition*, August 8–14, 1988, pp. 6–8.

5. Gordon Witkin, "Kids Who Kill," *U.S. News and World Report*, April 8, 1991, pp. 26–27.

6. "Murder Charge Might Set Legal Precedent," *The Columbus Dispatch*, August 27, 1989, p. A-9.

7. "Ten-Year-Old Boy Arrested in Alleged Rape of Four Children," *The [Baltimore] Sun*, September 14, 1989, p. A-15.

8. Witkin, "Kids Who Kill," p. 27.

9. "Killer Kids," WCMH, "Newswatch 4," Columbus, Ohio, June 22, 1991, 6:00 P.M. broadcast; Holly Goodman and Blair Boardman, "Juveniles Who Kill," *The Columbus Dispatch*, October 13, 1991, p. 1; Witkin, "Kids Who Kill."

10. Pete Hamill, "What Is Happening to Young People?" *The Columbus Dispatch*, December 8, 1981, p. B-3. The case that prompted Hamill's observations involved a 16-year-old who murdered his 14-year-old girlfriend and then hid her body in a wooden ravine outside Milpitas, California. The young man bragged to his friends about what he had done and when they doubted him, he took some of them to the ravine to see the body. Initially none of his friends, including those who

had seen the body, reported the murder to the police. For additional description of the case, see Wayne King, "Youths' Silence on Murder Victim Leaves a California Town Baffled," *The New York Times*, December 14, 1981, p. D-11.

11. FBI, *Crime in the United States: Uniform Crime Reports, 1990* (Washington, D.C.: U.S. Government Printing Office, 1991), pp. 8–42. The *Uniform Crime Reports* is issued each summer for the previous year. It is available in the reference section of most libraries.

12. The quickest way of finding recent and reasonably representative self-report data is Kathleen Maguire and Timothy Flanagan (eds.), *Sourcebook of Criminal Justice Statistics—1990* (Washington, D.C.: U.S. Government Printing Office, 1991), pp. 308–49. The *Sourcebook* is updated and issued annually. It is available in the reference section of most libraries.

13. FBI, *Crime in the United States*, p. 165.

14. Douglas A. Smith and Christy A. Visher, "Street-Level Justice: Situational Determinants of Police Arrest Decisions," in Thompson and Bynum (eds.), *Juvenile Delinquency*, pp. 438–51.

15. An enumeration of juveniles in public and private correctional facilities can be found in Bureau of Justice Statistics, *Children in Custody, 1975–85: Census of Public and Private Juvenile Detention, Correctional, and Shelter Facilities, 1975, 1977, 1979, 1983, and 1985* (Washington, D.C.: U.S. Department of Justice, Office of Justice Programs, Bureau of Justice Statistics, 1989), pp. 10–18. This report is updated periodically and can be found in the reference section of major public and university libraries.

16. FBI, *Crime in the United States*, p. 235. Also see Smith and Visher, "Street-Level Justice"; and Richard J. Lundman, Richard E. Sykes, and John P. Clark, "Police Control of Juveniles: A Replication," *Journal of Research in Crime and Delinquency* 15 (January 1978): 74–91.

17. Simha F. Landaw, "Juveniles and the Police: Who Is Charged and Who Is Referred to the Juvenile Bureau?" *British Journal of Criminology* 21 (January 1981): 27–46.

18. Snyder et al., *Juvenile Court Statistics, 1987*, pp. 12–15.

19. For an early example of the individual-treatment approach to the problem of juvenile delinquency, see William Healy, *The Individual Delinquent: A Text-Book of Diagnosis and Prognosis for All Concerned in Understanding Offenders* (Boston: Little, Brown, 1915).

20. For a description of the best-known example of the area-project approach, the Chicago Area Project, see Harold Finestone, *Victims of Change: Juvenile Delinquents in American Society* (Westport, Conn.: Greenwood Press, 1976), pp. 116–50.

21. Carolyn Needleman, "Discrepant Assumptions in Empirical Research," *Social Problems* 28 (February 1981): 247–62.

22. For a description and analysis of diversion programs written during the 1970s, see Robert M. Carter and Malcolm W. Klein (eds.), *Back on the Street: The Diversion of Juvenile Offenders* (Englewood Cliffs, N.J.: Prentice-Hall, 1976).

23. For a discussion of the origins of probation, see Blake McKelvey, *American Prisons: A History of Good Intentions* (Montclair, N.J.: Patterson Smith, 1977), pp. 247–49.

24. Snyder et al., *Juvenile Court Statistics*, pp. 12–15.

25. For a description and analysis of "scared straight" programs during the middle and late 1970s, see James O. Finckenauer, *Scared Straight! and the Panacea Phenomenon* (Englewood Cliffs, N.J.: Prentice-Hall, 1982).

26. For a general discussion of community-based treatment, see Vernon Fox, *Community-based Corrections* (Englewood Cliffs, N.J.: Prentice-Hall, 1977).

27. For an early and classic description of public juvenile correctional facilities, see Clifford R. Shaw, *The Jack-Roller: A Delinquent Boy's Own Story* (Chicago: University of Chicago Press, 1930), especially pp. 57–78 and pp. 103–14. For description of private institutions for juveniles, see David Shichar and Clemens Bartollas, "Private and Public Juvenile Placements: Is There a Difference?" *Crime and Delinquency* 36 (April 1990): 286–99.

28. For an overview of the incapacitation hypothesis, see James Q. Wilson, *Thinking About Crime*, rev. ed. (New York: Vintage Books, 1985), pp. 145–61.

29. For a discussion of deterrence theory as it applies to juvenile delinquency, see Anne L. Schneider, *Deterrence and Juvenile Crime: Results from a National Policy Experiment* (New York: Springer-Verlag, 1990).

30. For a brief overview of parole, see Norval Morris and Michael Tonry, *Between Prison and Probation: Intermediate Punishments in a Rational Sentencing System* (New York: Oxford University Press, 1990), pp. 24–27. Parole for juveniles is frequently called "aftercare."

PART ONE

PREDELINQUENT INTERVENTION

2

INDIVIDUAL TREATMENT

Physicians dominated early efforts to prevent delinquency by treating individual juveniles.[1] Among the most prominent was William Healy (1869-1963),[2] who devoted most of his long medical career to the diagnosis and treatment of juvenile delinquency. In his early years, Dr. Healy probed for the origins of delinquency. Later in his career, he turned his attention to the treatment of youthful offenders. In carrying out his diagnostic and treatment activities, Dr. Healy was a firm advocate of the idea that the causes of delinquency were to be found in the personalities of individual juveniles.

Dr. Healy's ideas about the largely individualistic origins of delinquency began to attract attention in 1909 when he was appointed director of the Juvenile Psychopathic Institute in Chicago. The Institute had been founded and funded by prominent residents of Chicago, and its task was "to undertake . . . an inquiry into the health of delinquent children in order to ascertain . . . in what degrees delinquency is caused or influenced by mental or physical defect or abnormality. . . ."[3] To discover the causes of delinquency, Dr. Healy and his colleagues assembled "social, medical, and psychological data"[4] on 1,000 repeat juvenile offenders in Cook County, Illinois.

William Healy's 1915 book, *The Individual Delinquent: A Text-Book of Diagnosis and Prognosis for All Concerned in Understanding Offenders*,[5] is a description of the results of his efforts as director of the Juvenile Psychopathic Institute. Dr. Healy asserted that delinquency is an individualistic problem with roots deep in the personalities of individual offenders. Abnormalities and pathologies ranging from "[m]ental dissatisfactions" to "fully-developed psychoses"[6] are the personality problems that propel juveniles in the direction of persistent involvement in delinquency (see Table 2.1).

Having asserted that persistent delinquency could be traced to individual personality disorders, Dr. Healy helped shape the logic of the individual-treatment approach to the prevention of delinquency.[7] Because it was not necessary or economically possible to treat all juveniles, the first logical step was early identification of juveniles experiencing personality problems. The second was provision of treatment services to identified juveniles to prevent otherwise inevitable involvement in delinquency.

Table 2.1   William Healy's Description of the "Bases of Delinquency" among 1,000 Repeat Juvenile Offenders in Cook County, Illinois, 1909–1914

Mental dissatisfactions; those developed from cravings of no special moral significance in themselves, or even from unfulfilled creditable ambitions.

Criminalistic imagery, sometimes fairly obsessional, which persists, and is strong enough to impel misconduct.

Irritative mental reactions to environmental conditions, seeking expression or relief in misdoing.

The development of habits of thought involving persistent criminalistic ideas and reactions.

Adolescent mental instabilities and impulsions.

Mental conflicts, worries, or repressions concerning various experiences or matters of mental content. These sometimes interfere with that smooth working of the inner life which fosters socially moral conduct. The misdeed here, too, may be a relief phenomena.

The chronic attitude of the offender representing himself to himself as one, like Ishmael, whose hand shall be against every man and every man's hand against him. The remarkable phenomenon of antisocial grudge may be included here.

Mental peculiarities or twists which are agents in the production of antisocial conduct, but which do not overwhelm the personality enough to warrant grading the subject as aberrational.

Aberrational mental states: all the way from fully-developed psychoses to temporary or border-line psychotic conditions.

Mental defect in any of . . . several forms.

Source: William Healy, *The Individual Delinquent: A Text-Book of Diagnosis and Prognosis for All Concerned in Understanding Offenders* (Boston: Little, Brown, 1915), p. 34.

This chapter probes the usefulness of the individual-treatment approach. It begins by examining attempts to identify juveniles headed for trouble with the law. Attention then is directed to the Cambridge-Somerville Youth Study, the single best-known example of an effort to prevent delinquency by treating individual juveniles. Last, a review of a replication of the Cambridge-Somerville Youth Study is undertaken.

EARLY IDENTIFICATION

Although there have been many attempts to identify juveniles headed for trouble with the law, two will be the focus of this section by reasons of size of effort and amount of attention received. The first is Starke R. Hathaway and Elio D. Monachesi's attempt to predict delinquency using the Minnesota Multiphasic Personality Inventory. The second is the Glueck Social Prediction Table.

THE MINNESOTA MULTIPHASIC PERSONALITY INVENTORY

The Minnesota Multiphasic Personality Inventory (MMPI)[8] emerged in the 1940s as an aid in the diagnosis of personality disorders. It was developed by asking questions of two groups of people—hospitalized psychiatric patients and over 1,000 normal residents of the state of Minnesota. The questions retained for use in the MMPI were those that best distinguished the patients from the normal group.

In evaluating responses to MMPI questions, attention is given to a person's score on the clinical scales named after the groups of patients used to develop the MMPI (see Table 2.2). Scale 1-Hs, or Hypochondriasis, for instance, is based on the responses of persons hospitalized because of acute anxieties about their health or recurrent complaints of imaginary illnesses. Scale 4-Pd, or Psychopathic deviation, is based on the responses of persons hospitalized because of their lack of moral and social feelings and their frequently impulsive, self-serving behavior.

Scoring of MMPI responses on the ten clinical scales is made simpler by the fact that each scale has an average, or mean, score of 50 and a standard deviation of 10. Accordingly, only 36 percent of the people taking the MMPI have scale scores above 54 and

Table 2.2   MMPI Clinical Scales

Scale Number	Scale Name	What the Scale Discloses
1	Hs—Hypochondriasis	Tired; inactive; lethargic; feels physically ill
2	D—Depression	Serious; low in morale; unhappy; self-dissatisfied
3	Hy—Hysteria	Idealistic; naïve; articulate; ill under stress; social
4	Pd—Psychopathic deviation	Rebellious; cynical; disregards rules; socially aggressive; selfish
5	Mf—Interest pattern of opposite sex	High score: sensitive. Low score: exaggerated own sex interest pattern. High score in males: gentlemanly; scholarly; feminine. High score in females: rough; ambitious.
6	Pa—Paranoia	Perfectionist; stubborn; hard to know; or, with moderate scores, socially acceptable
7	Pt—Psychasthenia	Dependent; desires to please; feelings of inferiority; indecisive; anxious
8	Sc—Schizophrenia	Negative; difficult; odd; pathetic; lacks social grace
9	Ma—Hypomania	Expansive; optimistic; decisive; not bound by custom
0	Si—Social introversion	Unassertive; self-conscious; shy; or, with low score, socially active

Source: Starke R. Hathaway and Elio D. Monachesi, *Adolescent Personality and Behavior: MMPI Patterns of Normal, Delinquent, Dropout, and Other Outcomes.* Minneapolis: The University of Minnesota Press, 1963, p. 228. Copyright © 1963 by The University of Minnesota. Reprinted by permission.

only 2 percent have scale scores above 70. Translated from the statistical, the higher a person's scale score, the less the person's responses resemble those of well-adjusted people taking the MMPI, and the more they approximate those of the hospitalized psychiatric patients used to develop the MMPI.

In clinical use, the MMPI is a diagnostic tool used to help identify a patient's problems. People with a Scale 8-Sc, or Schizophrenia, score of over 70, for instance, are different from most other people taking the MMPI because only 2 percent have the same high Sc score. At the outset of therapy, a clinician would likely use a high Scale 8 score as a starting point in exploring and planning treatment.

The MMPI as Predictor of Delinquency. In 1947, University of Minnesota researchers Starke R. Hathaway and Elio D. Monachesi began a project to determine whether it was possible to use the MMPI to predict delinquency.[9] They gave the MMPI to 1,290.[10] Minneapolis, Minnesota, public high school ninth-grade males. Four years after the ninth graders had taken the MMPI, Professors Hathaway and Monachesi checked police and county probation office records to see whether the names of any of these students appeared. If a juvenile's name appeared for an offense other than a traffic law violation,[11] that appearance was viewed as evidence of involvement in delinquency (see Box 2.1).

Table 2.3 contains MMPI clinical scale scores over 54 by percent delinquent four years after testing. Examination reveals that the single best predictor of delinquency is Scale 8-Sc, or Schizophrenia: 23.8 percent of the juveniles with a Scale 8 score above 54 were delinquent four years after testing. However, if predictions were made on the basis of a score over 54 on Scale 8, the data in Table 2.3 indicate that 76.2 percent of the predictions would be inaccurate.

Given the failure of any single score to reliably predict delinquency, Professors Hathaway and Monachesi turned their attention to combinations of two high scores among the three scales that most closely related to delinquency in Table 2.3—Scale 4-Pd, or Psychopathic deviation, Scale 8-Sc, or Schizophrenia, and Scale 9-Ma, or Hypomania. While none of these scales singly did a good job of predicting delinquency, it was possible that combinations of high scale scores might improve predictions.

Combinations of high scale scores did a slightly better job of predicting delinquency (see Table 2.4). Using the single best predictor (a score above 70 on two scales), the researchers found that 34.5 percent of the juveniles were delinquent four years after testing. Even with this improvement, however, 65.5 percent of the predictions made using the MMPI were still wrong.

As a result of the data in Table 2.3 and Table 2.4, Professors Hathaway and Monachesi concluded that the MMPI could not be used to predict delinquency. They observed: "No single MMPI code class dramatically predicted delinquency . . . and we seriously doubt that any one personality test pattern will be found to predict which individual children will do things called delinquent by those about them."[12]

Box 2.1   Official Measures as Indicators of Delinquency

All of the projects examined in this book use official measures, such as arrests, as indicators of involvement in delinquency. Although regularly used, official measures are plagued by serious problems of underestimation. Less than 10 percent of the delinquent acts committed by juveniles result in apprehension by police. Of those offenders unlucky enough to be caught, eight of ten are released rather than arrested.

Despite these problems, official measures remain useful indicators of involvement in delinquency in at least three respects:

1. Official measures reflect frequent and serious delinquency. The more often a juvenile commits seriously delinquent acts, the greater the probability of apprehension and arrest.

2. Official measures are usually assembled by persons and agencies unconnected with a project. This reduces unintentional bias or deliberate manipulation of outcome measures.

3. Regular use of official measures across many different projects permits assessment of relative effectiveness. Common measures of outcome allow comparison of the results of different projects.

Official measures, then, do not begin to fully indicate involvement in delinquency. They do, however, reflect frequent and serious delinquency, are free of project-related bias, and allow assessment of relative effectiveness. Although far from perfect, official measures are a useful way out of a difficult measurement situation.

Sources: Walter R. Gove, Michael Hughes, and Michael Geerken, "Are Uniform Crime Reports a Valid Indicator of the Index Crimes? An Affirmative Answer with Minor Qualifications," *Criminology* 23 (November 1985): 451–501; John T. Whitehead and Steven P. Lab, "A Meta-Analysis of Juvenile Correctional Treatment," *Journal of Research in Crime and Delinquency* 26 (August 1989): 276–295; and William S. Davidson II, Robin Redner, Richard L. Amdur, and Christina M. Mitchell, *Alternative Treatments for Troubled Youth: The Case of Diversion from the Justice System* (New York: Plenum, 1990), pp. 17–36.

Table 2.3   MMPI Clinical Scale Scores over 54 (high points) by Percent
Delinquent Four Years after Testing

High-Point Clinical Scale Number	High-Point Clinical Scale Name	Number of Juveniles	Number of Delinquents	Percent Delinquent
1	Hs—Hypochondriasis	48	10	20.8
2	D—Depression	67	9	13.4
3	Hy—Hysteria	39	7	17.9
4	Pd—Psychopathic deviation	276	65	23.6
5	Mf—Interest pattern of the opposite sex	88	10	11.4
6	Pa—Paranoia	38	7	18.4
7	Pt—Psychasthenia	89	17	19.1
8	Sc—Schizophrenia	202	48	23.8
9	Ma—Hypomania	317	68	21.5
0	Si—Social introversion	91	10	11.0
No high points	—	35	4	11.4
Totals		1,290	255	19.8

Source: Starke R. Hathaway and Elio D. Monachesi, "The Personalities of Predelinquent Boys," *Journal of Criminal Law, Criminology and Police Science* 48 (July-August 1957): 158. Copyright © 1957 by Starke R. Hathaway and Elio D. Monachesi. Revised and reprinted by permission of Livia Cuming.

THE GLUECK SOCIAL PREDICTION TABLE

In 1950, Sheldon and Eleanor Glueck published *Unraveling Juvenile Delinquency*,[13] a research monograph that described the results of their efforts to discover the "causal mechanisms of persistent delinquency."[14] The Gluecks reported that they had selected 500 juveniles serving time in Massachusetts correctional facilities and then matched them on residence in underprivileged inner-city neighborhoods, age, general intelligence, and ethnic origin with 500 nondelinquent males. By matching the juveniles, the Gluecks tried to make the two groups as much alike as possible save for the presence or absence of a record of delinquency.

The Gluecks then compared the delinquents with the nondelinquents. The comparisons seemed to suggest some possibly important differences, including the type of discipline afforded

Table 2.4   Maximum Predictive Power of MMPI: Clinical Scale Combination Scores over 54 and over 70 by Percent Delinquent Four Years after Testing

Clinical Scale Combinations	Score	Number of Juveniles	Number of Delinquents	Percent Delinquent
Combination of two among Scale 4-Pd, or Psychopathic deviation, Scale 8-Sc, or Schizophrenia, Scale 9-Ma, or Hypomania	>54[a]	391	111	28.4
Combination of two among Scale 4-Pd, or Psychopathic deviation, Scale 8-Sc, or Schizophrenia, Scale 9-Ma, or Hypomania	>70[a]	220	76	34.5

[a]Only 36 percent of the people taking the MMPI have scale scores over 54, and only 2 percent have scale scores over 70. In general, the higher a person's scale score, the less the person's responses resemble those of other people taking the MMPI, and the more the person's responses resemble those of the patients used to develop the particular MMPI scale.

Source: Starke R. Hathaway and Elio D. Monachesi, "The Personalities of Predelinquent Boys," *Journal of Criminal Law, Criminology and Police Science* 48 (July–August 1957): 159. Copyright © 1957 by Starke R. Hathaway and Elio D. Monachesi. Revised and reprinted by permission of Livia Cuming.

juveniles by their fathers (see Table 2.5): 41.6 percent of the fathers of delinquent juveniles provided "erratic" discipline as compared to 17.9 percent of the fathers of nondelinquents. Additionally, only 5.7 percent of the fathers of delinquents provided "firm but kindly" discipline as compared to 55.5 percent of the fathers of nondelinquents.

Table 2.5   Type of Father's Discipline of Son by Percent among Delinquents and Nondelinquents

Type of Father's Discipline	Percent among Delinquents	Percent among Nondelinquents
Lax	26.6	17.9
Overstrict	26.1	8.7
Erratic	41.6	17.9
Firm but kindly	5.7	55.5
Totals	100.0	100.0
	(459)[a]	(459)[a]

[a]Incomplete information reduced group sizes to 459.

Source: Sheldon Glueck and Eleanor Glueck, *Unraveling Juvenile Delinquency* (New York: The Commonwealth Fund, 1950), p. 131. Copyright © 1950 by The Commonwealth Fund. Reprinted by permission.

Having found "marked differences" such as those in Table 2.5, the Gluecks turned their attention to the use of these differences. Their goal was to create "predictive instrumentalities . . . to differentiate between potential juvenile offenders and nonoffenders very early in life, preferably at school entrance."[15]

The Gluecks selected five family-related factors: discipline of boy by father, supervision of boy by mother, affection of father for boy, affection of mother for boy, and family cohesiveness (see Table 2.6). These five factors were chosen because they differentiated the delinquents from the nondelinquents studied by the Gluecks; only 9.9 percent of the juveniles experiencing suitable supervision by their mothers were delinquent as compared to 83.2 percent of the juveniles receiving unsuitable maternal supervision. Additionally, these five factors were assumed to be well established by the time a child entered school.

Actual predictions of delinquency were made using the data in Tables 2.6 and 2.7. The first step was to assign a juvenile a "weighted failure score" using the percent delinquent figures in Table 2.6. Consider the hypothetical scoring example described by Sheldon and Eleanor Glueck: "If, for example, Johnny is always harshly disciplined by his father, he would be scored . . . [71.8][16] on this factor. If the mother generally leaves him to his own devices, letting him run around the streets and not knowing what he does or where he goes, her supervision would be rated 'unsuitable' and the score on this factor would be 83.2. If it is learned, further, that the father dislikes the boy, Johnny would be scored 75.9 on this factor. If the mother is shown to be indifferent to her son, expressing little warmth or feeling for him, or if she is downright hostile to him, the score on this item would be 86.2. Finally, if it is found that the family is unintegrated because, for example, the mother spends most of the day away from home, giving little if any thought to the doings of the children, and the father, a heavy drinker, spends most of his leisure hours in bars and cafes, ignoring his family, the score of this factor would be 96.9. Addition of these scores results in a total of . . . [414]."[17]

With this total, the Gluecks' research indicates that Johnny probably would be delinquent because 79 percent of the juveniles with scores of 250 and over actually were delinquent (see Table 2.7). Had Johnny received firm but kindly discipline from his father (score = 9.3), suitable supervision by his mother (score = 9.9),

Table 2.6   Family-Related Factors by Number of Juveniles, Number of Delinquents, and "Weighted Failure Scores" (percent delinquent juveniles)

Family-Related Factor	Number of Juveniles	Number of Delinquent Juveniles	"Weighted Failure Scores" (percent delinquent juveniles)
Discipline by father			
Overstrict or erratic	433	311	71.8
Lax	204	122	59.8
Firm but kindly	281	26	9.3
Supervision by mother			
Unsuitable	382	318	83.2
Fair	252	145	57.5
Suitable	355	35	9.9
Father's affection			
Indifferent or hostile	387	294	75.9
Warm (including over-protective)	585	198	33.8
Mother's affection			
Indifferent or hostile	160	138	86.2
Warm (including over-protective)	828	357	43.1
Family cohesiveness			
Unintegrated	127	123	96.9
Some elements of cohesion	483	296	61.3
Cohesive	389	80	20.6

Source: Sheldon Glueck and Eleanor Glueck, *Unraveling Juvenile Delinquency* (New York: The Commonwealth Fund, 1950), pp. 113, 115, 125, 126, and 131. Copyright © 1950 by The Commonwealth Fund. Reprinted by permission.

warm paternal and maternal affection (scores = 33.8 and 43.1), and lived in a cohesive family (score = 20.6), Johnny's score would have been 116.7. With a score of 116.7, Johnny probably would not be delinquent because only 16 percent of the juveniles with scores under 250 actually were delinquent.

Table 2.7   The Glueck Social Prediction Table

Score	Number of Juveniles	Number of Delinquents	Percent Delinquent	Prediction
Under 250	401	64	16	"Probably nondelinquent"
250 and over	489	387	79	"Probably delinquent"

Source: Sheldon Glueck and Eleanor Glueck, *Unraveling Juvenile Delinquency* (New York: The Commonwealth Fund, 1950), p. 262. Copyright © 1950 by The Commonwealth Fund. Revised and reprinted by permission.

Accuracy of the Glueck Social Prediction Table. The Gluecks were quick to caution that the accuracy of their predictions needed to be assessed using juveniles other than the ones studied for *Unravelng Juvenile Delinquency.* They noted that while their Social Prediction Table clearly distinguished between delinquent and nondelinquent juveniles in the two groups used to develop their instrument, there was no way of knowing whether it would do the same when applied to other juveniles.[18]

One effort to assess the accuracy of the Glueck Social Prediction Table began in New York City in the early 1950s.[19] The New York City Youth Board selected two public schools located in high-delinquency areas. Social workers were sent to the homes of all first-grade males, and predictions were made according to the procedures established by the Gluecks. The juveniles were then followed for seven years to assess the accuracy of those predictions.

Table 2.8 summarizes the predictions made by the New York City Youth Board using the Glueck Social Prediction Table. At first glance it appears that the Social Prediction Table is an extremely useful instrument because only 2.6 percent of the predictions of *nondelinquency* were inaccurate. However, when attention is directed to predictions of delinquency, the picture is far different: 74.6 percent of the predictions of delinquency were inaccurate.

The evidence of inaccuracy in predicting delinquency in Table 2.8 is not unique. Other applications of the Glueck Social Prediction Table have found much the same thing.[20] When applied to samples of juveniles other than the sample with which it was created, the Glueck Social Prediction Table does not accurately predict delinquency.

SUMMARY OF EFFORTS AT EARLY IDENTIFICATION

Two of the best-known and most ambitious efforts to identify juveniles headed for trouble with the law are Starke Hathaway and Elio Monachesi's analysis of the MMPI as a predictive instrument and Sheldon and Eleanor Glueck's Social Prediction Table. Review of the results of these two efforts, when combined with the results of more recent research,[21] reveals that prediction of delinquency is a stubbornly elusive task. In particular, *most*

Table 2.8 Accuracy of the Predictions Made by New York City Youth Board Using the Glueck Social Prediction Table Seven Years after Predictions Made

Score	Prediction	Number of Juveniles	Number of Delinquent Juveniles	Percent Accurate Predictions	Percent Inaccurate Predictions
Under 250	"Probably nondelinquent"	156	4	97.4	2.6
250 and over	"Probably delinquent"	67	17	25.4	74.6
Totals		223	21		

Source: Jackson Toby, "An Evaluation of Early Identification and Intensive Treatment Programs for Predelinquents," *Social Problems* 18 (Fall 1965): 169. Copyright © 1965 by the Society for the Study of Social Problems. Revised and reprinted by permission.

methods of predicting delinquency are inaccurate one-half to two-thirds of the time. Unless and until alternative research results are made available, this must be accepted as a summation of the current state of the predictive art.

THE CAMBRIDGE-SOMERVILLE YOUTH STUDY

The Cambridge-Somerville Youth Study[22] has been called the "best-known study of a prevention effort"[23] for juveniles identified as headed for trouble with the law. In addition, the Cambridge-Somerville Youth Study is representative of efforts to prevent delinquency by treating individual juveniles. Table 2.9 summarizes the major features of this widely discussed study and serves as a guide for the description and analysis that follow.

DESCRIPTION OF THE PROJECT

The Cambridge-Somerville Youth Study took place in Cambridge and Somerville, Massachusetts, two cities adjacent to Boston. When the study began in November 1937, Cambridge was a densely populated city with two faces. The first and smaller side of Cambridge consisted of Harvard, the Massachusetts Institute of Technology, and Radcliffe. The second and much larger side of Cambridge was industrial, less educated, and consisted primarily of white, working-class residents, one-quarter of whom were foreign born. Somerville, although smaller and less densely populated than Cambridge, was similar to Cambridge in its largely working-class population and moderate rate of delinquency.[24]

The original goal of the study was to provide ten years of uninterrupted treatment to juveniles identified as headed for trouble with the law. World War II, however, compromised that goal and forced considerable departure from it. Adult counselors providing treatment services were drafted, and as the war progressed the counselors' adolescent clients also were drafted. Because of these changes, the Cambridge-Somerville Youth Study ended on December 31, 1945, a point at which most of the juveniles had received far less than the intended ten years of treatment.

Table 2.9 Description of the Cambridge-Somerville Youth Study

Project Name:	The Cambridge-Somerville Youth Study
Locations:	Cambridge, Massachusetts, and Somerville, Massachusetts
Dates:	November 1937 to December 31, 1945
Subjects:	Juveniles identified by teachers, police officers, playground supervisors, and others as delinquency prone or average. All were male, their average age was approximately 11 at the start of the project, nearly all were white, and nearly all were from working-class backgrounds.
Type of treatment:	Adult counselors worked with the experimental juveniles to "bring about and foster . . . by intensive individual help and guidance a continuing social, physical, intellectual, and spiritual growth through which the boys will be assets to society and to themselves and in particular not sources of trouble or concern to others through their behavior."
Amount of treatment:	During the first two years of the project, the adult counselors averaged 11 contacts per year with the juvenile, 12 contacts per year with the juvenile's family, and 12 contacts per year with relevant social agencies, such as the school.
Evaluative design:	Experimental: Juveniles were randomly assigned to the treated and untreated groups.
Measures of results:	Initial measures of the results of the project were collected starting in 1942. Follow-up measures of results were collected in 1955 and again in 1976.
Replication:	The Cambridge-Somerville Youth Study has been replicated on numerous occasions, including Youth Consultation Service in New York City in the late 1950s.

Source: Edwin Powers and Helen Witmer, *An Experiment in the Prevention of Juvenile Delinquency: The Cambridge-Somerville Youth Study* (New York: Columbia University Press, 1951).

The study originally was to include Cambridge juveniles only. Cambridge public-school teachers were asked to identify males less than ten years of age displaying one or more of 32 different predelinquent behaviors. These behaviors included truancy, aggressiveness, sexual delinquency, and use of obscenities.

This request for identifications by teachers resulted in "unhappy public relations."[25] Teachers were unwilling to identify students displaying predelinquent characteristics. Some of the teachers were afraid their nominations might be incorrect. Others did not want to single out particular juveniles for potentially stigmatizing attention. Teacher resistance was so strong that it was quickly apparent that not enough juveniles would be identified to make up the treated experimental group and the untreated control group.

Because of resistance by teachers, several important changes were made in the method of securing subjects. The study was expanded to Somerville's teachers to increase the pool of possible referrals. Furthermore, teachers in Cambridge and Somerville were asked to nominate nondifficult or average juveniles with "no present signs of future delinquency."[26] Last, age limits were relaxed and referrals were sought from police officers, playground supervisors, and social work agencies. As a result of these politically necessary changes in the methods of securing subjects, the names of over 2,000 juvenile were eventually provided to Cambridge-Somerville Youth Study personnel.

For about 900 of the juveniles referred to the project, over 100 pieces of information were collected to establish whether they were headed for trouble with the law. Home visits were made by social workers to assess parental discipline, schoolteachers were tapped for additional descriptive information, physical examinations were performed by project physicians, and juveniles took paper and pencil personality assessment tests. The names of juveniles with complete informational dossiers were then sent to a Selection Committee for assignment to a treated experimental group or to an untreated control group.

By May 1939, a total of 650 subjects were involved in the study, with 325 in the experimental treatment group and 325 in the untreated control group. All were male, their average age was 11, nearly all were white, and nearly all were from working-class backgrounds. Reflective of initial teacher resistance, only about one-half of the subjects were identified as headed for trouble with the law.[27]

TYPE OF TREATMENT

The goal of the Cambridge-Somerville Youth Study was to prevent delinquency by treating individual juveniles. As shown in Figure 2.1, the treatment hypothesis was that assignment of adult counselors to work with juveniles in improving school performance, personality development, and family functioning would prevent juvenile delinquency.

FIGURE 2.1   The Cambridge-Somerville Youth Study's treatment
hypothesis in diagrammatic form

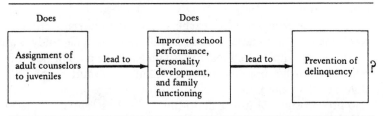

Sources: The treatment hypothesis is based on description of the Cambridge-Somerville
Youth Study in Edwin Powers and Helen Witmer, *An Experiment in the Prevention of
Delinquency: The Cambridge-Somerville Youth Study* (New York: Columbia University
Press, 1951), pp. 102–38. The diagrammatic representation of the treatment hypothesis in this
chapter and the chapters that follow is modeled after Carol Weiss, *Evaluation Research:
Methods of Assessing Program Effectiveness* (Englewood Cliffs, N.J.: Prentice-Hall, 1972),
p. 40.

Treatment activities began with the hiring of the adult counselors. Those hired were required to be of "good character" and to
have had some type of counseling experience, although they need
not have been professionally trained. During the course of the
study, 19 adult counselors—15 males and 4 females—were employed, but no more than 10 counselors were on staff at any time.
Of the 19, 8 had received graduate degrees in social work, 6 were
completing graduate degrees in social work, 2 were experienced
"boys' workers," 2 were psychologists, and 1 was a nurse.

Each counselor was assigned a 30-to-35 person caseload and
told to make contact with their largely unsuspecting juvenile
clients. Counselors knocked on doors, introduced themselves to
juveniles and their parents, and announced their intent to be-
friend and help them over a ten-year period. Juveniles and their
parents were not allowed to refuse this unsolicited friendship and
assistance. Too much time and money had been spent on identifying juveniles and assembling informational dossiers. As it
turned out, very few juveniles or parents were able to successfully
resist the sudden appearance of an adult with the announced
mission of providing individual treatment over the next decade.[28]

The adult counselors were instructed to provide friendship and
moral suasion and to engage in directed change activities to
improve school performance, personality development, and fam-

ily functioning. Toward these ends and toward the ultimate goal of preventing delinquency, the adult counselors:

Arranged for physical examinations.

Attempted to establish helpful relations with the family.

Took the juvenile on educational trips to "see things."

Arranged for camp and farm placements, and, in a few cases, foster homes.[29]

Found employment for the juvenile and family.

Advised and counseled the family with respect to the juvenile's problems (sex, discipline).

Gave specific tutorial help in school subjects.

Gave specific attention to analysis and correction of reading disability.

Arranged for intelligence and achievement tests.

Referred juvenile to other agencies for specific help.

Obtained legal advice for family.

Carried out "play therapy."

Invited the juvenile to spend a day at the counselor's home.

Procured psychiatric advice and treatment for the juvenile and family.

Interpreted the juvenile to the teacher.

Encouraged recreation by engaging in sports with the juvenile.

Placed, [the] family in contact with religious organizations.

Taught or encouraged hobbies.

Secured more information—through the juvenile's friends [and] other agencies.[30]

About the only thing counselors did not do was provide direct financial assistance to the juveniles or their families. The Cambridge-Somerville Youth Study was an attempt to prevent delinquency by treating individual juveniles, not by changing or improving their social environment. Counselors were therefore instructed to "refrain from radical alteration of the larger environment in which the boy lived."[31]

The amount of treatment received by the juveniles varied considerably. During the first two years of the study, counselors averaged 11 contacts per year with each juvenile. They also averaged 12 contacts per year with each client's family and 12 contacts per year with community agencies, such as the school.[32]

The original goal of the project was to maintain these levels of contact for all 325 treatment-group subjects over a full ten-year period.

However, the necessary public relations decision to include "nondifficult" juveniles in the study occasioned significant departure from the original goal, as did World War II. Starting in 1941, problems began to emerge in the treatment of the nondifficult cases included when teachers balked at identiying only delinquency-prone children. Average cases did not require the kind of treatment the largely social-work-trained counselors were prepared to provide. As one counselor stated: "You cannot solve problems that do not exist."[33] Because counselors were unprepared to treat these clients, 65 were dropped from the treatment group in the summer of 1942. Termination of these subjects along with two deaths and one move out of state reduced the number of active cases to 257.

Between 1943 and 1945 lingering problems with the remaining nondifficult cases, induction into the military of both counselors and subjects, and moves by adolescent clients to Maine to work in war-related shipyards further reduced the size of the treatment group. On July 15, 1943, 113 mostly nondifficult subjects were terminated (remaining $n = 144$), and during 1944 and 1945 an additional 72 subjects were terminated. At the end of the study on December 31, 1945, only 72 of the 325 experimental group juveniles were still receiving treatment.

EVALUATIVE DESIGN

Once the informational dossiers describing the backgrounds and characteristics of the juveniles had been assembled, a Selection Committee consisting of a psychiatrist and two social workers began a painstakingly elaborate matching procedure. Working with over 100 pieces of information for each juvenile and without the aid of a computer or even a card-sort machine, juveniles were first matched on six variables, including physical health and neighborhood environment. The juveniles were next matched on 13 variables, including standard of living and the home visit personality rating. Although clinical judgments were used to arrive at some matches, a long needle was also employed: "Cards were . . . placed in a file and with the aid of a long needle thrust through the holes it was possible to separate out of the pile those having similar contours or profiles in respect to each variable."[34] The end result of these procedures was the creation of 325 pairs of matched juveniles.

Once the 325 pairs of juveniles had been matched using clinical judgments and a long needle, they were assigned to the experimental treatment group or the untreated control group on the basis of a flip of a coin, a random assignment procedure. The Cambridge-Somerville Youth Study's experimental evaluative design (see Box 2.2) can therefore be summarized diagrammatically as:

$$
\begin{array}{lll}
 & & & \text{Treated subjects} \\
\text{Juvenile} & \text{Matched} & \text{Coin} & (n = 325) \\
\text{subjects} \rightarrow & \text{pairs} \rightarrow & \text{flip} & \\
(n = 900) & (n = 325) & & \text{Untreated subjects} \\
 & & & (n = 325)
\end{array}
$$

MEASURES OF RESULTS

Measures of the extent to which counselors had been able to improve school performance, personality development, and family functioning were initially collected in 1942. Sixty treated juveniles were randomly selected and then compared with the 60 juveniles with whom they had been matched prior to the coin flip. The comparisons showed few significant differences.[35] For example, treated subjects had a grade-point average of 2.83 as compared to a slightly higher grade-point average of 2.93 among untreated subjects.[36]

Measures of delinquency prevention were collected from police, court, and institutional sources.[37] Combined, they indicated that treated juveniles were no less delinquent than untreated juveniles (see Table 2.10). For example, essentially equal numbers had been to court, although on the average treated juveniles committed more court-recorded offenses than did untreated juveniles. The same applied to the 142 juveniles who received the most intensive treatment: They went to court more frequently and committed slightly more court-recorded offenses than did untreated juveniles.

Box 2.2   Experimental Evaluative Designs

The purpose of evaluation is to determine whether a project accomplished its announced goals. In the case of the Cambridge-Somerville Youth Study, the purpose of evaluation is to determine whether assignment of adult counselors to juveniles to improve school performance, personality development, and family functioning prevented juvenile delinquency.

An experimental evaluative design is an especially elegant way of determining whether a project accomplished its announced goals. An experimental design involves a control group of untreated juveniles. This makes it possible to compare the treated juveniles with the untreated juveniles and to answer questions such as: Is the treatment more effective than simply leaving the juveniles alone?

More important, experimental evaluative designs always involve random assignment procedures, such as the coin flip used in the Cambridge-Somerville Youth Study. Random assignment helps ensure that the treated and untreated groups of juveniles are equivalent at the start of a project. This pretreatment equivalency, in turn, helps ensure that any post-treatment differences between the experimental and control groups are the result of exposure to the project and not to other factors, such as simply growing older with the passage of time. No other type of evaluative design permits so much confidence in linking treatment with results, because no other type of evaluative design rules out so many alternative explanations for post-treatment differences between treated and untreated juveniles. When prevention and control projects such as the Cambridge-Somerville Youth Study are experimentally evaluated, we can be confident that differences between the experimental and control groups are the result of the experimental treatment and not some other factors.

Sources: Joan Petersilia, "Implementing Randomized Experiments: Lessons from the BJA's Intensive Supervision Project," *Evaluation Review* 13 (October 1989): 435–58; and Donald T. Campbell and Julian C. Stanley, *Experimental and Quasi-Experimental Designs for Research* (Chicago: Rand McNally, 1963).

Table 2.10   The Cambridge-Somerville Youth Study: Delinquent Behavior by Experimental and Control Juveniles as of July 1, 1948

Group	Percent That Went to Court[a]	Average Number of Offenses Committed by Those Going to Court[a]	Percent That Went to Court among 142 Most Extensively Treated Juveniles[b]	Average Number of Offenses Committed by 142 Most Extensively Treated Juveniles That Went to Court[b]
Experimental	29	2.75	42	2.85
	(96/325)	(264/96)	(60/142)	(171/60)
Control	28	2.36	34	2.52
	(92/325)	(218/92)	(48/142)	(121/48)

[a]Cases cleared through Massachusetts Commissioner of Probation as of July 1, 1948.
[b]Cases cleared through Massachusetts Commissioner of Probation as of July 1, 1948, for the 75 juveniles treated six or more years plus the 67 juveniles who received five years of treatment. Juveniles in the control group are those with whom the experimental juveniles had been matched prior to the random assignment of juveniles to the experimental and control groups.

Source: Edwin Powers and Helen Witmer, *An Experiment in the Prevention of Juvenile Delinquency: The Cambridge-Somerville Youth Study* (New York: Columbia University Press, 1951), pp. 326 and 328. Copyright © 1951 by Columbia University Press. Used by permission of the publisher.

The administrators and evaluators of the Cambridge-Somerville Youth Study drew one conclusion from the data in Table 2.10, and it serves as a useful summary of the initial measures of the results of the study: "The special work of the counselor was no more effective than the usual forces in the community in preventing boys from committing delinquent acts.[38]

Follow-up measures of the results (see Box 2.3) of the Cambridge-Somerville Youth Study were collected on two occasions. William and Joan McCord undertook the first of these follow-up measures as of December 31, 1955.[39] They found that nearly equal numbers of experimental- and control-group members had been convicted as adults of crimes against property, crimes against persons, and public drunkenness. The McCords concluded that the Cambridge-Somerville Youth Study had "failed to achieve its fundamental goal of preventing crime."[40]

Joan McCord undertook the second of these follow-up measures as of December 31, 1976.[41] Professor McCord secured the lifetime court, mental hospital, and alcoholism treatment center

---

Box 2.3   The Nature and Importance of Follow-Up Measures of Results

Follow-up measures of results are collected after initial measures of results have been assembled. For example, initial measures of the results of the Cambridge-Somerville Youth Study were assembled as of July 1, 1948. Follow-up measures of results were than collected by William and Joan McCord as of December 31, 1955, and by Joan McCord as of December 31, 1976.

Follow-up measures of results are important because they permit assessment of the stability of initial measures. They sometimes show that initial findings remain essentially unchanged with the passage of time, as was the case with the Cambridge-Somerville Youth Study. On other occasions, however, follow-up measures reveal that initial differences between experimental and control subjects "wash out," or disappear, with the passage of time. On still other occasions, follow-up measures reveal differences that were not apparent when initial measures were collected.

Sources: Peter W. Greenwood, "Promising Approaches for the Rehabilitation or Prevention of Chronic Juvenile Offenders," in Peter W. Greenwood (ed.), *Intervention Strategies for Chronic Juvenile Offenders: Some New Perspectives* (New York: Greenwood Press, 1986), pp. 222–24; and Carol Weiss, *Evaluation Research: Methods of Assessing Program Effectiveness* (Englewood Cliffs, N.J.: Prentice-Hall, 1972), pp. 31ff.

---

records of experimental- and control-group subjects. She found that 30 years after the official end of the Cambridge-Somerville Youth Study "none of the . . . measures confirmed hopes that treatment had improved the lives of those in the treatment group."[42]

REPLICATION: YOUTH CONSULTATION SERVICE

It is now possible to advance one conclusion about the Cambridge-Somerville Youth Study: It failed to prevent juvenile delinquency. What cannot be concluded on the basis of a single project is whether individual treatment is a generally ineffective method of preventing delinquency. The Cambridge-Somerville Youth Study was clearly compromised by teachers who refused to single out juveniles headed for trouble with the law and by World War II. It is entirely possible that another effort to treat individual juveniles, especially one less compromised by political and social forces, might produce more promising results.

In order to begin to advance a general conclusion, it is necessary to search for replicative confirmation (see Box 2.4) of the

---

Box 2.4   The Nature and Importance of Replication

To replicate is to repeat a previous project's treatment hypothesis in most of its essential elements. Replication is fundamental to the development of confidence in the generalizability of the results of earlier projects. As treatment hypotheses are repeated and similar results reported, we gain confidence in the general effectiveness of particular approaches to the prevention and control of juvenile delinquency.

The gain in confidence is greatest when replications do not repeat in exact detail all of the elements of a previous project. The question to be answered by searching for replicative studies is whether a treatment hypothesis implemented under a variety of circumstances is effective, not whether a project precisely repeated would have the same results. Diversity along dimensions such as location, dates, and subjects is important in assessing the general effectiveness of a particular approach to the problem of juvenile delinquency.

Additionally, previous projects have sometimes been seriously compromised by political and social forces. When this is the case, it is difficult to decide whether the treatment hypothesis or the compromises forced on the project explain its results. Replication is an opportunity to examine a treatment hypothesis under different political and social conditions and clarify the effectiveness of a particular approach to the prevention or control of juvenile delinquency.

Sources: William S. Davidson II, Robin Redner, Richard L. Amdur, and Christina M. Mitchell, *Alternative Treatments for Troubled Youth: The Case of Diversion from the Justice System* (New York: Plenum, 1990), pp. 103–21; and Norman K. Denzin, *The Research Act: A Theoretical Introduction to Sociological Methods* (Chicago: Aldine, 1970), pp. 32–33.

results of any particular project. Replication increases confidence in the generalizability of results by prying prevention and control hypotheses from the limits of location, time, and clients. Only with replication is it possible to be more confident that individual treatment is ineffective in places other than Cambridge-Somerville, during times other than 1937 to 1945, and with subjects other than white, working-class males.

The Cambridge-Somerville Youth Study's individual-treatment approach to the prevention of juvenile delinquency has been replicated on numerous occasions. Table 2.11 summarizes the major features of one of the most important of these replications, Youth Consultation Service,[43] a project that resembled the Cambridge-Somerville Youth Study in several important respects. School records were used to identify adolescents believed headed for trouble with the law. Once identified, juveniles were randomly assigned to experimental and control groups, and experimental juveniles were provided treatment services by professionally trained social workers.

However, Youth Consultation Service clearly differed from the Cambridge-Somerville Youth Study in several important respects. Youth Consultation Service was located in New York City, it began in 1955, and it involved young women, most of whom were African-American or Puerto Rican. These differences draw attention to the purpose of replication. The question to be answered is whether a delinquency prevention or control strategy implemented in different settings, at different times, and with different clients is effective. Clear differences in locations, dates, and subjects are desirable because the purpose of replicative analysis is to establish the general effectiveness of an approach to the prevention or control of delinquency.

The persons charged with measuring the results of Youth Consultation Service reported findings essentially similar to those advanced in the wake of the Cambridge-Somerville Youth Study: "No strong indications of effect are found and the conclusion must be stated in the negative when it is asked whether social work intervention with potential problem high school girls was in this instance effective."[44] As was true of the Cambridge-Somerville Youth Study, Youth Consultation Service also failed to prevent delinquency.

Table 2.11   Description of Youth Consultation Service

Project Name:	Youth Consultation Service ("Girls at Vocational High")
Location:	A vocational high school in New York City
Dates:	Fall 1955 to Spring 1960
Subjects:	Four successive cohorts of tenth-grade female students with "potential problems" as contained and identified in school records. Information taken as indicative of future problems included unsatisfactory student-teacher relations, difficulty with peers, evidence of formal disciplinary actions, absenteeism, unusual behaviors such as extreme shyness, and truancy. The total number of juveniles involved was 381. Three-quarters were African-American or Puerto Rican and the vast majority (89 percent) were from blue-collar backgrounds. Age at the start of the project for most of the young women was 15.
Type of treatment:	Potential problem cases were referred to a social work agency for group treatment by professionally trained social workers. The primary focus of the group was "on the individual member and her adjustment." Clients participated in one of three general types of groups: (1) family life groups concentrated on strengthening the family; (2) interview treatment groups helped clients experiencing "severe" conflict with parents or siblings; and (3) protective groups helped clients who functioned well but came from severely deprived family backgrounds. In all groups the topics discussed included sexual problems, acts of violence such as suicide and gang fights, and search for personal values.
Amount of treatment:	Treatment was available for the experimental subjects for an entire school year. Almost all (95 percent) received some treatment, one-half had 17 or more treatment contacts with the social workers, and 44 percent had more than 20 treatment contacts.
Evaluative design:	Experimental: Juveniles were randomly assigned to the treated and untreated groups.
Measures of results:	Initial measures of the results of the project were collected at the conclusion of each cohort's school year. Follow-up measures were collected to the normal point of high school graduation for each treatment cohort.

Source: Henry J. Meyer, Edgar F. Borgatta, and Wyatt C. Jones, in collaboration with Elizabeth P. Anderson, Hanna Grunwald, and Dorothy Headley, *Girls at Vocational High: An Experiment in Social Work Intervention* (New York: Russell Sage Foundation, 1965).

SUMMARY AND CONCLUSIONS

This chapter probed the usefulness of the individual-treatment approach to the prevention of juvenile delinquency. It began by examining attempts to identify juveniles headed for trouble with the law. Attention was then directed to the Cambridge-Somerville

Box 2.5   Other Assessments of the Individual Treatment Approach

Failure to prevent juvenile delinquency by treating individual juveniles is not limited to the projects examined in this chapter. Other assessments of the individual-treatment approach have reached the same conclusion. In the mid-1970s, for example, Jerry P. Walker, Albert P. Cardarelli, and Dennis L. Billingsley carefully examined 31 delinquency prevention projects, many of which involved individual treatment. They concluded that the "picture of delinquency prevention programs nationally is, with few promising but unproven exceptions, necessarily dismal. Generally speaking, prevention programs are ill conceived, poorly structured, and suffering from a lack of conceptual, definitional, and operational clarity in virtually all major aspects."

In 1981, Barry Krisberg's *National Evaluation of Delinquency Prevention* was published. Dr. Krisberg examined over 100 prevention programs in 68 cities. He concluded that "regardless of . . . type . . . of programs or intervention techniques . . . there is little positive evidence that they are effective in preventing delinquency."

More recently, "meta-analysis" of prevention and control projects reached precisely the same conclusion. John T. Whitehead and Steven P. Lab focused on well-designed projects and generated common measures of results—two of the distinguishing features of meta-analysis. They observed that their results "differ little from other reviews of the literature. . . . treatment has little effect." So too with the meta-analysis by William S. Davidson II and colleagues: "no overall evidence exists for the efficacy of current interventions."

Sources: Jerry P. Walker, Albert P. Cardarelli, and Dennis L. Billingsley, *The Theory and Practice of Delinquency Prevention in the United States: Review, Synthesis and Assessment* (Columbus, Ohio: Evaluation Division, Center for Vocational Education, The Ohio State University, January 1976), p. 207; Barry Krisberg, *The National Evaluation of Delinquency Prevention: Final Report* (San Francisco: Research Center, National Council on Crime and Delinquency, September 1981), p. 529; John T. Whitehead and Steven P. Lab, "A Meta-Analysis of Juvenile Correctional Treatment," *Journal of Research in Crime and Delinquency* 26 (August 1989), p. 291; and William S. Davidson II, Robin Redner, Richard L. Amdur, and Christina M. Mitchell, *Alternative Treatments for Troubled Youth: The Case of Diversion from the Justice System* (New York: Plenum, 1990), p. 36.

Youth Study, the single best-known example of an effort to prevent delinquency by treating individual juveniles. Last, a review of a replication of the Cambridge-Somerville Youth Study was undertaken.

The studies examined in this chapter cast grave doubts on the usefulness of the individual-treatment approach in the prevention of juvenile delinquency. Examination of the MMPI and the Glueck Social Prediction Table revealed that attempts to predict delinquency are inaccurate one-half to two-thirds of the time. Review of the Cambridge-Somerville Youth Study and Youth Consultation Service showed that both efforts failed to prevent delinquency.

Failure to prevent delinquency is not confined to the projects examined in this chapter (see Box 2.5). Robert Martinson and colleagues examined a relatively large number of similar projects and reported that it was highly unlikely that any had prevented delinquency.[45] Michael C. Dixon and William E. Wright also reviewed the results of a large number of projects and their conclusion serves as a useful summary of efforts to prevent delinquency by treating individual juveniles. Individual treatment, Professors Dixon and Wright concluded, "has not . . . proven effective."[46]

NOTES

1. Margo Horn, "Gee, Officer Krupke, What Are We to Do? The Politics of Professions and the Prevention of Delinquency, 1909-1940," *Research in Law, Deviance, and Social Control* 8 (Fall 1986): 57-81.

2. For a brief description of Healy and his work, see James R. Bennett, "Introduction," in Anthony Sorrentino, *Organizing Against Crime* (New York: Human Sciences Press, 1977), pp. 9-29. For an early statement of Healy's largely individualistic approach to the problem of juvenile delinquency, see William Healy, *The Individual Delinquent: A Text-Book of Diagnosis and Prognosis for All Concerned in Understanding Offenders* (Boston: Little, Brown, 1915). For a similar and equally individualistic statement from about the same time period, see Thomas Travis, *The Young Malefactor: A Study in Juvenile Delinquency, Its Causes and Treatment* (New York: Thomas Y. Crowell, 1908).

3. Barry Krisberg and James Austin, *The Children of Ishmael: Critical Perspectives on Juvenile Justice* (Palo Alto, Calif.: Mayfield, 1978), p. 29.

4. Ibid., p. 29.

5. Healy, *The Individual Delinquent.*

6. Ibid., p. 34.

7. See especially ibid., pp. 166–82.

8. Description of the MMPI is based on Patricia King, Ellison Good, and John P. Brantner, *A Practical Guide to the MMPI: An Introduction for Psychologists, Physicians, Social Workers, and Other Professionals* (Minneapolis, Minn.: The University of Minnesota Press, 1974); Starke R. Hathaway and Elio D. Monachesi, *Adolescent Personality and Behavior: MMPI Patterns of Normal, Delinquent, Dropout, and Other Outcomes* (Minneapolis: the University of Minnesota Press, 1963); and Starke R. Hathaway and Elio D. Monachesi, "The Personalities of Predelinquent Boys," *Journal of Criminal Law, Criminology and Police Science* 48 (July–August 1957): 149–63.

9. This discussion is based on Hathaway and Monachesi, "The Personalities."

10. This includes only those juveniles with valid and determinate MMPI profiles. See ibid.

11. Ibid.

12. Hathaway and Monachesi, *Adolescent Personality*, p. 99.

13. Discussion of the Glueck Social Prediction Table is based on Sheldon Glueck and Eleanor Glueck, *Unraveling Juvenile Delinquency* (New York: The Commonwealth Fund, 1950); Sheldon Glueck and Eleanor Glueck, *Predicting Delinquency and Crime* (Cambridge, Mass.: Harvard University Press, 1959); Ralph Whelen, "An Experiment in Predicting Delinquency," *Journal of Criminal Law, Criminology and Police Science* 45 (September–October 1954): 432–41; Maude M. Craig and Selma Glick, "Ten Years Experience with the Glueck Prediction Table." *Crime and Delinquency* 9 (July 1963):249–61; and Jackson Toby, "An Evaluatiuon of Early Identification and Intensive Treatment Programs for Predelinquents," *Social Problems* 13 (Fall 1965): 160–75.

14. Glueck and Glueck, *Unraveling Juvenile Delinquency*, p. ix.

15. Ibid., p. 257.

16. In ibid., p. 261, a "weighted failure score" of 71.8 was assigned male juveniles disciplined by their fathers in an "overstrict or erratic" manner. In Glueck and Glueck, *Predicting Delinquency and Crime*, pp. 118 and 233, a weighted failure score of 72.5 was assigned male juveniles disciplined by their father in an overstrict or erratic manner. There is no explanation for this discrepancy. I used the weighted failure score appearing in *Unraveling Juvenile Delinquency*, p. 261, on the assumption that it was the one the Gluecks intended to advance in *Predicting Delinquency and Crime*. This is the reason the weighted failure score appears in brackets.

17. Glueck and Glueck, *Predicting Delinquency and Crime*, pp. 118-19.

18. Ibid., p. 127.

19. See Whelen, "An Experiment"; Craig and Glick, "Ten Years Experience"; and Toby, "An Evaluation."

20. Craig and Glick, "Ten Years Experience"; Walter C. Reckless, *The Crime Problem*, 5th ed. (New York: Appleton-Century-Crofts, 1973), p. 694.

21. Donna Martin Hamparian et al., *The Violent Few: A Study of Dangerous Juvenile Offenders* (Lexington, Mass.: Lexington Books, 1978), pp. 54-55 and 133-35; Brent B. Benda, "Predicting Juvenile Recidivism: New Method, Old Problem," *Adolescence* 32 (Fall 1987): 691-704; Emmy E. Werner, "Vulnerability and Resiliency in Children at Risk for Delinquency: A Longitudinal Study from Birth to Young Adulthood," in John D. Burchard and Sara N. Burchard (eds.), *Prevention of Delinquent Behavior* (Newbury Park, Calif.: Sage, 1987), pp. 16-43; George Spivack and Norma Cianci, "High-Risk Early Behavior and Later Delinquency," in Burchard and Burchard, *Prevention*, pp. 44-74; Rolf Loeber and Thomas J. Dishion, "Antisocial and Delinquent Youths: Methods for Their Early Identification," in Burchard and Burchard, *Prevention*, pp. 75-89; Delbert S. Elliot, Franklyn W. Dunford, and David Huizinga, "The Identification and Prediction of Career Offenders Utilizing Self-Reported and Official Data," in Burchard and Burchard, *Prevention*, pp. 90-121; and Peter W. Greenwood, "Predictors of Chronic Criminal Behavior," in Peter W. Greenwood (ed.), *Intervention Strategies for Chronic Juvenile Offenders: Some New Perspectives* (New York: Greenwood Press, 1987), pp. 75-89.

22. Description fo the Cambridge-Somerville Youth Study is based on Edwin Powers and Helen Witmer, *An Experiment in the Prevention of Delinquency: The Cambridge-Somerville Youth Study* (New York: Columbia University Press, 1951); and William McCord and Joan McCord, with Irving Kenneth Zola, *Origins of Crime: A New Evaluation of the Cambridge-Somerville Youth Study* (New York: Columbia University Press, 1959).

23. LaMar T. Empey and Mark C. Stafford, *American Delinquency: Its Meaning and Construction*, 3rd. ed. (Belmont, Calif.: Wadsworth, 1991), p. 375.

24. For description of delinquency and rates of delinquency in Cambridge and Somerville 1927-1930, see Clifford R. Shaw and Henry D. McKay, *Juvenile Delinquency and Urban Areas: A Study of Rates of Delinquency in Relation to Differential Characteristics of Local Communities in American Cities*, rev. ed. (Chicago: The University of Chicago Press, 1969), pp. 223-54.

25. Powers and Witmer, *An Experiment*, p. 30.

26. Ibid., p. 31.

27. Ibid., p. 79.

28. Ibid., pp. 102–10.

29. For an analysis of the effects of foster-home placements made during the Cambridge-Somerville Youth Study, see Joan McCord, William McCord, and Emily Thurber, "The Effects of Foster-Home Placement in the Prevention of Adult Antisocial Behavior," *Social Service Review* 34 (December 1960): 415–20.

30. Powers and Witmer, *An Experiment*, p. 115.

31. Ibid., p. 99.

32. Ibid., p. 125.

33. Ibid., p. 138.

34. Ibid., p. 65.

35. Ibid., pp. 293–307.

36. Additional measures of school performance, personality development, and family functioning were collected at the end of 1943 with precisely the same results. See Powers and Witmer, *An Experiment*, pp. 307–09.

37. Powers and Witmer, *An Experiment*, pp. 323–38.

38. Ibid., p. 337.

39. McCord and McCord, *Origins*, pp. 1–61.

40. Ibid., p. 61.

41. Joan McCord, "A Thirty-Year Follow-Up of Treatment Effects," *American Psychologist* 33 (March 1978): 284–89. For a highly critical and, in my opinion, largely misguided assessment of Professor McCord's follow-up, see William W. Vosburgh and Leslie B. Alexander, "Long-Term Follow-Up as Program Evaluation: Lessons from McCord's 30-Year Follow-Up of the Cambridge-Somerville Youth Study," *American Journal of Orthopsychiatry* 50 (January 1980): 109–24.

42. McCord, "A Thirty-Year Follow-Up," p. 288. For additional follow-ups of the Cambridge-Somerville Youth Study by Professor McCord, see Joan McCord, "Alcoholism and Criminality: Confounding and Differentiating Factors," *Journal of Studies on Alcohol* 42 (September 1981): 739–48; Joan McCord, "A Forty-Year Perspective on Effects of Child Abuse and Neglect," *Child-Abuse and Neglect* 7 (Summer 1983): 265–70; Joan McCord, "Drunken Drivers in Longitudinal Perspective," *Journal of Studies on Alcohol* 45 (July 1984): 316–20; Joan McCord, "Identifying Developmental Paradigms Leading to Alcoholism," *Journal of Studies on Alcohol* 49 (July 1988): 357–62; Joan McCord, "Parental Behavior in the Cycle of Aggression," *Psychiatry* 51 (February 1988): 14–23; Joan McCord, "Alcoholism: Toward Understanding Genetic and Social Factors," *Psychiatry* 51 (May 1988): 131–41.

43. Henry J. Meyer, Edgar F. Borgatta, Wyatt C. Jones, in collabora-

tion with Elizabeth P. Anderson, Hanna Grunwald, and Dorothy Headley, *Girls at Vocational High: An Experiment in Social Work Intervention* (New York: Russell Sage Foundation, 1965).

44. Ibid., p. 180.

45. Robert Martinson, "What Works? Questions and Answers About Prison Reform," *The Public Interest* 35 (Spring 1974): 22-54. Also see Douglas Lipton, Robert Martinson, and Judith Wilks, *The Effectiveness of Correctional Treatment: A Survey of Treatment Evaluation Studies* (New York: Praeger, 1975).

46. Michael C. Dixon and William E. Wright, *Juvenile Delinquency Prevention Programs: An Evaluation of Policy-Related Research on the Effectiveness of Prevention Programs* (Washington, D.C.: National Science Foundation, 1975), p. 18. Also see William E. Wright and Michael C. Dixon, "Community Prevention and Treatment of Delinquency," *Journal of Research in Crime and Delinquency* 14 (January 1978): 35-67.

3

AREA PROJECTS

This chapter examines the effectiveness of area projects in the prevention of juvenile delinquency. It begins by establishing the theoretical origins of the area-project approach to the prevention of delinquency. Attention is then directed to the Chicago Area Project, the single best-known attempt to prevent delinquency by changing areas of the city. Last, a review of a replication of the Chicago Area Project is undertaken.

THEORETICAL ORIGINS

During the early part of the 1900s, the Department of Sociology at the University of Chicago was the leading sociology department in the United States.[1] Its faculty included many of the best-known representatives of the then new discipline of sociology. Its graduate students went on to establish themselves and the "Chicago School of Sociology" at a variety of prestigious universities and colleges.

Also during the early part of this century, the state of Illinois started the Institute for Juvenile Research and, as part of the Institute, a Department of Research Sociology. Clifford R. Shaw was head of this department, and Henry D. McKay was one of Shaw's early associates. Close professional and friendship ties linked sociologists at the University of Chicago and the Institute for Juvenile Research. Clifford Shaw and Henry McKay had been sociology graduate students at the University of Chicago,[2] and when they left graduate school to work at the Institute for Juvenile Research, they maintained close contact with their former faculty mentors. In addition, sociologists at the University of Chicago routinely sent their graduate students to work with and learn from Shaw and McKay.

These close linkages helped produce a remarkable series of studies of the ecology and origins of urban delinquency. Shaw and McKay first established the ecology of urban delinquency by mapping patterns of adolescent crime in Chicago. They then collected life histories from young adults who previously had engaged in delinquent behavior as youthful residents of high-delinquency areas. Ultimately, Shaw and McKay used these materials to advance a clear theoretical explanation of the origins of urban delinquency.

THE ECOLOGY OF URBAN DELINQUENCY

The animating assumption of the sociologists at the Institute for Juvenile Research and at the University of Chicago was that city neighborhoods shape the behavior and beliefs of local residents.[3] Particular neighborhoods, especially when they are ethnically or racially homogeneous, develop distinctive values and traditions that are passed from generation to generation, from established resident to newcomer, and from older to younger juveniles. On occasion these values and traditions are supportive of criminal deviance.

The sociologist's first task was to identify high-delinquency neighborhoods. In Clifford Shaw's words: "The study of such a problem as juvenile delinquency necessarily begins with a study of its geographic location. This first step reveals the areas in which delinquency occurs most frequently, and therefore marks off the communities which should be studied intensively for the factors related to delinquent behavior."[4]

As reported in 1929 in their book *Delinquency Areas: A Study of the Geographic Distribution of School Truants, Juvenile Delinquents, and Adult Offenders in Chicago*,[5] Shaw and McKay used school and court information to plot the home residences of truants, delinquents, and adult offenders on maps of the city of Chicago. Figure 3.1 is one of Shaw and McKay's "rate maps." Examination reveals that in certain areas of the city large num-

FIGURE 3.1 "Rate map": rate per 100 male juveniles brought to the attention of police in 1926 by areas of Chicago

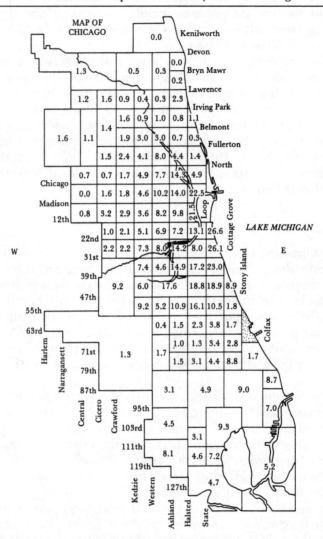

bers of juveniles had been brought to the attention of police. In other areas of the city many fewer juveniles had experienced police contact. In the area directly west of Chicago's downtown, or Loop, for example, 21.5 of every 100 adolescent males had come to the attention of police in 1926. By contrast, in the area in the far northwest side of the city, the rate was only about 1 of every 100 male juveniles.

Shaw and McKay did not limit their data to 1926 or to the delinquent actions solely of males. They also mapped delinquency rates from as early as 1900 and for females as well as males. The various maps, however, contained basically the same information: "There are marked variations . . . between areas in Chicago. Some areas are characterized by very high rates, while other areas show very low rates. These differences are seen in all of the . . . [maps] . . . studied. . . . "[6]

Shaw and McKay then turned their attention to describing the origins of urban delinquency (see Figure 3.2). They noted that high-delinquency areas generally were located in neighborhoods experiencing "invasion" by business and industry. High-delinquency areas also contained large number of European immigrants or African-American inmigrants. Neighborhood adults generally came from rural environments far different from the intensely urban life they were living, worked long hours at

FIGURE 3.2   Diagrammatic representation of Shaw and McKay's description of the origins of urban delinquency

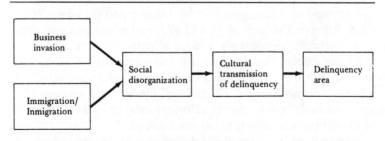

Source: Clifford R. Shaw, Frederick M. Zorbaugh, Henry D. McKay, and Leonard S. Cottrell, *Delinquency Areas: A Study of the Geographic Distribution of School Truants, Juvenile Delinquents, and Adult Offenders in Chicago* (Chicago: The University of Chicago Press, 1929), pp. 205–06.

dehumanizing jobs, and had little time to parent their children. In such socially disorganized environments,[7] children escaped the control of weary adults to participate in the delinquent street life of their neighborhoods. In these ways, Shaw and McKay reasoned, neighborhoods became high-delinquency areas.

LIFE HISTORIES

Having advanced a tentative description of the origins of urban delinquency, Shaw and McKay were quick to note that their description should be empirically assessed using techniques such as "detailed case studies of individual delinquents."[8] These individual case studies, or life histories (see Box 3.1), as they came to be called, were among the research interests of Shaw and McKay in the years immediately following their initial analysis of the ecology of urban delinquency.

Shaw, McKay, and other sociologists at the Institute for Juvenile Research secured over 200[9] life histories from young adults who previously had engaged in delinquent behavior as youthful residents of high-delinquency areas. A minority of these life histories were published, including *The Jack-Roller* (1930),[10] *The Natural History of a Delinquent Career* (1931),[11] and *Brothers in Crime* (1938).[12] Of the three, *The Jack-Roller* was the first and has become the best known.

The Jack-Roller is "Stanley's" life history.[13] Stanley was first arrested in 1914 at the age of 6 for sleeping under a doorstep. By age 8 Stanley had been arrested nine more times, primarily for truancy and running away. During the next three years, Stanley was arrested 16 times, generally for truancy and occasionally for theft. Between the ages of 11 and 17, Stanley was arrested eight times for such increasingly serious offenses as "jack-rolling"— clubbing public drunkenness offenders and then taking their money. Although Stanley was not convicted or incarcerated following every arrest, he did spend 5 of the 11 years between 1914 and 1924 in detention centers, reformatories, and, toward the end of his delinquent career, penal institutions.

Stanley lived in a high-delinquency area of the city of Chicago known as the "Back of the Yards." Clifford Shaw described Stanley's neighborhood as: "One of the grimiest and most unat-

---

Box 3.1   The Life History

A life history is a person's own story written at the request and with the guidance of a sociologist. The sociologist selects a particular individual, generally because that person is available, is somewhat representative of the type of people the sociologist is interested in learning more about, and is capable of preparing a written life history. The sociologist secures an objective description of the individual's life including places of residence, family structure, arrests, and incarcerations. The individual is then asked to describe his or her life as it relates to the information collected by the sociologist and in response to questions posed by the sociologist. The sociologist and individual then discuss and edit the life history with the individual adding and deleting sections in response to the suggestions and questions of the sociologist. The end result is a document that in large part is a person's own story.

Sources: James F. Short, Jr., "Life History, Autobiography, and the Life Cycle," in The Jack-Roller and Jon Snodgrass, with Gilbert Geis, James F. Short, Jr., and Solomon Kobrin, *The Jack-Roller at Seventy: A Fifty-Year Follow-Up* (Lexington, Mass.: Lexington Books, 1982), pp. 135–52; Solomon Kobrin, "The Uses of the Life-History Document for the Development of Delinquency Theory," in The Jack-Roller et al., *The Jack-Roller at Seventy: A Fifty-Year Follow-Up* (Lexington, Mass.: Lexington Books, 1982), pp. 153–65; and Howard S. Becker, "Introduction," in Clifford R. Shaw, *The Jack-Roller* (1930; reprint, Chicago: The University of Chicago Press, 1966), pp. v–xviii.

---

tractive neighborhoods in the city, being almost completely surrounded by packing plants, stock yards, railroads, factories and waste lands. The life in the neighborhood is largely dominated by, and economically dependent upon, the larger industrial community of which it is a part. The population is composed largely of families of unskilled laborers, most of whom depend upon the stock yards and local industries for employment. The air in the neighborhood is smoky and always filled with a disagreeable odor from the stock yards."[14]

Stanley's mother and father were born in rural Poland. They immigrated to the United States as young adults essentially unprepared for the harshly urban conditions characteristic of their Back of the Yards neighborhood. They spoke little English because nearly all of their neighbors also had immigrated to urban Chicago from rural Poland.

Stanley's neighborhood was characterized by what Shaw and McKay believed was social disorganization. Because it was not a pleasant place in which to live, only the poorest of immigrant families lived Back of the Yards, and most moved as soon as they were able. Parents worked long hours in nearby stockyards and packing plants and raised large families—Stanley was one of 15 children. There were few opportunities to develop a sense of community and precious little time for children.

Driven from a home that weary and confused parents could not make pleasant, Stanley escaped to sidewalks, streets, and gangways rich in delinquent traditions. Stanley wrote of the streets and the delinquent friends he made: "The life in the streets and alleys became fascinating and enticing. I had two close companions that I looked up to with childish admiration and awe. . . . They were close friends, four years older than me and well versed in the art of stealing."[15]

A CLEAR THEORETICAL EXPLANATION

Although *The Jack-Roller* provided strong support for Shaw and McKay's description of the origins of urban delinquency, there remained three troublesome issues. First, their findings were limited to the years 1900–1926, a period of intense European immigration and African-American inmigration from the rural South to the urban North. This raised the possibility that as immigration and inmigration decreased, delinquency areas would disappear. Second, their data were confined to Chicago, and there was no method of determining whether similar patterns existed in other cities. Most important, there was no clear theoretical explanation of why delinquent traditions emerged in socially disorganized neighborhoods.

Shaw and McKay addressed all three issues in their 1942 book *Juvenile Delinquency and Urban Areas*.[16] First, they updated their analysis of the ecology of urban delinquency in Chicago by providing comparable data through 1940. Using rate and other maps, Shaw and McKay demonstrated that high- and low-delinquency areas could still be easily identified even though immigration had significantly decreased.

Second, *Juvenile Delinquency and Urban Areas* examined the ecology of urban delinquency in 22 other cities and reported patterns similar to those first reported for Chicago.[17] All of the cities had distinctive high- and low-delinquency areas, with the former characterized by business invasion, foreign-born or African-American residents, and evidence of what Shaw and McKay had termed social disorganization.

Most important, *Juvenile Delinquency and Urban Areas* clearly explained the emergence of criminal and delinquent traditions in socially disorganized neighborhoods. Shaw and McKay noted that residents of socially disorganized neighborhoods lacked easy access to conventional means of reaching important cultural goals. Frustrated in their efforts to reach those goals using legitimate means, the urban poor turned to crime in an effort to obtain the money and property their low-paying jobs could not provide. Shaw and McKay explained that crime "may be regarded as one of the means employed by people to acquire, or attempt to acquire, the economic and social values generally idealized in our culture, which persons in other circumstances acquire by conventional means."[18]

SUMMARY OF THEORETICAL ORIGINS

Sociologists at the Illinois Institute for Juvenile Research and the University of Chicago, especially Clifford R. Shaw and Henry D. McKay, contributed a great deal to the search for the origins of urban delinquency. They carefully plotted rates of delinquency by area of the city, secured hundreds of life histories, and extended their work to other cities. Ultimately, they explained the emergence of delinquent and criminal traditions in socially disorganized neighborhoods.

Equally important, Shaw and McKay established the logic of the area-project approach to the prevention of juvenile delinquency. They observed that "reduction in the volume of delinquency in large cities probably will not occur except as general changes take place which effect improvements in the economic and social conditions surrounding children in those areas in which delinquency rates are relatively high."[19]

THE CHICAGO AREA PROJECT

The Chicago Area Project[20] was a continuation of the efforts of Clifford Shaw and, to a much lesser extent, Henry McKay. Having explained the origins of urban delinquency, Shaw set about the task of attempting to prevent delinquency by stimulating development of neighborhood self-help community committees. The Chicago Area Project was thus a nobly intended effort to give the inner-city poor control over their lives. However, the Chicago Area Project also has never been adequately assessed. Table 3.1 summarizes the major features of this important project and serves as a guide for the description and analysis that follow.

Description of the Project

The Chicago Area Project began in three white, ethnically homogeneous neighborhoods in 1932. The "Near North" and "Near West" area projects were located directly north and directly west of Chicago's central business district, or Loop.[21] Both were high-delinquency areas, having recorded the seventh and sixth highest rates of court appearances for male adolescents in Chicago during the years 1927–1933.[22] Near North and Near West also were in the top 7 percent in rates of male school truancy (1927–1933), infant mortality (1928–1933), tuberculosis (1931–1937), and mental illness (1922–1934).[23] The predominant nationality of family heads in both areas in 1930 was Italian-American.[24]

The third of the initial area projects was carried out in Russell Square on Chicago's southeast side. Russell Square abuts Lake Michigan on the east and was a heavily industrialized area consisting primarily of steel mills and railroad operations. However, as compared to the Near North and Near West areas, Russell Square had a lower delinquency rate: It had the 48th highest delinquency rate in the city of Chicago during the years 1927–1933.[25] Russell Square occupied essentially similar positions in rates of school truancy, tuberculosis, and mental illness.[26] The only exception to this pattern was in the rate of infant mortality. Portions of Russell Square were in the top 9 percent in the rate of infant mortality.[27] The predominant nationality of family heads in Russell Square in 1930 was Polish-American.[28]

Table 3.1   Description of the Chicago Area Project

Project Name:	The Chicago Area Project
Location:	Chicago, Illinois
Dates:	1932 to early 1960s
Subjects:	The focus of project efforts was neighborhoods rather than individual juveniles. The areas chosen for attention were generally high-delinquency areas as measured by arrests, court appearances, and commitments to juvenile institutions. The project neighborhoods also generally displayed high rates of school truancy, infant mortality, tuberculosis, and mental illness. In addition, the heads of families in most cases were foreign born or African-American.
Type of treatment:	Chicago Area Project staff members organized local self-help community committees consisting of existing community groups, such as churches and labor unions, as well as indigenous community leaders. The community committees then recruited large numbers of local adults. Although committee activities varied considerably dependent upon the neighborhood in question, most launched three major types of activities: (1) a standard recreational program for area youth; (2) community improvement campaigns that focused on sanitation, health care services, and education; and (3) the assignment of local adults as detached workers to neighborhood gangs.
Amount of treatment:	In each neighborhood the area project staff consisted of a full-time director, recruited from the local community, and one full-time detached gang worker, also recruited from the local community. Added were large numbers of adult volunteers who did most of the work.
Evaluative design:	Although Shaw and McKay were in a position to evaluate the Chicago Area Project quasi-experimentally, they undertook no visible evaluative efforts.
Measures of results:	Although McKay continued to collect the police arrest data that would permit assessment of the results of the Chicago Area Project, the only materials thus far released consist of the subjective assessments of those associated with the project.
Replication:	Because the Chicago Area Project was unique in both its philosophy and its operation, there is no easily identified replication. However, several projects constitute partial replications. One of the most important is the Midcity Project carried out in Boston in the mid-1950s.

Sources: Harold Finestone, *Victims of Change* (Westport, Conn.: Greenwood Press, 1976), pp. 116–50; James F. Short, Jr., "Introduction," Clifford R. shaw and Henry D. McKay, *Juvenile Delinquency and Urban Areas*, rev. ed. (Chicago: The University of Chicago Press, 1969), pp. xlvi–liv; Anthony Sorrentino, *Organizing Against Crime: Redeveloping the Neighborhood* (New York: Human Sciences Press, 1977); and Southside Community Committee, *Bright Shadows in Bronzetown* (Chicago: Southside Community Committee, 1949).

Throughout the years, other area projects were launched. In the 1940s, for example, projects were begun in African-American southside neighborhoods.[29] However, Near North, Near West, and Russell Square were the first and they lasted the longest.[30] The Near North and Russell Square projects operated for nearly 30 years and were abandoned in the early 1960s.[31] The Near West project was closed at about the same time that its land was taken by the Chicago Circle Campus of the University of Illinois.[32] Primary attention will therefore be directed at the efforts and accomplishments of the Near North, Near West, and Russell Square area projects.

Type of Treatment

The Chicago Area Project's goal was to prevent juvenile delinquency. The treatment hypothesis was that organization of local self-help community committees concerned with recreational programs, neighborhood improvement campaigns, and area youth gangs would prevent involvement in delinquency (see Figure 3.3).

The sequence of treatment activities began with visits by Clifford Shaw to high-delinquency areas to meet with small groups

FIGURE 3.3   The Chicago Area Project's treatment hypothesis in diagrammatic form

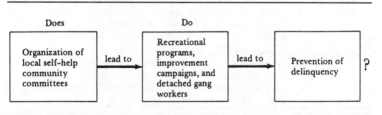

Sources: The treatment hypothesis is based on description of the Chicago Area Project in Harold Finestone, *Victims of Change* (Westport, Conn.: Greenwood Press, 1976), pp. 116–50; Clifford R. Shaw and Henry D. McKay, *Juvenile Delinquency and Urban Areas*, rev. ed. (Chicago: The University of Chicago Press, 1969), pp. xivi–liv; Anthony Sorrentino, *Organizing Against Crime* (New York: Human Sciences Press, 1977); and Southside Community Committee, *Bright Shadows in Bronzetown* (Chicago: Southside Community Committee, 1949).

of community leaders. Shaw told these groups what he and McKay had found as a result of their analyses of the ecology and origins of urban delinquency. Anthony Sorrentino, a youthful resident of Near West, recalls Shaw's visit and message: "Our first introduction to . . . [the Chicago Area Project] . . . was one Sunday afternoon when Clifford Shaw spoke to our group at a meeting at Hull House. He first spoke about the problems of delinquency, presenting some of his findings from *Delinquency Areas*. He indicated that the earlier immigrant groups in the city had high rates of delinquency which tended to go down as these groups improved their social and economic position. He stated that although the rates of delinquency and crime were high among Italians, in time they too would decrease. . . . His views were refreshing, since we Italians were then being stigmatized by the public and the press. For some time we have been hoping that we could do something to improve the reputation of our area."[33]

Residents of the African-American neighborhoods organized by Shaw in the early 1940s heard much the same message. Shaw told them that delinquency "results from the conditions that obtain in the community rather than from any inherent delinquency producing qualities in the population. . . . The greater volume of delinquency in low-income areas may be regarded as a symptom of the conditions of life surrounding children, and not as evidence of any inferiority or peculiarity in the children or their parents."[34]

Shaw then suggested that "the methods now employed for treating boys already delinquent do not yield the results desired."[35] These methods concentrated attention on individual juveniles after they were already in trouble with the law and ignored the role of the community in the origins of delinquency. Individual juveniles, Shaw argued, were the symptom rather than the cause.

Shaw went on to state that local self-help community organizations were needed to improve neighborhood life. Shaw explained that all communities had the resources and skills necessary to bring about meaningful change, asserted that leadership was present but dormant, and proposed the formation of community committees. One resident of the Near West area recalled that Shaw "talked about the importance of self-help, expressing great faith in the ability of our people to solve their problems if they would band together and work cooperatively. . . ."[36] Shaw then promised that the Chicago Area Project would provide community workers to help organize neighborhoods, and limited financial assistance if initial organizational efforts proved successful. He noted, however, that responsibility for the continued viability and operation of the community committees would rest in the hands of the people. The Chicago Area Project would serve only as a catalyst.

From these meetings there slowly emerged broadly based self-help community committees.[37] The community workers assigned to neighborhoods by Shaw contacted existing organizations, such as local businesses, labor unions, and churches, to solicit financial support and promises of cooperation. Local adults were urged to join community committees, elect committee leaders, and initiate fund-raising activities, such as dances and raffles. The funds raised were then used to hire the indigenous detached gang workers who were assigned to neighborhood youth gangs, refurbish rented storefront community centers, and buy the sports equipment used in the recreational programs run by adult volunteers. As a result of efforts such as these, relatively large numbers of residents[38] became involved in self-help activities stimulated by Clifford Shaw's successful efforts at community organization (see Box 3.2).

Once community committees were formed they generally did three things.[39] First, they sponsored a standard recreation program for area children using existing but underutilized neighborhood park facilities. Several of the community committees also built summer camps outside the city and sponsored extensive summer camping programs for neighborhood juveniles.

Second, community committees sponsored vitally needed community improvement campaigns. The areas selected for attention suffered from a variety of problems including high infant mortality and crime rates. Attention was therefore directed to improving or making available health care, sanitation, and law enforcement services to local residents.

Third, community committees engaged in specific activities intended to prevent and control juvenile delinquency. Most important, indigenous detached gang workers were assigned to neighborhood youth gangs. Gang workers, staff members, and adult volunteers also acted as advocates for neighborhood juve-

---

Box 3.2 Clifford Shaw's Success as a Community Organizer

The reasons for Clifford Shaw's success as a community organizer require brief explanation. Clifford Shaw was a charismatic figure sincerely troubled by the problems of delinquency and convinced that local residents of all communities could be organized for purposes of community improvement. He firmly believed that people could be motivated to help themselves and especially their children. Additionally, Shaw brought residents of the local communities an appealing message. Popular theories of crime emphasized the criminal inclinations of particular ethnic or racial groups. Shaw explained that all immigrant and inmigrant groups experienced high rates of delinquency and crime when they first settled in the inner city, indicated that these rates inevitably declined as these groups gained modest economic advantage, and suggested that this process could be accelerated by forming local self-help community committees. Shaw thus helped free members of ethnic and racial minorities from stereotypical and racist theories of crime that paralyzed meaningful action.

Sources: Harold Finestone, *Victims of Change* (Westport, Conn.: Greenwood Press, 1976), pp. 127–29; Anthony Sorrentino, *Organizing Against Crime: Redeveloping the Neighborhood* (New York: Human Sciences Press, 1977), p. 73; and Southside Community Committee, *Bright Shadows in Bronzetown* (Chicago: Southside Community Committee, 1949), p. 74.

---

niles in contact with the juvenile justice system. They tried to prevent the arrest of juveniles picked up by the police, the petitioning to juvenile court of those arrested, and incarceration of adolescents adjudicated delinquent by the juvenile court. When advocacy failed, staff members and volunteers visited incarcerated adolescents to emphasize that the community stood ready to provide acceptance and assistance upon their return.

The amount of activity taking place in area-project neighborhoods varied considerably.[40] In neighborhoods such as Russell Square (see Box 3.3), large numbers of adults became involved in project activities, considerable money was raised, and, consequently, the lives of relatively large numbers of juveniles were affected. In other project neighborhoods community organiza-

Box 3.3   Russell Square

Russell Square on Chicago's southeast side was one of three original area projects and perhaps the most successful. Working through the local Catholic Church, Clifford Shaw's community organizers established a widely used Boys' Club in the basement of the church that later was opened to young women as well as young men. With a full-time staff of six and some 200 active adult volunteers, the Russel Square Community Committee assigned detached workers to 15 neighborhood gangs, sponsored extensive recreation programs, community improvement campaigns, and advocacy programs, and provided English-language classes for the Polish immigrants who resided in Russell Square.

Indicators of the apparent success of Clifford Shaw's efforts in Russell Square are several. It is reported that project-sponsored talent shows put on by neighborhood youth regularly attracted over 1,000 local residents. Additionally, local adults raised $5,000, purchased 27 acres on a lake near Michigan City, Indiana, and built a summer camp for neighborhood youth. Camp Lange (named after the local parish priest) was opened July 4, 1939, and over 3,000 residents—approximately 20 percent of the community—made the long journey to attend the opening ceremony. The camp was attended by 300 Russell Square juveniles each summer.

Sources: Dominic A. Pacyga, "The Russell Square Community Committee: An Ethnic Response to Urban Problems," *Journal of Urban History* 15 (February 1989): 159–84; Steven Schlossman and Michael Sedlack, *The Chicago Area Project Revisited* (Santa Monica, Calif.: Rand, January 1983 [N-1944-NIE]; Steven Schlossman, *Studies in the History of Early 20th Century Delinquency Prevention* (Santa Monica, Calif.: Rand, January 1983 [N-1945-NIE]; and Steven Schlossman and Michael Sedlak, "The Chicago Area Project Revisited," *Crime and Delinquency* 29 (July 1983): 398–462.

tion efforts were less successful, with less money raised and fewer juveniles assisted. However, all community committees had a full-time project director recruited from the local neighborhood and one or more detached gang workers also recruited from the local community. Added to these paid personnel were adult volunteers who did most of the work.

EVALUATIVE DESIGN

Clifford Shaw and colleagues made no visible effort to evaluate the Chicago Area Project. This lack of visible evaluative effort is curious in light of Shaw's commitment to evaluation and the ease with which a quasi-experimental evaluative design could have been implemented.

Clifford Shaw stated on several occasions that he was committed to evaluating his pioneering efforts to prevent delinquency by organizing community committees. Writing in 1944, for instance, Shaw stated: "It is our hope that *The Chicago Area Project* may continue to operate in the spirit of experimentation and inquiry. If we operate in this spirit, we should be willing to record and accept our failures as well as our successes. In fact, we are not truly scientific unless we are willing to face complete and absolute failure in our attempt to deal with the problem of delinquency. It is my profound conviction that experimentation is necessary to discover the most fruitful way to serve the interests of delinquent children and offers the greatest prospect for discovering methods or procedures by which the volume of delinquency may be reduced."[41]

Additionally, Shaw was in an excellent position to evaluate the Chicago Area Project quasi-experimentally (see Box 3.4). Shaw and McKay had previously mapped rates of delinquency, truancy, infant mortality, and population characteristics for the entire city of Chicago. It would have been easy for Shaw to use this information to create comparison groups by matching project with nonproject neighborhoods and thus create a quasi-experimental evaluative design.

MEASURES OF RESULTS

Measurement of the extent to which the Chicago Area Project accomplished its delinquency prevention goal has repeatedly been approximated using the insights and opinions of persons associated with the project. In addition to these subjective assessments (see Box 3.5), people associated with the Institute for Juvenile Research, especially Henry McKay, continued to collect information on rates of arrest of juveniles by areas of the city of Chicago. However, these official delinquency statistics have

Box 3.4   Quasi-Experimental Evaluative Designs

More often than most researchers would prefer, the conditions that foster the use of true experimental designs simply do not exist. In some projects there are not enough "extra" juveniles to randomly fill both the treated and untreated comparisons groups. In other situations, strong objections surface to randomly assigning juveniles believed to be in need of treatment to an untreated control group. Additionally, researchers sometimes are not brought into a project early enough to push for random selection and assignment procedures.

Quasi-experimental evaluative designs are a viable alternative to true experimental designs because they permit assessment of the results of a project. Quasi-experimental evaluative designs involve creation of comparison groups using other than random assignment or selection techniques. The most common nonrandom assignment or selection technique is matching subjects (or areas of the city) on factors such as race, social class, and extent of delinquency to ensure equivalence on the matched characteristics.

However, because quasi-experimental evaluative designs involve creation of comparison groups using nonrandom techniques, the resulting groups may be nonequivalent. Even with matching, it is nearly impossible to equate individuals or groups on more than a few important dimensions, and on occasion matching is limited to a single important attribute. It therefore is very important to use caution when interpreting the results of quasi-experimentally evaluated projects.

Source: Donald T. Campbell and Julian C. Stanley, *Experimental and Quasi-Experimental Designs for Research* (Chicago: Rand McNally, 1963).

never been reported in ways that permit outsiders to assess the extent to which the Chicago Area Project accomplished its announced goal of preventing delinquency.

A relatively large number of people and agencies have issued reports descriptive of the results of the Chicago Area Project, and there exists subjective agreement that it accomplished its announced goals. One of these reports is a 1954 United States government publication, *The Effectiveness of Delinquency Prevention Programs,* prepared by Helen Witmer and Edith Tufts.[42]

Box 3.5 Subjective Assessment of the Results of a Project

The opinions and insights of project administrators, staff members, and juvenile subjects are potentially biased in ways that make exclusive reliance upon their perceptions unacceptable. Project administrators spend considerable amounts of time and money amid a swirl of political and social forces and must, according to Carol Weiss, "be suspected of bias . . . in the direction of seeing improvement where none exists, or placing high value on tiny, subtle shifts that seem trivial to others." The perceptions of juvenile subjects also are not reliable. Donald T. Campbell has called such perceptions "grateful testimonials" and noted: "Human courtesy and gratitude being what it is, the most dependable means of assuring a favorable evaluation is to use voluntary testimonials from those who have had the treatment. If the spontaneously produced testimonials are in short supply, these should be solicited from recipients with whom the program is still in contact. The rosy glow resulting is analogous to the professor's impression of . . . teaching success when it is based solely upon the comments of those students who come up and talk . . . after class."

It thus is necessary to move beyond subjective assessments of the results of a project. While we may want to assume that administrators, treatment staff, and juvenile clients are honest people capable of accurately reporting the results of a project, it should be recognized that their opinions and insights are potentially distorted by considerable personal involvement. It is not necessary to automatically reject subjective assessments of success. But it is necessary to insist that objective support for subjective assessments be available.

Sources: Carol Weiss, *Evaluation Research: Methods of Assessing Program Effectiveness* (Englewood Cliffs, N.J.: Prentice-Hall, 1972), pp. 40–41; and Donald T. Campbell, "Reforms as Experiments," in James A. Caporaso and Leslie T. Roos (eds.), *Quasi-Experimental Approaches: Theory Testing and Evaluating Policy* (Evanston, Ill.: Northwestern University Press, 1973), p. 217.

The two researchers advanced three observations: "(1) Residents of low income areas can and have organized themselves into effective working units for promoting and conducting welfare programs. (2) These community organizations have been stable and enduring. They raise funds, administer them well, and adapt

the programs to local needs. (3) Local talent, otherwise un-
tapped, has been discovered and . . . mobilized in the interest of
children's welfare.''[43]

A second and more recent assessment of the Chicago Area
Project is a book written by Anthony Sorrentino.[44] The book,
Organizing Against Crime, is Sorrentino's life history, especially
as it relates to his 40-year association with the Chicago Area
Project. In his life history Sorrentino advances three positive
statements: ''(1) The development of stable and vital citizens'
organizations in low-income areas is feasible. (2) Community
committees and affiliated citizen groups perform many varied
and useful functions. (3) Community committees have attacked
the problem of delinquency.''[45]

In addition to these subjective assessments, Henry D. McKay
and others associated with the Institute for Juvenile Research
continued to collect information on police contacts and rates of
arrest by areas of the city of Chicago. However, this information
has never been presented in ways that permit assessment of the
results of the Chicago Area Project (see Box 3.6). For example,
instead of using the 140 areas of the city to report their data as
was the case prior to the start of the Chicago Area Project (see
Figure 3.1), these researchers have based their data on 75 Chicago
communities.[46]

This change in the unit used to report arrests makes it impossible to assess the results of the Chicago Area Project. Unless one is
willing to accept the subjective assessments of persons associated
with the project, there simply is no method of determining
whether the Chicago Area Project accomplished its announced
goal of preventing juvenile delinquency. Replication therefore
assumes extraordinary importance.

REPLICATION: THE MIDCITY PROJECT

The Chicago Area Project was unique in its philosophy of stimulating organization of community committees and its policy of
respecting the autonomy of the community committees once they
had been created. As a result, there is no true replication of its
efforts.[47] Most other projects have little or no faith in the ability
of residents of inner-city neighborhoods to deal effectively with

---

Box 3.6 Delinquency Rates in Russell Square and Adjoining Communities

Henry D. McKay and others associated with the Institute for Juvenile Research continued to collect information on rates of delinquency by areas of the city of Chicago. Clifford Shaw made use of these data in *unpublished* papers that seemed to show that delinquency rates in Russell Square were significantly lower than in several adjoining communities. Shaw reported in one unpublished paper that police contacts with Russell Square juveniles had declined from 60 per 1,000 in 1932 to 20 per 1,000 in 1942. In several adjoining neighborhoods there had been no change in rates of police contacts during that same time period.

However, Shaw and others associated with the Chicago Area Project never published these papers. Why they elected not to do so is unclear, but two possible explanations can be advanced. Shaw reported in his unpublished papers that communities without area projects also had experienced considerable decrease in rates of delinquency. Additionally, Shaw apparently developed some misgivings about the accuracy and hence the utility of official measures, such as police contacts and arrests. Shaw's failure to publish his papers along with the change in the unit to report arrests by Henry McKay combine to make it impossible to assess the results of the Chicago Area Project.

Sources: Steven Schlossman and Michael Sedlack, *The Chicago Area Project Revisited* (Santa Monica, Calif.: Rand, January 1983 [N-1944-NIE]), pp. 100-23; Christopher B. Keys, "Synergy, Prevention and the Chicago School of Sociology," *Prevention in Human Services* 5 (Spring–Summer 1987), p. 27; and Ronald J. Berger and Cherylynne E. Berger, "Community Organization Approaches to the Prevention of Juvenile Delinquency," *Journal of Sociology and Social Welfare* 12 (March 1985), p. 133.

---

their own problems and therefore place responsibility for delinquency prevention in the hands of experts.

Consider the Midcity Project[48] summarized in Table 3.2. Midcity is an example of a delinquency prevention and control project that tried to do many of the things attempted by the Chicago Area Project without placing trust in the people living

Table 3.2   Description of the Midcity Project

Project Name:	The Midcity Project
Location:	Boston, Massachusetts
Dates:	1954–1957
Subjects:	Seven juvenile gangs with a total of 205 members. Gangs were located in a lower-class, inner-city community. Four of the gangs consisted of white males, one of African-American males, one of white females, and one of African-American females. Ages of gang members ranged from 12 to 21.
Type of treatment:	Attention was directed to the community, the family, and the gang. At the community level, effort was directed at developing and strengthening local citizens' groups and youth service agencies. "Chronic-problem families" were provided with psychiatrically oriented casework. Gangs were assigned professionally trained detached gang workers.
Amount of treatment:	The major thrust of the project was directed at the seven target gangs. Seven social workers, five male and two female, worked with the gangs across a three-year period, with an intensive contact period of not less than ten months. The detached gang workers averaged 3.5 contacts with their gangs per week, and each contact period averaged five hours.
Evaluative design:	Quasi-experimental: Juveniles in the seven target gangs were matched with juveniles in other gangs not receiving services on age, sex, ethnicity, and social class.
Measures of results:	A variety of measures were collected, including frequency of court appearance.

Source: Walter B. Miller, "The Impact of a 'Total Community' Delinquency Control Project," *Social Problems* 10 (Fall 1962): 168–91.

in high-delinquency areas. The Midcity Project began in inner-city Boston in 1954, largely in response to widely publicized gang violence. The primary focus of the project was seven neighborhood gangs. Most of the gangs consisted of white males, although African-American and female gangs also received services.

Type and Amount of Treatment. The Midcity Project directed its efforts at three of the factors thought to play a causal role in urban delinquency: the community, the family, and the neighborhood gang. Efforts directed at the community included developing and strengthening existing citizens groups as well as extensively utilizing existing professional agencies, such as settlement houses. Families with long histories of repeated use of welfare services were identified and then "subjected to a special and intensive program of psychiatrically-oriented case-work."[49]

The major thrust of the Midcity Project, however, was assignment of detached workers to seven target gangs. Unlike the Chicago Area Project's indigenous workers, the workers in the Midcity Project were social workers with graduate degrees. The detached gang workers changed the gangs from loosely organized near-groups to formal clubs, served as intermediaries between gang members and adult institutions, such as employers, schools, police, and other professional agencies, and encouraged law-abiding behavior through group-work techniques, through persuasion, and by acting as middle-class role models. According to the project evaluator, the techniques employed by the gang workers "were based on a sophisticated rationale, used both sociocultural and psychological concepts . . . encompassed an unusually wide range of practice techniques, and were executed with care, diligence, and energy by competent and professionally trained workers."[50]

The amount of treatment received by the seven target gangs was considerable. The detached workers contacted the gangs an average of 3.5 times per week, and each of these contacts lasted between five and six hours. The remainder of the gang workers' time each week was devoted to other actions on behalf of the gang members, such as conferences with teachers and police officers. This level of service was maintained between 10 and 34 months.

Evaluative Design.   A true experimental evaluative design was impossible because of the circumstances surrounding the emergence of the Midcity Project. Following a widely publicized murder of a prominent adult by members of a local gang, the project was quickly initiated.[51] Once the project had begun, however, some of the urgency and much of the publicity surrounding the gang problem subsided and the project was "reconceptualized as a 'demonstration' project. . . . This meant . . . the Project also assumed responsibility for testing the efficacy of these methods."[52] Walter B. Miller was charged with the evaluation, and it was obviously too late to implement a true experimental evaluative design.

Professor Miller solved his evaluative dilemma by creating a quasi-experimental design. He matched the juveniles in the gangs assigned detached workers with juveniles in other gangs not receiving these services on "age, sex, ethnic status, and social status."[53] Professor Miller then went on to call for caution in interpreting the results of the Midcity Project because of the problems of nonequivalency that threatens all quasi-experimentally evaluated projects: "The use of a control population entailed certain risks—primarily the possibility that service and control populations might not be adequately matched in some respect."[54]

Measures of Results. Numerous measures of results were collected,[55] including the number of court appearances by juveniles in project and nonproject gangs. The various measures combined to indicate that the Midcity Project failed to prevent delinquency, something Walter B. Miller was quick to admit: "It is . . . possible to provide a definite answer to the principal evaluative research question—'Was there a significant measurable inhibition of law-violating . . . behavior as a consequence of Project efforts?' The answer, with little necessary qualification, is 'No.'"[56]

SUMMARY AND CONCLUSIONS

This chapter examined the effectiveness of area projects in the prevention of juvenile delinquency. It began by establishing the theoretical origins of the area-project approach to the prevention of delinquency. Attention was then directed to the Chicago Area Project, the single best-known attempt to prevent delinquency by changing areas of the city. Last, a review of a replication of the Chicago Area Project was undertaken.

It is very difficult to draw any firm conclusion about the effectiveness of the area-project approach to the prevention of juvenile delinquency. The single best-known example of this approach, the Chicago Area Project, was not designed and measured in ways that permit assessment of its results by outsiders. Additionally, there have not been any completely satisfactory replications of the Chicago Area Project.

However, it is possible to advance a tentative conclusion on the basis of the results of prevention projects that approximate the Chicago Area Project. Assigning detached workers to juvenile gangs, a central component of both the Chicago Area Project and the Midcity Project, has been relatively common. And, we already know that the Midcity Project failed to prevent delinquency. What is important is that the results of the Midcity Project are not unique. Other projects involving community organization and detached gang workers have produced similar results. Michael C. Dixon and William E. Wright are among those who have examined these other projects and here is their conclusion: "The traditional street-corner worker approach has not proved successful in reducing delinquent behavior. . . ."[57]

In light of this evidence, it seems most accurate to conclude that the Chicago Area Project also failed to prevent juvenile delinquency. It is recognized that this conclusion is based on the results of projects that only approximate the pioneering efforts of Clifford Shaw and Henry McKay. Nonetheless, it seems highly unlikely that the Chicago Area Project alone succeeded when other similar efforts have failed.

NOTES

1. See Robert E. L. Faris, *Chicago Sociology: 1920-1932* (Chicago: The University of Chicago Press, 1970).

2. Ibid., pp. 74-75; and Don Gibbons, *The Criminological Enterprise: Theories and Perspectives* (Englewood Cliffs, N.J.: Prentice-Hall, 1979), pp. 25, 40, and 135.

3. Clifford Shaw, Frederick M. Zorbaugh, Henry D. McKay, and Leonard S. Cottrell, *Delinquency Areas: A Study of the Geographic Distribution of School Truants, Juvenile Delinquents, and Adult Offenders in Chicago* (Chicago: The University of Chicago Press, 1929), pp. 1-10.

4. Ibid., p. 10.

5. Ibid.

6. Ibid., p. 198.

7. Ibid., pp. 205-06.

8. Ibid., p. 206.

9. Clifford R. Shaw, *The Jack-Roller* (1930; reprint, The University of Chicago Press, 1966), p. 1. Also see Harold Finestone, *Victims of Change* (Westport, Conn.: Greenwood Press, 1976), p. 111.

10. Shaw, *The Jack-Roller.*

11. Clifford R. Shaw and Maurice E. Moore, *The Natural History of a Delinquent Career* (Chicago: The University of Chicago Press, 1931).

12. Clifford Shaw, Henry D. McKay, and James F. McDonald, *Brothers in Crime* (Chicago: The University of Chicago Press, 1938).

13. Discussion of "Stanley's" background and delinquent career is based on Shaw, *The Jack-Roller*.

14. Shaw, *The Jack-Roller*, p. 34. For a far more complete and sympathetic description of Back of the Yards, see Robert A. Slayton, *Back of the Yards: The Making of a Local Democracy* (Chicago: The University of Chicago Press, 1986).

15. Shaw, *The Jack-Roller*, p. 50. To find out what happened to Stanley during his adult years, see The Jack-Roller and Jon Snodgrass, with Gilbert Geis, James F. Short, Jr., and Solomon Kobrin, *The Jack-Roller at Seventy: A Fifty-Year Follow-Up* (Lexington, Mass.: Lexington Books, 1982). Professor Snodgrass reports in a postscript (p. 173) that "Stanley . . . died on 25 April 1982 at age seventy-five. He is buried in San Fernando Mission Cemetery, Grenada Hills, California."

16. Clifford R. Shaw and Henry D. McKay, *Juvenile Delinquency and Urban Areas* (Chicago: The University of Chicago Press, 1942).

17. Ibid., pp. 193–314.

18. Ibid., p. 439. It is interesting to compare Shaw and McKay's argument with Robert K. Merton, "Social Structure and Anomie," *American Sociological Review* 3 (August 1938): 672–82. For a recent assessment of Shaw and McKay's theory of the origins of urban delinquency, see Jerzy Sarnecki, "Delinquency Networks in Sweden," *Journal of Quantitative Criminology* 6 (March 1990): 31–50; Robert J. Sampson, "Community Structure and Crime: Testing Social-Disorganization Theory," *American Journal of Sociology* 94 (January 1989): 774–802; and Robert J. Sampson, "Urban Black Violence: The Effect of Male Joblessness and Family Disruption," *American Journal of Sociology* 93 (September 1987): 348–82.

19. Shaw and McKay, *Juvenile Delinquency*, p. 441.

20. Description of the Chicago Area Project is based on Dominic A. Pacyga, "The Russell Square Community Committee: An Ethnic Response to Urban Problems," *Journal of Urban History* 15 (February 1989): 159–84; Slayton, *Back of the Yards*; Finestone, *Victims of Change* pp. 116–50; Solomon Kobrin, "The Chicago Area Project—a 25-Year Assessment," *The Annals of the American Academy of Political and Social Science* 322 (March 1959): 19–29; James F. Short, Jr., "Introduction to the Revised Edition," Clifford R. Shaw and Henry D. McKay, *Juvenile Delinquency and Urban Areas: A Study of Rates of Delinquency in Relation to Differential Characteristics of Local Communities in American Cities*, rev. ed. (Chicago: The University of Chicago Press, 1969), pp. xlvi–liv; Anthony Sorrentino, *Organizing Against Crime:*

Redeveloping the Neighborhood (New York: Human Sciences Press, 1977); and Southside Community Committee, *Bright Shadows in Bronzetown* (Chicago: Southside Community Committee, 1949).

21. These locations are approximate. I did not find any precise identification of project areas in the materials I consulted. The approximate locations are based on passages in Sorrentino, *Organizing Against Crime*, pp. 47, 76, 143, and 149-150.

22. Shaw and McKay, *Juvenile Delinquency*, p. 54.

23. Ibid., pp. 91-154.

24. Ibid., p. 41.

25. Ibid., p. 54.

26. Ibid., pp. 91-154.

27. Ibid., p. 100.

28. Ibid., p. 41.

29. See Southside Community Committee, *Bright Shadows*.

30. James R. Bennett, "Introduction," in Sorrentino, *Organizing Against Crime*, p. 26.

31. Sorrentino, *Organizing Against Crime*, p. 231.

32. Ibid., p. 225.

33. Ibid., p. 73.

34. Southside Community Committee, *Bright Shadows*, p. 39.

35. Ibid., pp. 39-40.

36. Anthony Sorrentino, *How to Organize the Neighborhood for Delinquency Prevention* (New York: Human Sciences Press, 1979), pp. 159-60.

37. See Sorrentino, *Organizing Against Crime*; and Southside Community Committee, *Bright Shadows*.

38. Southside Community Committee, *Bright Shadows*.

39. Kobrin, "Chicago Area Project," p. 26.

40. Ibid., pp. 25-26; Finestone, *Victims of Change*, pp. 139-49.

41. Cited in Finestone, *Victims of Change*, pp. 128-29.

42. Helen L. Witmer and Edith Tufts, *The Effectiveness of Delinquency Prevention Programs* (Washington, D.C.: U.S. Government Printing Office, 1954).

43. Ibid., p. 15.

44. Sorrentino, *Organizing Against Crime*.

45. Ibid., pp. 247-48. Also see Kobrin, "Chicago Area Project."

46. Shaw and McKay, *Juvenile Delinquency*, pp. 329-73.

47. In a letter to the author dated September 29, 1983, James F. Short, Jr., argues that there has never been a true replication of the Chicago Area Project. However, there have been several projects that have come close, including Mobilization for Youth (MFY) and Harlem Youth Op-

portunities Unlimited (HARYOU). Unfortunately, these other projects were not experimentally or quasi-experimentally evaluated and objectively measured. For description of MFY, see George A. Brager and Francis P. Purcell (eds.), *Community Action Against Poverty: Readings from the Mobilization Experience* (New Haven, Conn.: College and University Press, 1967); Daniel Knapp and Kenneth Polk, *Scouting the War on Poverty: Social Reform Politics in the Kennedy Administration* (Lexington, Mass.: Heath Lexington Books, 1971); Peter Marris and Martin Rein, *Dilemmas of Social Reform: Poverty and Community Action in the United States* (New York: Atherton Press, 1969); Daniel P. Moynihan, *Maximum Feasible Misunderstanding: Community Action in the War on Poverty* (New York: Free Press, 1969); and Harold H. Weissman (ed.), *Community Development in the Mobilization for Youth Experience* (New York: Association Press, 1969). For a description of HARYOU, see Kenneth B. Clark, *Dark Ghetto: Dilemmas of Social Power* (New York: Harper & Row, 1965).

48. Discussion of the Midcity Project is based on Walter B. Miller, "Inter-Institutional Conflict as a Major Impediment to Delinquency Prevention," *Human Organization* 17 (Fall 1958): 20–23; and Walter B. Miller, "The Impact of a 'Total Community' Delinquency Control Project," *Social Problems* 10 (Fall 1962): 168–91.

49. Miller, "Impact," p. 169.

50. Ibid., p. 176.

51. See Miller, "Inter-Institutional Conflict."

52. Miller, "Impact," p. 176.

53. Ibid., p. 185.

54. Ibid., p. 185.

55. Ibid.

56. Ibid., p. 187.

57. Michael C. Dixon and William E. Wright, *Juvenile Delinquency Prevention Programs: An Evaluation of Policy Related Research on the Effectiveness of Prevention Programs* (Washington, D.C.: National Science Foundation, 1975), p. 22. Also see William C. Berleman, James R. Seaberg, and Thomas W. Steinburn, "The Delinquency Prevention Experiment of the Seattle Atlantic Street Center: A Final Evaluation," *Social Service Review* 46 (September 1972): 323–46; Jerry P. Walker, Albert P. Cardarelli, and Dennis L. Billingsley, *The Theory and Practice of Delinquency Prevention in the United States: Review, Synthesis and Assessment* (Columbus, Ohio: Evaluation Division, Center for Vocational Education, The Ohio State University, January 1976), p. 207; Barry Krisberg, *The National Evaluation of Delinquency Prevention: Final Report* (San Francisco: Research Center, National Council on Crime and Delinquency, September 1981), p. 529; John T. Whitehead

and Steven P. Lab, "A Meta-Analysis of Juvenile Correctional Treatment," *Journal of Research in Crime and Delinquency* 26 (August 1989), p. 291; and William S. Davidson II, Robin Redner, Richard L. Amdur, and Christina M. Mitchell, *Alternative Treatments for Troubled Youth: The Case of Diversion from the Justice System* (New York: Plenum, 1990), p. 36.

PART TWO

PREADJUDICATION
INTERVENTION

4

DIVERSION

Diversion of juvenile offenders away from the juvenile justice system into short-term treatment emerged as a major delinquency-control strategy during the 1970s.[1] Diversion is premised on the belief that juvenile justice system processing does more harm than good, with primary attention directed at two specific negative consequences.

First, juvenile justice system processing provides juveniles with a delinquent self-image.[2] Whereas prior to arrest and intake, most juvenile offenders see themselves as basically good kids who shoplift overpriced items from big stores that can easily afford the loss, or as one of many out for an innocent Friday night of group-based beer and fun, arrested juveniles sent to intake are treated as if they are delinquent. Being treated as delinquent causes some adolescents to view themselves as delinquent and invites more rather than less delinquency.

Second, juvenile justice system processing stigmatizes juveniles in the eyes of significant others.[3] Schoolteachers, police officers, and potential employers are understandably wary of juveniles with formal records of delinquency. So, too, with potential friends, lovers, and spouses. Although a formal record is not automatically or uniformly stigmatizing, delinquent labels cause at least some of the important people around a juvenile to hesitate in assisting in the transition to adulthood. This hesitation reduces linkages between adolescence and adulthood and prolongs involvement in delinquency.

For many juvenile offenders, therefore, the best treatment is little or no treatment.[4] This is especially the case when the juvenile is young and charged with nothing more serious than a status or minor property offense. For these types of youthful offenders and perhaps others, diversion away from formal juvenile justice system processing is hypothesized to be the most effective method of controlling delinquency.

This chapter probes the effectiveness of diversion. The chapter begins by demonstrating that efforts to control delinquency by diverting juveniles are based on labeling theory. Attention is then directed to the Sacramento County Diversion Project, an exemplary program that attempted to control delinquency by diverting juveniles into short-term treatment. Examined last are the results of three replications of the Sacramento County Diversion Project.

LABELING THEORY

Efforts to control delinquency by diverting juveniles are grounded in labeling theory.[5] Labeling theorists assert that persistent delinquency is the result of treating minor offenders as if they are about to become persistently delinquent. Labeling theorists therefore advance a radical nonintervention solution to the problem of delinquency: "leave kids alone whenever possible."[6]

FRANK TANNENBAUM

The ideas of Frank Tannenbaum are a useful starting point for understanding labeling assertions and solutions. Writing in 1938, Professor Tannenbaum noted that juveniles who break windows, shoplift, and annoy adults with their loud music, define their behavior as "play, adventure, excitement, interest, mischief, fun."[7] Adults almost always see this behavior differently and view the juveniles responsible for such actions as "evil." Some juveniles internalize this judgment and come to see themselves as evil. In addition, adults "dramatize the evil" of delinquent juveniles by pushing them into the juvenile justice system where negative self-images are reinforced and isolation from conforming others increased. Professor Tannenbaum therefore asserted that the "process of making the . . . [delinquent] . . . is a process of tagging, defining, identifying, segregating, emphasizing, making conscious and self-conscious; it becomes a way of stimulating, suggesting, emphasizing and evoking the very traits that are complained of."[8] Professor Tannenbaum had a solution as well: "The way out is through a refusal to dramatize the evil. The less said about it the better. The more said about something else, still better."[9]

HOWARD S. BECKER

It was not until the 1960s, however, that labeling theory emerged as a major explanation of deviant behavior within academic sociology. Among those at the cutting edge of the development of labeling theory was Northwestern University sociologist Howard S. Becker. Writing in 1963, Professor Becker argued: "One of the most crucial steps in the process of building a stable pattern of deviant behavior is . . . the experience of being caught and publicly labeled as deviant."[10] Labeling, according to Professor Becker, causes a "drastic change in the individual's public identity."[11] In the context of delinquency, others around a labeled juvenile see only the label and assume the worst. In addition, being labeled frequently results in the person being "treated in accordance with the popular diagnosis . . . and treatment itself may produce increasing deviance."[12] For some labeled juveniles, diagnosis and treatment mean time in a detention center followed by still more time in a correctional facility, experiences labeling theorists believe make juveniles more rather than less delinquent.

SUMMARY OF LABELING THEORY

Labeling theorists assert that the juvenile justice system is a big part of the delinquency problem. The big solution, according to labeling theorists, is to keep as many kids out of the system as possible.

THE SACRAMENTO COUNTY DIVERSION PROJECT

The purpose of the Sacramento County Diversion Project[13] was to determine whether status offenders could be "handled better through short-term family crisis therapy than through the traditional procedures of the juvenile court."[14] Table 4.1 summarizes the major features of this exemplary[15] project and serves as a guide for the description and analysis that follow.

DESCRIPTION OF THE PROJECT

The Sacramento County Diversion Project began receiving status offenders on October 26, 1970. In November 1973 the experimen-

Table 4.1 Description of the Sacramento County Diversion Project

Project Name:	Sacramento 601 Diversion Project
Location:	Sacramento County, California
Dates:	October 26, 1970, to present
Subjects:	Juveniles accused of status offenses (runaway, beyond control of parents, truancy) and referred to probation intake by police, parents, and schools. Three-quarters of these offenders had no previous record of arrest, 59 percent were under 15 years of age, 59 percent were female, 76 percent were white, and the family income of 62 percent was less than $9,999 per year.
Type of treatment:	Specially trained deputy probation officers worked to avoid detention of juveniles, resolve the case short of referral to juvenile court, and provide short-term crisis intervention and family crisis counseling.
Amount of treatment:	Juveniles and parents agreeing to become involved in the short-term crisis intervention and family crisis counseling were limited to a maximum of five counseling sessions, with each session lasting one to two hours.
Evaluative design:	Experimental: Juveniles were randomly assigned to diversion intake or regular probation intake.
Measures of results:	Initial measures were collected after the juveniles assigned to the specially trained deputy probation officers had been out of treatment for seven months. Follow-up measures were collected when the juveniles assigned to the specially trained probation officers during the first 12 months of the project had been out of treatment for 12 months.
Replication:	The Sacramento County Diversion Project has been replicated on numerous occasions, including the California Youth Authority's Evaluation of Juvenile Diversion Projects, the National Evaluation of Diversion Projects, and the Adolescent Diversion Project.

Sources: Roger Baron, Floyd Feeney, and Warren Thornton, "Preventing Delinquency Through Diversion," *Federal Probation* 37 (March 1973): 13–18; and Roger Baron and Floyd Feeney, *Juvenile Diversion Through Family Counseling* (Washington, D.C.: U.S. Government Printing Office, February 1976).

tal diversion intake became the standard procedure for all status offenders in Sacramento County. Evaluation, however, was directed at juveniles diverted during the first year of the experimental intervention. Our analysis is therefore confined to juveniles processed between October 26, 1970, and October 25, 1971.

All of the Sacramento County Diversion Project's subjects were accused of status offenses. Juveniles were excluded if they were accused of other than status offenses, if they resided outside Sacramento County, or if they had previously been adjudicated delinquent for "drug offenses, robbery, burglary, grand theft auto . . . [or] . . . offenses involving violence or sexual assault."[16] The majority of alleged offenders meeting these admission criteria were white females brought to Juvenile Hall for their first offense.

Most of the status offenses involved family problems. Consider "Susan L." and her parents: "During Easter vacation her father hit her for wearing a girlfriend's skirt, calling her a liar and a bitch. The parents indicated they did not want Susan wearing the girl's skirt, that they do not like Susan in those kind of clothes. Susan admits that she deliberately turned up the hem of her already short dress to be kicked out of the house by her parents so she could come to juvenile hall. She stated that they are constantly fighting and picking on her over everything."[17]

TYPE OF TREATMENT

The goal of the Sacramento County Diversion Project was to control delinquency by diverting juveniles into short-term treatment. The treatment hypothesis was that special training of deputy probation officers to encourage use of crisis intervention and family counseling skills in place of overnight detention and referral to juvenile court would reduce labeling and stigmatization and thereby control delinquency (see Figure 4.1).

The college-educated deputy probation officers received a week of special training prior to the start of the project. Using group workshops, demonstrations, role playing, and occasional lectures, the probation officers were taught "the concepts of family process and family rules and the extent to which the way families make decisions is often as important as the decisions themselves; the concept of the family as a system and the ways in which the

FIGURE 4.1   The Sacramento County Diversion Project's treatment
            hypothesis in diagrammatic form

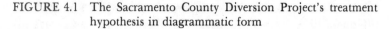
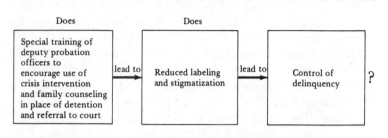

Sources: The treatment hypothesis is based on descriptions of the Sacramento
County Diversion Project in Roger Baron, Floyd Feeney, and Warren Thornton,
"Preventing Delinquency Through Diversion," *Federal Probation* 37 (March
1973): 13–18; and Roger Baron and Floyd Feeney, *Juvenile Diversion Through
Family Counseling* (Washington, D.C.: U.S. Government Printing Office, Febru-
ary 1976).

actions of one family member affect other members of the family;
how to enlist the family's own efforts to work on its problems;
how understanding one's self and one's own family system is
important to becoming an effective family counselor."[18]

The probation officers also received special in-service training.
They observed professionally trained family therapists counsel
juveniles and their parents, engaged in role playing with other
colleagues, and analyzed videotapes of actual counseling sessions. Additionally, project psychiatrists and clinical psychologists were available for consultation.

The special training was put to use the moment an eligible
case was referred to intake. Probation officers contacted the juvenile's parents and asked that they come to Juvenile Hall for an
immediate counseling session. In talking with parents, probation officers were instructed to use the following approach:
"Hello, Mrs. Brown? I'm from the family crisis intervention unit.
Your son has just been brought in here by the police. He is very
upset. I've set an appointment for you in a half hour and I look
forward to seeing you and your husband then so we can make
some sort of decision about what to do in this situation."[19] Most
parents contacted in this manner agreed to come to Juvenile
Hall.

When the parents arrived, probation officers read juveniles their Miranda warning and explained that participation was voluntary. They noted, however, that if parents or a juvenile chose not to volunteer for an immediate counseling session, their case would have to be referred to juvenile court.[20] Parents and juveniles also were told that once the initial counseling session had been completed, they could return for a limited number of additional sessions, although they were under no obligation to do so. After weighing the options, most parents and juveniles decided to volunteer for immediate treatment without trial (see Box 4.1) rather than risk going to court.

Once juveniles had waived their rights, a counseling session began. Using the family counseling techniques they had been taught, probation officers "sought to develop the idea that the problem was one that should be addressed by the family as a whole. Locking up the youth as a method of solving problems was discouraged and a return home with a commitment by all to try to work through the problem was encouraged."[21]

The amount of treatment received by juveniles and parents was left to the discretion of family members. Probation officers usually concluded the first session by saying: "Well, I feel really good about the way you and your husband conveyed your feelings to your son and about the way he expressed himself to you. I see a great improvement in the way you communicate with one another. I feel a lot of concern on your part, a lot of caring and a lot of closeness, and it seems to me that if we were to work for two or three more sessions that things would really improve dramatically. I would really enjoy seeing you next week at the same time. How do you feel about that?"[22] If parents and juveniles elected to return, they were limited to a maximum of five sessions to avoid the labeling and stigmatization thought to result from more protracted treatment efforts.

EVALUATIVE DESIGN

The Sacramento County Diversion Project was experimentally evaluated. Starting on October 26, 1970, and continuing through October 25, 1971, project personnel handled the intake of status offenders meeting admission criteria four days per week. Regular probation officers handled status offender intake three days per

Box 4.1 "Treatment Without Trial"

In March 1946 Paul Tappan's classic paper "Treatment Without Trial" was published. In his paper, Professor Tappan, a lawyer and sociologist, argued that adolescents appearing in juvenile court lacked legal protection that adults appearing in traffic court took for granted. Juveniles, for example, had no real right to an attorney.

On May 15, 1967, the United States Supreme Court agreed with Professor Tappan when it ruled *In re Gault*. The case involved Gerald Gault, a 14-year-old Arizona boy adjudicated delinquent for making an obscene phone call and sentenced to six years at the State Industrial School. The essence of the Gault decision was that because adolescents in juvenile court clearly risked severe punishment, they were entitled to some of the same legal protections afforded adults—including counsel, a transcript of the hearing, and the right to confront and cross-examine witnesses, remain silent, and appeal.

The Gault decision, however, had no effect on the treatment without trial afforded juveniles during preadjudication diversion programs. In the context of the Sacramento County Diversion Project, for example, juveniles accused of status offenses but convicted of nothing received treatment by specially trained deputy probation officers.

Treatment without trial presents several serious problems. Treatment always is coercive for it necessarily involves trying to change people in ways they might not choose if left alone. Additionally, the choice juveniles and parents make can hardly be described as voluntary. Most waive due process protections under difficult circumstances without really knowing that if they took the chance and went to court, the case would probably be dismissed. Last, diversion represents a step back to a time when large numbers of juveniles routinely received treatment without trial. Professor Tappan would not be pleased.

Sources: Paul Tappan, "Treatment Without Trial," *Social Forces* 24 (March 1946): 306–11; *In re Gault* (1967, 387 U.S. 1); and Alan Neigher, "The Gault Decision: Due Process and the Juvenile Courts," *Federal Probation* 31 (December 1967): 421–27.

week. Days of the week handled by project and nonproject probation officers were rotated on a monthly basis. This practice of
rotating intake days of the week across a full year was equivalent
to a random assignment procedure and thus helped ensure
equivalency of the juvenile subjects assigned to diversion or
regular probation intake services.

MEASURES OF RESULTS

Specially trained deputy probation officers were able to substi-
tute crisis intervention and family crisis counseling skills for
detention and referral to juvenile court (see Table 4.2). Only 13.9
percent of the juveniles experiencing diversion intake were detained overnight as compared to 55.5 percent of the juveniles
processed by regular intake. In addition, only 3.7 percent of the
diversion intake referrals resulted in a petition to juvenile court
as compared to 19.8 percent of the regular probation intake
referrals.

The specially trained deputy probation officers also were able
to control delinquency (see Table 4.3). After subjects had been out
of treatment for 12 months, fewer of the juveniles experiencing
diversion intake had been rebooked: 46.3 percent as compared to

Table 4.2 Sacramento County Diversion Project: Percent of
Diversion and Regular Intake Referrals Detained Overnight
and Petitioned to Juvenile Court

Percent of Referrals[a]	Diversion Intake ($n = 977$)	Regular Intake ($n = 612$)
Detained overnight	13.9	55.5
Petitioned to juvenile court	3.7	19.8

[a]*Referrals* during the first 12 months of the project. It is important to note
that these are referrals, not individual juveniles, because it was possible for an
individual juvenile to be referred to intake more than once. Thus, the 674
diversion intake juveniles accumulated 977 referrals and the 526 regular
intake juveniles accumulated 612 referrals. The percent figures represent the
number of overnight detensions and petitions to juvenile court in each group
divided by the number of referrals.

Sources: Roger Baron, Floyd Feeney, and Warren Thorton, "Preventing Delinquency Through Juvenile Diversion," *Federal Probation* 37 (March
1973):13-18; and Roger Baron and Floyd Feeney, *Juvenile Diversion Through
Family Counseling* (Washington, D.C.: U.S. Government Printing Office,
February 1976).

Table 4.3   Sacramento County Diversion Project: Percent of
Diversion and Regular Intake Juveniles Rebooked for Status
and Criminal Offenses Twelve Months after Intervention

Percent Rebooked	Diversion Intake ($n = 674$)	Regular Intake ($n = 526$)
For status or criminal offense	46.3	54.2
For criminal offense	22.4	29.8

Source: Roger Baron and Floyd Feeney, *Juvenile Diversion Through Family
Counseling* (Washington, D.C.: U.S. Government Printing Office, February
1976), p. 10.

54.2 percent of the juveniles processed by regular intake personnel. Diverted juveniles were rebooked for criminal offenses at a
slightly lower rate as well: 22.4 percent as compared to 29.8
percent of the juveniles experiencing regular intake processing.
Although the differences are small, the Sacramento County Diversion Project was able to reduce recidivism (see Box 4.2).

REPLICATION: EVALUATION OF
JUVENILE DIVERSION PROJECTS

Replication of the Sacramento County Diversion Project has
been frequent, including the Evaluation of Juvenile Diversion
Projects[23] (see Table 4.4). These 11 replicative efforts took place
in California and were quasi-experimentally evaluated starting
in 1974. Review of the information in Table 4.4 reveals that these
projects were similar to the Sacramento County Diversion Project. They substituted individual and family counseling for detention and referral to juvenile court. In addition, the amount of
treatment juveniles received was similar. Last, diversion intake
was made standard procedure in these 11 jurisdictions as well.

However, there also were important differences between Sacramento County's early effort and the replicative projects. More of
the juveniles in the replicative projects were male, Hispanic, or
African-American, and were diverted following arrest for a criminal rather than status offenses. These sex, ethnic, race, and offense differences permit preliminary assessment of effectiveness
of diversion with other than the predominantly white and female
status offenders involved in the Sacramento County Diversion
Project.

Box 4.2 Net Widening

There is a problem with the modest reduction in recidivism associated with the Sacramento County Diversion Project. The net of social control was widened to include a large number of juveniles who otherwise would have been left alone. Please look again at Table 4.2. Slightly less than one of five (19.8 percent) of the status offenders experiencing regular intake were petitioned to juvenile court. The majority (80.2 percent) were released, although a little more than half (55.5 percent) were detained before they were released. Because assignment was random, it is safe to assume that approximately 80 percent of the juveniles diverted into short-term treatment would have been released had it not been for the existence of the project.

Net widening is not unique to the Sacramento County Diversion Project. Large numbers of juveniles who would have been left alone were instead diverted in the three replications examined in the remainder of this chapter.

Net widening occurs for understandable reasons. Street cops and probation officers regularly encounter juveniles who need something less than a visit to intake or court and something more than outright release. Diversion programs provide a third alternative and street cops and probation officers use it for juveniles they otherwise would have released.

Sources: William S. Davidson II, Robin Redner, Richard L. Admur, and Christina M. Mitchell, *Alternative Treatments for Troubled Youth: The Case of Diversion from the Justice System* (New York: Plenum, 1990), pp. 190–91; Franklyn W. Dunford, D. Wayne Osgood, and Hart F. Weichselbaum, *National Evaluation of Diversion Projects: Final Report* (Washington, D.C.: The National Institute of Juvenile Justice and Delinquency Prevention, U.S. Department of Justice, May 1981), pp. 39 and 376; and Ted Palmer, Marvin Bohnstedt, and Roy Lewis, *The Evaluation of Juvenile Diversion Projects: Final Report* (Sacramento, Calif.: Division of Research, California Youth Authority, Winter 1978), pp. 44–55.

Measurement of the results of Evaluation of Juvenile Diversion Projects was undertaken six months after the quasi-experimental intervention (see Table 4.5). Juveniles processed by diversion intake were once again arrested slightly less frequently than juveniles processed by regular intake. Apparently, projects lo-

Table 4.4 Description of Evaluation of Juvenile Diversion Projects

Project Name:	Evaluation of Juvenile Diversion Projects
Locations:	Compton, El Centro, Fremont, Fresno, Irvine, La Colonia, Mendocino, Simi Valley, Stockton, Vacaville, and Vallejo, California
Dates:	1974 to present
Subjects:	Juveniles referred to diversion projects by police or probation officers because of status or criminal law violations. Slightly over 75 percent of the juveniles were 16 years of age and under; 58 percent were male; 57 percent were white; 23 percent were Hispanic; 9 percent were African-American; 29 percent had a previous arrest; and 50 percent were diverted following an arrest for a criminal (as opposed to status) offense.
Type of treatment:	The 11 separate diversion projects offered a limited variety of services. These services in order of frequency were individual counseling, family counseling, and group counseling.
Amount of treatment:	Diverted juveniles averaged between four and six weeks of project contact and nearly six hours of direct contact services.
Evaluative design:	Quasi-experimental: Juveniles in each of the 11 diversion programs were matched with juveniles processed by the police and probation departments in each community in the year prior to the creation of the local diversion project on age, sex, ethnicity, prior arrests, and referral source.
Measures of results:	Measures of the results of these projects were collected for the diverted juveniles for the six months following the arrest that brought them to the attention of the diversion program. For the juveniles in the quasi-experimentally created control groups, rearrest measures were collected for the six months following the arrest that brought them to the attention of police or probation intake officers.

Source: Ted Palmer, Marvin Bohnstedt, and Roy Lewis, *The Evaluation of Juvenile Diversion Projects: Final Report* (Sacramento, Calif: Division of Research, California Youth Authority, Winter 1978).

Table 4.5 Evaluation of Juvenile Diversion Projects: Percent Diversion and Regular Intake Juveniles Rearrested for Status and Criminal Offenses Six Months after Intervention

Percent Rearrested[a]	Diversion Intake ($n = 1,345$)	Regular Intake ($n = 1,192$)
For status offense	14.0	15.4
For criminal offense	15.7	20.3
For status or criminal offense	25.4	30.7

Source: Ted Palmer, Marvin Bohnstedt, and Roy Lewis, *The Evaluation of Juvenile Diversion Projects: Final Report* (Sacramento, Calif.: Division of Research, California Youth Authority, Winter 1978), pp. 81–83. Modified and reprinted by permission.

cated in places other than Sacramento County and diverting male as well as female, Hispanic and African-American as well as white, and criminal as well as status offenders are also modestly effective.

REPLICATION: NATIONAL EVALUATION OF DIVERSION PROJECTS

As diversion projects increased, social scientists raised important questions. Some argued that quasi-experimental designs confounded assessment of diversion.[24] Others thought it time to divert criminal juveniles, not just adolescents accused of status offenses.[25] Still others urged radical nonintervention to learn what happens when offenders are simply left alone.[26]

In response to these concerns, the federal government's Office of Juvenile Justice and Delinquency Prevention (OJJDP) made $10 million available for a National Evaluation of Diversion Programs[27] (see Table 4.6). To receive OJJDP funding, diversion projects were required to include an experimental design to help overcome the evaluative problems that confounded assessment of diversion. It was also hoped that the availability of federal funds would encourage a bolder and broader evaluative agenda,[28] perhaps focusing on other than status offenders and embracing radical nonintervention as an important question worthy of a precise answer.

By 1976, four jurisdictions—Kansas City, Missouri, Memphis, Tennessee, Orange County, Florida, and New York City—had experimentally designed diversion projects underway. Equally important, all four projects excluded status offenders and included radical intervention among the important questions their experimental designs could precisely answer.

Referrals to the diversion projects came from several sources. In Kansas City and New York City, police officers made referral decisions. In Memphis, court intake personnel made the referral decision, whereas in Orange County, Florida, a state attorney made the decision. Irrespective of the referral source, the juveniles involved shared one important characteristic: had it not been for the existence of the diversion projects, they would have further penetrated the juvenile justice system.

Diverted juveniles in all four projects received individual and family counseling. In Orange County, however, recreational ser-

Table 4.6   Description of National Evaluation of Diversion Projects

Project Name:	National Evaluation of Diversion Projects
Locations:	Kansas City, Missouri; Memphis, Tennessee; Orange County, Florida; and New York City
Dates:	1976–1979
Subjects:	Juveniles referred by police, intake personnel, or state attorney for other than index crimes against persons or status offenses, who otherwise would have further penetrated the juvenile justice system. Slightly over 75 percent were 14 years old or more; 82 percent were male; 53 percent were African-American; 47 percent had a previous arrest; and 62 percent were referred for a misdemeanor offense.
Type of treatment:	Diverted juveniles received individual and family counseling along with employment, educational, and recreational services.
Amount of treatment:	Services were provided between two and six months with between 13 and 48 service contacts per juvenile.
Evaluative design:	Experimental: Eligible offenders were randomly assigned to one of three comparison groups: (1) release with no services; (2) diversion services; or (3) further penetration of the juvenile justice system.
Measures of results:	Measures of official delinquency were collected 6 and 12 months following intervention.

Source: Franklyn W. Dunford, D. Wayne Osgood, and Hart F. Weichselbaum, National Evaulation of Diversion Projects: Final Report (Washington, D.C.: The National Institute of Juvenile Justice and Delinquency Prevention, Office of Juvenile Justice and Delinquency Prevention, U.S. Department of Justice, May 1981).

vices were emphasized, whereas in Kansas City some diverted juveniles were assigned adult counselors who also acted as advocates before public agencies such as the schools. Additionally, employment and educational services were available in all four projects.

The experimental design was more detailed than most because of the important radical nonintervention question. Instead of the usual two-group comparison, juveniles were randomly assigned to one of three comparison groups: (1) release without services ("radical nonintervention"); (2) diversion services; and (3) further penetration of the juvenile justice system. Juveniles assigned to the first comparison group were released without treatment or further intervention by the juvenile justice system. Juveniles in the second group were diverted away from the juvenile justice system into the counseling, employment, educational, and recreational services made available by the diversion projects. Juveniles in the third group were sent back to the referral source where some, but not all,[29] experienced further penetration of the juvenile justice system.

Numerous measures of results were collected, including the official arrest information in Table 4.7. Only one finding emerges, but that finding is very important: there was no difference in rearrest between the groups 6 and 12 months following intervention.

The "no difference" finding is significant for two reasons. First, it suggests diversion can safely be extended to other than status offenders. Both of the previous diversion projects examined included large numbers of status offenders. In Sacramento County, only status offenders were included. Half of the subjects included in the California Youth Authority's Evaluation of Juvenile Diversion Projects' were status offenders. The National Evaluation of Diversion Projects excluded status offenders and therefore included only juveniles accused of criminal acts. Even with a more serious group of offenders, diversion was just as effective as further penetration of the juvenile justice system. Assuming replicative confirmation, no difference is clearly a very important finding.

Second, the no difference finding suggests doing less may be just as effective as doing more. Of the three comparison groups, one involved radical nonintervention. The juveniles in this group were accused of criminal acts and had been ushered through the front door of the juvenile justice system. Their "treatment" was a quick, no-strings exit. Once released, abso-

Table 4.7 National Evaluation of Diversion Projects: Percent Release, Diversion, and Penetration Comparison Groups with One or More Rearrests 6 and 12 Months Following Intervention

Percent with One or More Rearrests	Comparison Groups		
	Release[a] ($n = 848$)	Diversion ($n = 936$)	Penetration ($n = 804$)
After 6 Months	22	22	22
After 12 Months	30	31	32

[a]"Radical nonintervention"

Source: Franklyn W. Dunford, D. Wayne Osgood, and Hart F. Weichselbaum, *National Evaluation of Diversion Projects: Final Report* (Washington, D.C.: The National Institute of Juvenile Justice and Delinquency Prevention. Office of Juvenile Justice and Delinquency Prevention, U.S. Department of Justice, May 1981). Constructed from tables 2-24, pp. 98-101.

lutely nothing more was done to or for them, yet they were no more likely to be rearrested. Is less more?

REPLICATION: ADOLESCENT DIVERSION PROJECT

The Adolescent Diversion Project[30] (see Table 4.8) was an exceptional project. It included juveniles accused of criminal acts. It

Table 4.8   Description of the Adolescent Diversion Project

Project Name:	Adolescent Diversion Project
Location:	Ingham County (Lansing and East Lansing), Michigan
Dates:	Study I: fall 1976 to spring 1981; Study II: fall 1979 to spring 1981
Subjects:	Juveniles admitting status and criminal acts, excluding those accused of index crimes against persons and those already on probation. The two most common offenses were larceny-theft (34 percent) and breaking and entering (24 percent). Average age was a little over 14 years, 84 percent were male, and a little under 30 percent were African-American or Hispanic.
Type of treatment:	During Study I, juveniles were randomly assigned to one of six interventions: two involved individual and family-focused behavioral contracting and child advocacy by university students who received special training; one involved behavioral contracting and child advocacy by trained students and a member of the juvenile court; one involved relationship building by trained students; one involved "minimal training" with students left on their own to determine how to intervene; and in one control group juveniles were returned to court intake for "standard . . . processing." During Study II, juveniles were randomly assigned to one of four interventions: three involved individually focused behavioral contracting and child advocacy by three types of trained volunteers—university students, community college students, and volunteers from the local community; in the fourth group juveniles were returned to court intake for standard processing.
Amount of treatment:	With the exception of juveniles returned to court, each offender was assigned a student or volunteer who worked with them 6 to 8 hours per week for 18 weeks.
Evaluative design:	Experimental: Eligible offenders were randomly assigned to a group.
Measure of results:	New court petitions in the two years following random assignment.

Source: William S. Davidson II, Robin Redner, Richard L. Admur, and Christina M. Mitchell, *Alternative Treatments for Troubled Youth: The Case of Diversion from the Justice System* (New York: Plenum, 1990).

implemented a variety of diversion interventions. It asked and was designed to answer important questions. It was experimentally evaluated and objectively measured.

One-third of the subjects of the Adolescent Diversion Project had been accused of larceny-theft and another one-quarter had been accused of breaking and entering. Because most of the project's subjects were criminal offenders, it provides another opportunity to determine whether diversion can safely be extended to other than status offenders.

The Adolescent Diversion Project implemented a variety of diversion interventions (see Box 4.3). Study I, which began in the fall of 1976 and ended in the spring of 1981, offered six distinct interventions ranging from behavioral contracting and child advocacy to standard court processing. Diversion services were provided by undergraduate university students working for course grades. All were specially trained and each had their own juvenile "client" for 6 to 8 hours per week across 18 weeks. The undergraduate students were monitored and evaluated by graduate students, by their juvenile clients, and by the professors running the study and assigning the grades. Study II, which started in the fall of 1979 and ended in the spring of 1981, limited diversion intervention to behavioral contracting and child advocacy but reached beyond grade-driven undergraduates to volunteers as providers of diversion services. All the volunteers were carefully trained, each had their own client for 6 to 8 hours per week across 18 weeks, and each was carefully monitored and evaluated.

The Adolescent Diversion Project asked and was designed to answer important questions, with some based directly on labeling theory and others intended to probe whether less is more. Is it true, as labeling theorists assert, that court processing causes more delinquency? The designed comparisons between the diversion interventions (AC, AC-FF, RC, UV, CCV, and CV) and the control condition (CC) contain answers. Is diversion treatment delivered in the standard court setting, as labeling theory would suggest, less effective than diversion treatment free of court contamination? The designed comparison in Study I between the AC-CS and AC interventions holds the answer. Is less more? Answers can be found in the APC versus AC, AC-FF, and RC comparisons in Study I.

Box 4.3 Description of Adolescent Diversion Project Interventions

Study I started in the fall of 1976 and ended in the spring of 1981. It offered six distinct interventions and except for return to court intake, each juvenile had their own counselor:

1. *Action Condition, Individual Focus* (AC): 76 juveniles were placed with university students trained in behavioral contracting and advocacy. The student identified the needs and problems of their client, wrote a contract specifying changes, and mobilized community resources to increase the odds of successful changes.

2. *Action Condition, Family Focus* (AC-FF): 24 juveniles were placed with university students trained in behavioral contracting and advocacy with a focus on the family as a unit.

3. *Action Condition, Court Setting* (AC-CS): 12 juveniles were placed with university students and a juvenile court staff member trained in behavioral contracting and advocacy. All contacts took place in the court setting.

4. *Relationship Condition* (RC): 12 juveniles were placed with university students trained in building relationships. The primary goal was to create a positive relationship and then move in the direction of agreed upon change.

5. *Attention-Placebo Condition* (APC): 29 juveniles were placed with university students who received "minimal training" and were simply left on their own to figure out what to do with and for their juvenile. Most thought recreation was a good idea and that is mostly what they did.

6. *Control Condition* (CC): 60 juveniles were referred to the project and then returned to court intake for standard processing.

Study II started in the fall of 1979 and ended in the spring of 1981. All three of the experimental interventions involved behavioral contracting and advocacy, with a focus on the individual. All of the service providers received special training. The only difference was that the people doing the contracting and advocacy were volunteers and except for return to court intake, each juvenile had their own counselor:

1. *University Volunteer Condition* (UV): 47 juveniles received services from university volunteers.
2. *Community College Volunteer* (CCV): 36 juveniles received services from community college volunteers.
3. *Community Volunteer Condition* (CV): 19 juveniles received services from volunteers from the local community.
4. *Control Condition* (CC): 27 juveniles were referred to the project and then returned to court intake for standard processing.

Source: William S. Davidson II, Robin Redner, Richard L. Admur, and Christina M. Mitchell, *Alternative Treatments for Troubled Youth: The Case of Diversion from the Justice System* (New York: Plenum, 1990), pp. 57–66 and 75–76.

The Adolescent Diversion Project was experimentally evaluated. Eligible juveniles who "admitted . . . having committed the offense"[31] and their parents were told about the project by the Ingham County juvenile court intake referee. If they expressed interest, project staff then explained to juveniles and their parents the type and amount of treatment. Project staff also told juveniles and their parents that participation was voluntary but if they chose not to participate, the juvenile would be immediately "returned to the court's intake referee for another disposition."[32] Most agreed to participate. Juveniles were then randomly assigned to one of the project's comparison groups.

The Adolescent Diversion Project was objectively measured using a number of different indicators of delinquency. Representative of the official measures collected by the project evaluators are the court petition data in Figure 4.2. Three observations are important.

First, the data confirm that diversion can safely be extended to other than status offenders. Most of the project's offenders admitted criminal acts and yet all of the community-based diversion interventions involved less delinquency than did return to court intake. For example: only 39 percent of the juveniles randomly assigned to individually focused behavioral contracting and child advocacy (AC in Figure 4.2) had at least one new court

FIGURE 4.2   Adolescent Diversion Project: Percent of offenders with at least one new court petition in the two years following intervention, by type of intervention, intervention setting, and amount of intervention

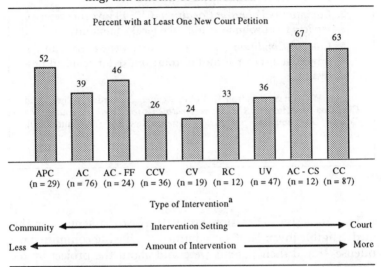

Percent with at Least One New Court Petition

52	39	46	26	24	33	36	67	63
APC	AC	AC - FF	CCV	CV	RC	UV	AC - CS	CC
(n = 29)	(n = 76)	(n = 24)	(n = 36)	(n = 19)	(n = 12)	(n = 47)	(n = 12)	(n = 87)

Type of Intervention[a]

Community ←——————— Intervention Setting ———————→ Court

Less ←——————— Amount of Intervention ———————→ More

[a]See Box 4.3 for a description of the interventions. The CC group is composed of juveniles in the control condition in Study I and Study II. The APC and CC interventions were placed at the left and right extremes, respectively. The AC-CS intervention was placed second right next to the CC intervention. All of the other interventions were placed alphabetically by acronym from second from left to third from right.

Source: William S. Davidson II, Robin Redner, Richard L. Admur, and Christina M. Mitchell, *Alternative Treatments for Troubled Youth: The Case of Diversion from the Justice System* (New York: Plenum, 1990). Constructed from table 6-1 on p. 96, table 5-9 on p. 75, and table 7-11 on p. 118. Modified and reprinted by permission of Plenum Press.

petition as compared to 63 percent of the juveniles returned for standard intake processing (CC in Figure 4.2).

Second, labeling assertions and suggestions are strongly supported by the data in Figure 4.2. In addition to the clear superiority of diversion over return to intake, the AC versus AC-CS[33] comparison is of special interest. For both the AC and AC-CS interventions, treatment involved behavioral contracting and child advocacy. In both interventions, services were provided by specially trained university students. There also were two important differences. Unlike AC sessions, AC-CS sessions took place at the Ingham County juvenile court. And the university students providing AC-CS services were supervised by a member of the court who frequently participated in treatment sessions. The result was clear: the AC-CS intervention produced a 67 percent recidivism rate, the highest of any of the interventions.

Third, the evidence with respect to whether less is more yields contradictory answers and both are correct. Consider first the answer harbored in the APC versus AC, AC-FF, and RC comparisons in Study I. The APC intervention was deliberately unfocused and left the university students mostly on their own when it came to treatment. Training, for example, directed attention to sociological and psychological theories of delinquency,[34] not to the specifics of behavioral contracting and child advocacy. Left alone to determine what to do, most of the students concluded that recreation was a good idea and spent 6 to 8 hours per week across 18 weeks shooting baskets and kicking soccer balls with their juvenile clients. Almost certainly it was fun stuff but doing less was not as effective as doing more. As compared to the other diversion interventions in Study I, the APC intervention yielded a 52 percent recidivism rate, the highest of the diversion interventions.

However, all of the diversion interventions, including APC, yielded less delinquency than the CC intervention. When juveniles have committed other than index crimes against persons, doing less was just as effective as further penetration of the juvenile justice system.

SUMMARY AND CONCLUSIONS

This chapter probed the effectiveness of diversion. It began by demonstrating that efforts to control delinquency by diverting juveniles are grounded in labeling theory. Attention was then directed to describing and assessing the Sacramento County Diversion Project. Examined last were the results of three replications, starting with the Evaluation of Juvenile Diversion Projects, continuing with the National Evaluation of Diversion Projects, and ending with the Adolescent Diversion Project.

The four projects examined and the results of other assessments of diversion in the control of delinquency[35] combine to yield one firm conclusion. Diversion of juveniles accused of status and property crimes is at least as effective as further penetration of the juvenile justice system.

But not without cost. Diversion always involves treatment without trial. Diversion also means widening the net of social control to include juveniles who otherwise would have been left alone.

NOTES

1. William S. Davidson II, Robin Redner, Richard L. Admur, and Christina M. Mitchell, *Alternative Treatments for Troubled Youth: The Case of Diversion from the Justice System* (New York: Plenum, 1990); Franklyn W. Dunford, D. Wayne Osgood, and Hart F. Weichselbaum, *National Evaluation of Diversion Projects: Final Report* (Washington, D.C.: The National Institute of Juvenile Justice and Delinquency Prevention, Office of Juvenile Justice and Delinquency Prevention, U.S Department of Justice, May 1981); Michelle Bauer, Gilda Bordeaux, John Cole, William S. Davidson, Arnoldo Martinez, Christina Mitchell, and Dolly Singleton, "A Diversion Program for Juvenile Offenders: The Experience of Ingham County, Michigan," *Juvenile and Family Court Journal* 17 (August 1980): 58–61; Ted Palmer, Marvin Bohnstedt, and Roy Lewis, *The Evaluation of Juvenile Diversion Projects: Final Report* (Sacramento, Calif.: Division of Research, California Youth Authority, Winter 1978); Roger Baron and Floyd Feeney, *Juvenile Diversion Through Family Counseling* (Washington, D.C.: U.S. Government Printing Office, February 1976); and Roger Baron, Floyd Feeney, and Warren Thornton, "Preventing Delinquency Through Diversion," *Federal Probation* 37 (March 1973): 13–18.

2. Robert M. Carter and Malcolm Klein (eds.), *Back on the Street: The Diversion of Juvenile Offenders* (Englewood Cliffs, N.J.: Prentice-Hall, 1976).

3. Edwin M. Schur, *Radical Nonintervention: Rethinking the Delinquency Problem* (Englewood Cliffs, N.J.: Prentice-Hall, 1973).

4. Ibid.

5. For an early statement, see Frank Tannenbaum, *Crime and the Community* (New York: Columbia University Press, 1938). For a recent empirical assessment of labeling theory, see Douglas A. Smith and Raymond Paternoster, "Formal Processing and Future Delinquency: Deviance Amplification as Selection Artifact," *Law and Society Review* 24 (December 1990): 1109–31.

6. Schur, *Radical Nonintervention*, p. 155.

7. Tannenbaum, *Crime and the Community*, p. 17.

8. Ibid., p. 18.

9. Ibid., p. 19.

10. Howard S. Becker, *Outsiders: Studies in the Sociology of Deviance* (New York: The Free Press of Glencoe, 1963), p. 31.

11. Ibid., p. 32.

12. Ibid., p. 34.

13. Baron, Feeney, and Thornton, "Preventing Delinquency Through Diversion"; Baron and Feeney, *Juvenile Diversion*.

14. Baron, Feeney, and Thornton, "Preventing Delinquency Through Diversion," p. 13.

15. Thomas G. Blomberg, "Diversion's Disparate Results and Unresolved Questions: An Integrative Evaluation Perspective," *Journal of Research in Crime and Delinquency* 20 (January 1983): 26.

16. Baron, Feeney, and Thornton, "Preventing Delinquency Through Diversion," p. 15.

17. Baron and Feeney, *Juvenile Diversion*, p. 52.

18. Ibid., p. 32.

19. Ibid., p. 44.

20. Ibid., p. 43.

21. Ibid., p. 3.

22. Ibid., pp. 44–45.

23. Palmer, Bohnstedt, and Lewis, *Evaluation of Juvenile Diversion Projects*.

24. Blomberg, "Diversion's Disparate Results."

25. Richard J. Lundman, "Will Diversion Reduce Recidivism?" *Crime and Delinquency* 22 (October 1976): 428–37.

26. Schur, *Radical Nonintervention*.

27. Dunford, Osgood, and Weichselbaum, *National Evaluation of Juvenile Diversion Projects*.

28. Ira M. Schwartz, *(In) Justice for Juveniles: Rethinking the Best Interests of the Child* (Lexington, Mass.: Lexington Books, 1989), pp. 110–118. Professor Schwartz was administrator of the OJJDP in 1980.

29. Dunford, Osgood, and Weichselbaum, *National Evaluation*, pp. 39ff.

30. Davidson et al., *Alternative Treatments*.

31. Ibid., p. 53.

32. Ibid., p. 55.

33. The AC-CS comparison group involved only 12 offenders. This is a very small *n* and it is a good idea to be careful with this finding.

34. Davidson et al., *Alternative Treatments*, p. 65.

35. Deborah J. Denno, "Impact of a Youth Service Center: Does Diversion Work? *Criminology* 18 (November 1980): 347–62; Mark Lipsey, David Cordray, and Dale E. Berger, "Evaluation of a Juvenile Diversion Program: Using Multiple Lines of Evidence," *Evaluation Review* 5 (June 1981): 283–306; Sharla Rausch, "Court Processing Versus Diversion of Status Offenders: A Test of Deterrence and Labeling Theories," *Journal of Research in Crime and Delinquency* 20 (January 1983): 39–54; James G. Emshoff, "The Diversion of Delinquent Youth: Family-Focused Intervention," *Children and Youth Services Review* 5 (December 1983): 343–56; Robert Regoli, Elizabeth Wilderman, and Mark Pogrebin, "Using an Alternative Measure for Assessing Juvenile Diversion Programs," *Children and Youth Services Review* 7 (January 1985): 21–38; J. Randy Koch, "Community Service and Outright Release as Alternatives to Juvenile Court: An Experimental Evaluation" (Ph.D. diss., Michigan State University, 1985).

PART THREE

POSTADJUDICATION
INTERVENTION

5

PROBATION AND PAROLE

Probation is an alternative to incarceration that permits convicted juvenile offenders to serve their sentences in the community. Attached to probation are special conditions, such as regular school attendance or employment, that probationers must comply with to remain in the community. In an effort to ensure compliance with the conditions of probation, juvenile courts employ probation officers to supervise and assist probationers.

Parole is a conditional release from an institution. Unlike probationers who serve their time in the community, parolees first serve part of their sentences in a correctional facility for juvenile offenders. They then are released to the community to serve the remainder of their sentences. Like probationers, parolees must comply with special conditions to remain in the community. Parole officers enforce the conditions of parole and attempt to keep parolees out of further trouble with the law.

This chapter examines the effectiveness of probation and parole in the control of juvenile delinquency. It begins by describing probation and parole services for juvenile offenders, including the recent and widespread popularity of intensive supervision programs (ISPs). Examined next is California's Community Treatment Project, an ISP that anticipated the current wave of interest by almost forty years. Last, brief replication of the Community Treatment Project is presented.

PROBATION AND PAROLE SERVICES
FOR JUVENILE OFFENDERS

Probation and parole services for juvenile offenders have different historical origins. Probation for juveniles traditionally is traced to the pioneering efforts of John Augustus, a social reformer who almost single-handedly shaped the basic parameters of probation as we know it today. Parole for juvenile offenders has its roots in the houses of refuge established in the early 1800s. After serving one or two years in these special institutions, offenders were bound to adult masters to serve the remainder of their sentences in the community.

Although their historical origins are different, contemporary probation and parole services are parallel in most respects. Probation and parole are both conditional releases to the community that require compliance with special conditions. Additionally, probation and parole officers experience conflict between the law enforcement and social work demands of their job. Most importantly, intensive supervision programs are bringing new hope to both probation and parole.

PROBATION

Origins.   Distinctly modern probation is traditionally traced to the pioneering efforts of John Augustus (1784–1859).[1] A shoemaker by vocation and a social reformer by avocation. Augustus was active in many reform groups, including the anti-liquor Washington Total Abstinence Society.[2] This interest almost certainly led to his first involvement in "bailing on probation": "In the month of August, 1841, I was in court one morning when the door communicating with the lock-room was opened and an officer entered, followed by a ragged and wretched looking man. . . . I imagined from the man's appearance, that his offense was that of yielding to his appetite for intoxicating drinks, and . . . I found that . . . the man was charged with being a common drunkard. . . . I conversed with him for a few moments and found that he was not yet past all hope of reformation, although his appearance and his looks precluded a belief in the minds of others that he would ever become a man again. . . . I bailed him, by permission of the Court. He was ordered to appear for sentence in three weeks. . . . He signed the pledge and became a sober man; at the expiration of this period of probation, I accompanied him into the court room; his whole appearance was changed and no one . . . could have believed he was the same person. . . . The judge expressed himself much pleased . . . and instead of the usual penalty—imprisonment in the House of Correction—he fined him one cent and costs, amounting in all to $3.76. . . . The man continued industrious and sober, and without doubt had been by this treatment, saved from a drunkard's grave."[3]

Justifiably encouraged by his first success, Augustus continued to bail on probation large numbers of male public drunkenness offenders. He also added to his "caseload" female public drunkenness offenders and then juveniles accused of a variety of offenses. During his lifetime, Augustus bailed on probation nearly 2,000 people, and it is said that only ten failed to reappear in court.[4]

Although Augustus was never an official member of the court, he established the basic parameters of probation as we know it today. Augustus carefully investigated the backgrounds of candidates for probation: "Great care was observed . . . to ascertain whether the prisoners were promising subjects for probation, and to this end it was necessary to take into consideration the previous character of the person, his age and the influences by which he would in the future be likely surrounded, and although these points were not rigidly adhered to, they were the circumstances which usually determined my action."[5] Augustus also supervised his probationers, provided them with counsel and assistance, and reported their behavior to the court: ". . . it was agreed on my part, that I would note their general conduct, see that they were sent to school or supplied with some honest employment, and . . . make an impartial report to the court whenever they should desire it."[6] Last, Augustus, like most contemporary probation officers, was overworked because of multiple responsibilities and a large caseload: "That year [1845] I made 1,500 calls and received more than this number at my house. I bailed in both courts one hundred and thirty-three, forty-five of whom were females."[7]

When John Augustus died on June 21, 1859, his efforts lacked one essential element: They were not officially recognized by the courts. Massachusetts remedied that situation in 1878 when it passed the first probation law in the United States. The law required that the mayor of Boston appoint "a suitable person whose duty it shall be to attend the sessions of the courts of criminal jurisdictions, to investigate the cases of persons charged with or convicted of crimes and misdemeanors and to recommend to such courts the placing on probation of such persons as may reasonably be expected to be reformed without punishment."[8] In 1880, probation was extended to all courts in Massachusetts although implementation was left optional.[9] In 1890, probation and probation officers were made mandatory in all criminal courts in Massachusetts.[10]

Other states slowly followed Massachusetts in establishing probation as a sentencing alternative and probation officers as members of the court.[11] In 1897, Missouri passed a law that authorized its courts to grant probation. In 1898, Vermont required that probation officers be appointed in each county. Minnesota and Rhode Island passed similar laws in 1899.

However, it was passage by Illinois in 1899 of the first juvenile court law in the nation (see Box 5.1) that resulted in the general availability of probation services for juvenile offenders. The Illinois law required that probation officers "be present in court to present the interests of the child . . . to furnish to the court such information and assistance as the judge may require . . . and to take charge of any child before and after trial as may be directed by the court."[12] Other states quickly passed laws modeled after the Illinois law, including its provisions for probation and probation officers. By 1925, all states except Wyoming had passed juvenile court laws that included probation services.[13]

Contemporary Probation Services.   Probation officers provide three important services[14] to the juvenile court: (1) intake screening; (2) preparation of a social history or presentence investigation (PSI); and (3) supervision and assistance of offenders sentenced to probation.

Probation officers providing intake screening make two fateful decisions. The first is whether the juvenile will be referred to juvenile court. After learning more about the complaint from police, parents, or school officials, the officer checks the juvenile's record and listens to the juvenile's side of the story. In checking and listening, the officer is deciding whether to handle

Box 5.1   "An Act to Regulate the Treatment and Control of
          Dependent, Neglected, and Delinquent Children"

Troubled by the fact that juvenile offenders were tried in adult
courts and sentenced to adult correctional facilities, a group of
wealthy and largely female reformers—sometimes called the
"child savers"—successfully lobbied the Illinois legislature for the
passage of the nation's first juvenile court law in 1899. That law
required that circuit court judges in counties with a population of
over 500,000 "designate one or more of their number, whose duty
it shall be to hear all cases coming under this act. A special court
room to be designated as the juvenile court room, shall be provided for the hearing of such cases, and the findings of the court
shall be entered in a book or books to be kept for that purpose, and
known as the 'Juvenile Record,' and the court may for convenience be called the 'Juvenile Court.'"

Sources: Anthony M. Platt, *The Child Savers: The Invention of Delin-*
quency, 2nd ed. (Chicago: The University of Chicago Press, 1977); and
Robert Bremner (ed.), *Children and Youth in America: A Documentary*
History, Volume II: 1866–1932, parts 1–6 (Cambridge, Mass.: Harvard
University Press, 1970), p. 507.

the case informally or refer to juvenile court for formal processing. Available research indicates that prior record, the seriousness
of the offense, family status, and "attitude" all shape intake
decisions.[15] Juveniles repeatedly in trouble with the law, those
who have committed major offenses, juveniles without homes to
be sent back to, and juveniles who are disrespectful and defiant
are far more likely to be referred to juvenile court.

Once a decision has been made to refer a juvenile, probation
officers working intake must then decide whether to temporarily
detain the youth until a formal detention hearing can be held.
Here too the decision is based on the probation officer's perception of the strength of the informal controls surrounding the
juvenile.[16] Accordingly, prior record, the seriousness of the offense, family status, and attitude shape this decision as well.

Much probation work is paperwork, and the social history or
presentence investigation is the major paperwork burden of con-

temporary probation officers.[17] The PSI is prepared by probation officers and used by judges to dispose of cases involving juveniles adjudicated delinquent by the court. PSIs are burdensome because they require checking school, court, and police records; listening to the juvenile, parents, siblings, teachers, employers, and complainants; and assessing medical, psychiatric, and psychological reports. The PSI concludes with the probation officer's dispositional recommendation to the judge. In approximately 80 percent of cases, the judge's disposition follows the probation officer's recommendation.[18]

The probation officer's final service to the court is supervision and assistance of offenders conditionally released to the community. Offenders sentenced to probation are supposed to abide by special conditions intended to minimize the possibility of further trouble with the law (see Box 5.2). Probation officers enforce the conditions of probation and assist their youthful clients.

There is genuine drama and excitement in the day-to-day work of probation officers, and very little of what they do is easy.[19] Like

---

Box 5.2   The Conditions of Probation

Mark D. Jacobs, in his book *Screwing the System and Making It Work: Juvenile Justice in the No-Fault Society*, notes that probation officers are expected to "reduce repeat criminal activity by enforcing the written and signed rules governing each probationer's travel, curfew, personal associations, compliance with specific court orders, and respect for other forms of authority." These "conditions of probation" mean that a probationer cannot leave the county without permission of the probation officer, must comply with local curfew laws for juveniles, stay clear of other delinquent youth, abide by special rules such as regular school attendance, employment, and restitution or community service, and do as they are told by parents, teachers, and other responsible adults.

Source: Mark D. Jacobs, *Screwing the System and Making It Work: Juvenile Justice in the No-Fault Society* (Chicago: The University of Chicago Press, 1990), p. 111.

street cops,[20] probation officers working intake see kids when they are scared, hurt, and dangerous. Probation officers writing PSIs help make important decisions, ranging from who gets probation to who does hard time in tough training schools. Probation supervision means long hours of trying to help kids who desperately need help, responding to emergencies involving probationers in trouble at school, at home, and with the law, trying to maintain professional distance but ending up attached to some kids, looking for public and private funds to get kids badly needed services, and tracking down parents who do not want to be found because, perhaps, they are drug addicts or they have abused their children physically or sexually. Most of all, probation supervision means working with kids and families on the economic, educational, and health care fringes of our society and trying to find ways of helping them move a little closer toward the center.

In performing these difficult tasks, probation officers experience conflict between the "law enforcement" and "social work" demands of their job.[21] Probation officers are agents of the court charged with the task of protecting the community from additional crimes by their probationers. Probation officers are law enforcers, but they also are social workers who are expected to help their youthful clients identify their problems, work with them in the search for viable solutions, and assist them in implementing strategies for staying out of trouble with the law. These casework efforts require intimacy and caring and do not easily mesh with the law enforcement aspects of the probation officer's role. Some probation officers emphasize one or the other of these conflicting expectations, putting community protection ahead of client growth or promoting client interests at the occasional expense of the community. Others vacillate, not quite sure what they should be doing, or why. Still others artfully alternate and combine law enforcement and social work based on their perception of the immediate needs of the young people placed in their care.[22]

Apart from the ways probation officers do their work, nearly all probation officers are assigned large caseloads and carry multiple responsibilities, including PSIs and other paperwork.[23] Probation officers can devote sustained attention and effort to only some of their probationers and even then, only for short periods of time. For many probationers, regular probation necessarily consists of little more than "an occasional contact with an overworked probation officer."[24]

PAROLE

Origins. Parole for juveniles, also called aftercare, can be traced to the houses of refuge established in the 1820s.[25] The first of these special institutions for juvenile offenders, the New York City House of Refuge, was opened in 1825.[26] Founded by prominent philanthropists and funded by the city and the state, the refuge, in addition to sheltering dependent and neglected children, accepted juveniles convicted by the criminal courts. In 1826 the Boston City Council established the Boston House of Reformation for juveniles, and in 1828 Philadelphia's House of Refuge opened.[27]

These early institutions took only white, male juveniles. Separate facilities were eventually established for African-American males and for young women. Philadelphia opened the Colored House of Refuge in the late 1840s and Baltimore opened its House of Reformation and Instruction for Colored Children during that same time.[28] The Western House of Refuge for young women was opened in Rochester, New York, in the 1850s.[29]

The houses of refuge for white males worked to teach the juveniles how to read, write, and "cipher" (do arithmetic), acquire job-related skills, and, most important, establish habits of obedience and conformity. A typical day at the New York City House of Refuge began at sunrise with "the children . . . warned by the ringing of a bell to rise from their beds. Each child makes his own bed, and steps forth, on a signal, into the Hall. They then proceed, in perfect order, to the Wash Room. Thence they are marched to parade in the yard, and undergo an examination as to their dress and cleanliness; after which, they attend morning prayer. The morning school then commences, where they are occupied in summer, until 7 o'clock. A short intermission is allowed, when the bell rings for breakfast; after which they proceed to their respective workshops, where they labor until 12 o'clock, when they are called from work . . . for dinner. At one, they again commence work . . . until five. . . . Half an hour is allowed for washing and eating . . . and at half-past five, they are conducted to the school room where they continue at their studies until 8 o'clock. Evening prayer is performed by the Superintendent; after which, the children are conducted to their dormitories, which they enter, and are locked up for the night, when perfect silence reigns throughout the establishment."[30]

The separate institutions for African-American juveniles and young women were products of their places and their times. In the North, "white boys were trained as farmers and skilled artisans and provided with academic instruction. . . . blacks were prepared for manual labor and discouraged from pursuing academic education."[31] In the South "white boys [were] taught some useful occupation and [African-American] boys [were] compelled to work and support the institution."[32] At houses of refuge for white girls inmates learned how to take care of their own homes. African-American girls were trained as domestics.[33] The separate houses of refuge reflected the society in which they existed and mirrored racist and sexist assumptions and stereotypes.

Most juveniles were sentenced to houses of refuge until their majority, age 21 for young men and 18 or 19 for young women. In practice, however, most were kept one or two years and then released under a procedure known as "binding out." Gustave de Beaumont and Alexis de Tocqueville studied the houses of refuge in the early 1830s and described this early method of parole for juvenile offenders: "Absolute and complete liberty is not restored . . . because what would become of him in the world, alone, without support, unknown by anybody?—He would find himself in precisely the same situation in which he was, before he entered the house. This great danger is avoided: the superintendent waits for a good opportunity to bind him out as apprentice with some mechanic, or to place him as a servant in some respectable family; he avoids sending him into a city, where he would relapse into his bad habits, and find again the companions of his disorderly life; and every time an opportunity offers, employment for him, with farmers, is preferred. At the moment he leaves the establishment, a writing is given to him, which, in kind words, contains advice for his future conduct; the present of a Bible is added."[34]

The earliest houses of refuge in New York, Boston, and Philadelphia served as models for the responses of states to criminal, neglected, and dependent children and adolescents. In 1847, Massachusetts opened the Lyman School for boys at Westborough.[35] Reformatories and training schools spread rapidly, especially in the north and west. Maine, Ohio, and Rhode Island opened correctional facilities for juvenile offenders in 1850, Connecticut did so in 1854, Maryland in 1855, Michigan and Missouri in 1856, and Wisconsin in 1857.[36] By 1900, 36 states had separate correctional facilities for juvenile offenders. Only the South lagged behind the rest of the nation in creating separate facilities for troubled youth.[37]

These new institutions were called reformatories and later schools,[38] but they were little different than the houses of refuge that had preceded them. The legislation establishing the first of these new institutions, Massachusetts' Lyman School For Boys, instructed the school's superintendent and managers to "cause the boys under their charge to be instructed in piety and morality, and in such branches of useful knowledge as shall be adapted to their ages and capacity; they shall also be instructed in some regular course of labor . . . as may seem to them best adapted to secure the reformation, amendment, and future benefit, of the boys."[39] Once juveniles had been exposed to an institution's programs for one or two years, they were bound to adult masters.

As the number of juveniles bound to adult masters increased, states began to make provisions for investigating and monitoring the placements of indentured juveniles. In 1869, Massachusetts passed a law making "visiting agents" responsible for investigating and monitoring parole placements: "All applications to take . . . children . . . by indenture . . . shall be referred to the . . . agent, who shall investigate the character of each applicant, and the expediency of so disposing of the child applied for, and report the result to the board or magistrate having jurisdiction over the child, and no such child shall be indentured . . . until such report is received. . . . It shall be his duty to visit the children . . . at least once in three months, to inquire into their treatment, their health and associations, and especially to ascertain whether their legal rights have been invaded, and whether all contracts or stipulations made in their behalf have been duly observed, and to collect such other information respecting them as the board of state charities may direct; and, for this purpose, he shall have the right to hold private interviews with the children, whenever he may deem it advisable."[40]

However, as was true of probation, parole received its greatest impetus with the passage by Illinois of the nation's first juvenile court law in 1899. The law required the superintendents of state institutions for juvenile offenders to appoint parole officers to "examine the homes of . . . [paroled] . . . children . . . to assist children paroled or discharged . . . in finding suitable employment, and to maintain a friendly supervision over paroled inmates during . . . their parole."[41] Because other states modeled their juvenile court statutes after the Illinois law, "parole was legalized in virtually every state as a part of the juvenile court movement."[42]

Contemporary Parole Services. Probation and parole offer parallel services[43] (see Figure 5.1). Prior to the decision to release a juvenile offender from a correctional facility, institutional personnel assemble a preparole report that includes information similar to that contained in the probation officer's presentence investigation. The actual decision to grant parole is made by the superintendent of the institution, other members of a state's

FIGURE 5.1   Probation and parole as parallel services

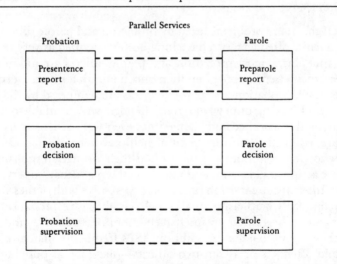

Source: Howard Abadinsky, *Probation and Parole: Theory and Practice*, 4th ed., p. 154. © 1991. Adapted by permission of Prentice-Hall, Englewood Cliffs, New Jersey.

department of juvenile corrections, or by the judge who originally sentenced the juvenile. Once early release has been granted, the offender is supervised and assisted by a parole officer.

Because probation and parole offer parallel services, procedures and problems are similar. Parolees are conditionally released to the community and expected to abide by conditions of parole little different from those associated with probation. Parole officers also experience conflict between the law enforcement and social work aspects of their job.[44] Some choose to focus on their law enforcerment duties, and are quick to revoke parole for even minor violations of the conditions of parole. Others are more comfortable with the social work aspects of their job and ignore minor violations as long as their youthful clients are making sincere efforts to change their ways of thinking and acting. Further, most parole officers, like most probation officers, have large caseloads and multiple responsibilities. Last, parole officers, like probation officers, try to help juveniles and their families more from the fringes of society toward the mainstream. As with probation, very little of what parole officers do is easy.

INTENSIVE SUPERVISION PROGRAMS

Of the many problems faced by probation and parole officers for juvenile offenders, two have long been recognized as very important.[45] First, most probation and parole officers are too busy to see their clients more often than once a month for brief meetings. Second, probation and parole services are hampered by the haphazard linking of newly arrived offenders with available officers. Juveniles who need and sometimes even want strict supervision are assigned to officers good at helping, not policing. Officers who view community protection as their primary responsibility are assigned kids who need more social services than supervision.

Intensive supervision programs (ISPs) solve both of these problems. ISPs emphasize small caseloads that give probation and parole officers time to intensively monitor, supervise, and treat their young clients. In addition, ISPs frequently match officers and offenders or assign two officers—one good at policing, the other at helping—to each small caseload.

However, there is much more to current ISPs than simply solving long-recognized problems of large caseloads and haphazard placements. ISPs are intermediate interventions, that is, they stand midway between routine probation and institutionalization, and between institutionalization and routine parole[46] (see Figure 5.2). ISPs therefore fill important gaps in the range of existing responses to delinquent juveniles. Juvenile court judges regularly encounter offenders who require something more than routine probation, yet something less than institutionalization. Intensive probation fills this need. For the correctional officials and judges who make parole decisions, intensive parole allows for the earlier release of juveniles who require options other than regular parole with its large caseloads and infrequent contacts.

ISPs are intended to relieve overcrowding of correctional facilities.[47] Instead of sending juveniles who require something more than routine probation to an institution, juvenile court judges sentence offenders to an intensive probation program emphasizing close monitoring and supervision. Intensive parole programs permit earlier release of offenders not quite ready for regular parole but ready enough for closely monitored and enforced aftercare.

FIGURE 5.2 Intensive supervision programs as intermediate interventions standing midway between existing responses to delinquent juveniles

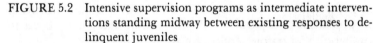

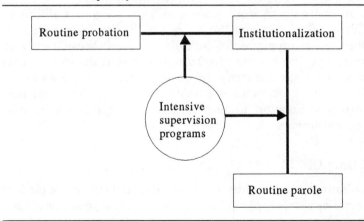

Source: This figure is based on a description of intermediate interventions in Norval Morris and Michael Tonry, *Between Prison and Probation: Intermediate Punishments in a Rational Sentencing System* (New York: Oxford University Press, 1990).

ISPs are an example of the United States' current "get tough" policy with respect to adolescent crime.[48] Intensive probation and intensive parole programs are *tough* ways of doing time in the community. Small caseloads allow for the strict enforcement of the routine conditions of probation and parole. Officers have time to make sure clients are in school or at work each weekday and at home each night and weekend. Electronic monitoring devices enhance surveillance of client compliance with educational, work, and curfew conditions. Frequently scheduled, random urine checks for drugs dramatically increase the odds that offenders who continue to abuse drugs or alcohol will be detected. New conditions can be added to probation and parole in ISPs, including fines, restitution, community service, and treatment for substance abuse, with offenders paying some of the costs of their supervision and treatment. Tough and intrusive supervision, surveillance, and control are central and deliberate features of contemporary ISPs.

ISPs have breathed new life into probation and parole for juveniles.[49] Just a few short years ago, probation and parole were overwhelmed by too many clients, too few officers, and too little attention. ISPs are bringing more money, officers, and attention to probation and parole. ISPs also are bringing new hope to probation and parole services for juvenile offenders.

Intensive supervision, however, is not a new idea. California's Community Treatment Project, one of the first intensive parole supervision programs for juvenile offenders, began nearly 40 years ago. The Community Treatment Project therefore teaches lessons that speak directly and clearly to the new hope surrounding current probation and parole services for juveniles. We now turn our attention to that early project, including its still-relevant lessons.

COMMUNITY TREATMENT PROJECT

California's Community Treatment Project[50] was one of the first intensive parole supervision programs involving juvenile offenders. To make certain that supervision was intensive, caseloads were reduced to no more than 12 offenders. Additionally, offenders were matched with parole officers thought able to meet their particular needs. Table 5.1 summarizes the major features of the

Table 5.1 Description of the Community Treatment Project

Project Name:	The Community Treatment Project
Locations:	Sacramento, Stockton, and San Francisco, California
Dates:	1961–1969
Subjects:	Juveniles adjudicated delinquent and sentenced to California Youth Authority correctional facilities. Offenders averaged 5.8 arrests prior to their commitment, primarily for property offenses, such as burglary, and status offenses, such as incorrigibility. Most were from lower-class backgrounds and about half were white.
Type of treatment:	Experimental subjects were released back to the community for intensive parole supervision by specially selected parole officers responsible for caseloads no larger than 12. Control subjects were sent to California Youth Authority correctional facilities for about 8 months and then released to regular nonintensive parole supervision.
Amount of treatment:	Experimental juveniles were intensively treated and supervised by their specially selected parole officers for up to three years. Control subjects spent approximately eight months in a correctional facility for juvenile offenders and then approximately three years on standard nonintensive parole.
Evaluative design:	Experimental: At least through April 1966 eligible subjects were randomly assigned to the experimental and control groups.
Measures of results:	Parole suspensions and revocations, favorable and unfavorable discharges from parole, and arrests following discharge from parole status were used to measure results.
Replication:	Community-based efforts to control delinquency including intensive supervision programs have been quite common. At the end of this chapter, brief replicative attention is directed at one of those projects. Other projects are examined in detail in the chapters that follow.

Sources: Ted B. Palmer, "California's Community Treatment Project for Delinquent Adolescents," *Journal of Research in Crime and Delinquency* 8 (January 1971): 74–92; Ted Palmer, "Youth Authority's Community Treatment Project," *Federal Probation* 38 (March 1974): 3–14.

Community Treatment Project and serves a a guide for the description and analysis that follow.

DESCRIPTION OF THE PROJECT

Starting in 1961 and continuing through 1969, the California Youth Authority operated the Community Treatment Project in Sacramento, Stockton, and San Francisco.[51] The primary purpose of the project was to determine whether intensive parole supervision and matching of parolees with parole officers could be used in place of commitment to a correctional facility. The Community Treatment Project was thus one of the first efforts to provide a special form of community treatment for offenders who otherwise would have been institutionalized.

Juveniles involved in the Community Treatment Project had been adjudicated delinquent by Sacramento, Stockton, and San Francisco juvenile court judges and committed to the California Youth Authority for placement in a correctional facility. Prior to their commitment to the Youth Authority they had averaged 5.8 arrests, primarily for property offenses, such as burglary and auto theft, and status offenses, such as incorrigibility and running away. Nearly all were from disadvantaged social backgrounds, 80 percent were male, about one-half were white, one-quarter were Hispanic, and one-quarter were African-American. The average age was 15½.

Not all offenders committed to the Youth Authority from Sacramento, Stockton, and San Francisco were eligible for inclusion in the Community Treatment Project. Some offenders were excluded because they had been adjudicated delinquent for committing serious crimes, such as murder, armed robbery, and rape. Others were excluded when local officials, primarily police and probation officers, objected to the nearly immediate return of an offender to the community. Overall, 35 percent of the male and 17 percent of the female commitments to the Youth Authority from Sacramento, Stockton, and San Francisco were declared ineligible on the basis of these two criteria.[52]

TYPE OF TREATMENT

Almost all delinquency control projects experience some slippage between intended and actual treatment services.[53] Plans and ideas that look good on paper and in meetings are inevitably altered by day-to-day problems of administering and delivering treatment services. In the case of the Community Treatment Project, however, slippage was so great that it is necessary to first examine what treatment was supposed to involve and then what it became.

Intended Treatment Program. The Community Treatment Project was intended to be a relatively benign mixture of community-based program elements delivered in the context of small parole caseloads and matching of parolees with parole officers. It was hypothesized that intensive parole supervision and assistance would improve parole services and thereby control delinquency (see Figure 5.3).

The Community Treatment Project made the following community-based program elements available to its parolees: (1) group and other out-of-home placements; (2) individual, group, and family counseling; (3) frequent parolee-parole officer meetings, including daily contacts as necessary; (4) extensive surveillance during the day, at night, and on weekends; (5) educational and recreational programs at the Community Treatment Project's community center; and (6) "short-term, treatment- and/or control-oriented detention at a nearby . . . facility."[54]

Small caseloads of between six and eight offenders were considered crucial to the success of the Community Treatment Project.[55] With small caseloads, parole officers could meet the needs of individual parolees by selectively exposing them to the community-based program elements made available by the project. Equally important, with small caseloads parole officers could intensively supervise their parolees.

The amount of treatment provided parolees was intended to be divided into three stages. Stage A, or *intensive treatment,* was to

FIGURE 5.3 Community Treatment Project: *intended* treatment hypothesis in diagrammatic form

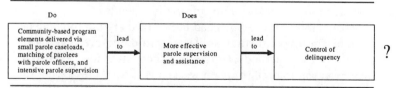

Sources: The intended treatment hypothesis is based on description of the Community Treatment Project in Ted B. Palmer, "California's Community Treatment Program for Delinquent Adolescents," *Journal of Research in Crime and Delinquency* 8 (January 1971): 74–92; and Marguerite Q. Warren, "The Case for Differential Treatment of Delinquents," *The Annals of the American Academy of Political and Social Science* 38 (January 1969): 47–59.

last about eight months and average two to five parolee–parole officer contacts per week. It was also to involve "full or partial day programming,"[56] utilizing the community-based program elements made availabe by the Community Treatment Project. Stage B, or *transitional treatment*, limited contacts to an average of one per week with a focus on "any difficulties arising from the decrease in amount of support and supervision"[57] by parole officers. Stage C, or *minimum treatment*, was to resemble the routine parole supervision provided control group subjects following their approximately eight months in a Youth Authority correctional facility. Contacts were therefore to be limited to an average of one per month.

Actual Treatment Program.   Many aspects of the Community Treatment Project were implemented as intended. Offenders were matched with parole officers in a successful effort to link those who needed help with officers who liked helping and those who needed strict enforcement with officers who liked policing. Some aspects of the project were changed only slightly. Caseload sizes, for example, were nudged up to 12 to increase the number of experimental subjects. Other aspects of the project, however, were dramatically different from what was intended, with three of prime importance.

First, analysis in advance of the project had suggested that only 12 percent of the experimental subjects would need to be removed from their own homes and placed in foster or group homes.[58] By April 1966, however, Community Treatment Project parole officers had placed 67 percent of the experimental subjects in foster or group homes.[59] In practice, the Community Treatment Project was far more *instrusive* than originally intended.

Second, initial projections had indicated that only about 40 percent of the experimental subjects would require detention,[60] primarily as a method of grabbing their attention. Even then, detention was to occur only on weekends. Actual use of detention was far more frequent and of much greater duration. By April 1966, nearly eight of ten experimental subjects had been sent to local detention facilities at least once, and the average was 2.8 detentions per experimental subject. Once detained, experimental subjects averaged 20 days per detention.[61] In practice, the

Community Treatment Project was far *tougher* than originally intended.

The third important change in the intended design of the Community Treatment Project involved the intensity of the supervision and assistance provided experimental subjects. As originally projected, experimental subjects were to receive intensive supervision for about eight months, transitional supervision for a brief period of time, and then minimum supervision for the remainder of their time on parole, usually two to three years. Almost four years into the project on July 1, 1965, however, 85 percent of the experimental subjects were still receiving intensive supervision.[62] Some eight months later on March 31, 1966, 90 percent of the experimental subjects were receiving intensive supervision.[63] In practice, the Community Treatment Project was far more *intensive* than originally intended.

Actual treatment, then, was more intrusive, far tougher, and more intensive than originally intended. Most experimental subjects were taken from their own homes and placed in foster or group homes by their parole officers. Most also spent considerable time locked up in local detention facilities. All were intensively exposed to these and other program elements during the full term of their parole, usually two to three years. Figure 5.4 shows what actually happened during the course of the Community Treatment Project.

FIGURE 5.4   Community Treatment Project: *actual* treatment hypothesis in diagrammatic form

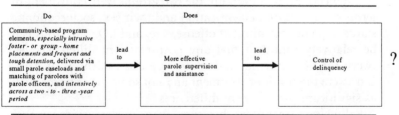

Source: The actual treatment hypothesis is based on description of the Community Treatment Project in Paul Lerman, *Community Treatment and Social Control: A Critical Analysis of Juvenile Correctional Policy* (Chicago: The University of Chicago Press, 1975), pp. 30–54.

EVALUATIVE DESIGN

The Community Treatment Project was intended to be evaluated experimentally. Offenders sentenced to the California Youth Authority by juvenile courts in Sacramento, Stockton, and San Francisco were first sent to the Youth Authority's Northern Reception Center and Clinic. At the clinic, ineligible offenders were excluded and eligible offenders classified[64] for later matching with parole officers. Eligible offenders were then randomly assigned to either the Community Treatment Project or a Youth Authority correctional facility. Normally, such procedures would produce two equivalent groups of roughly comparable size.

However, the policy of providing intensive supervision and asistance during the full term of parole meant that the experimental caseloads did not turn over as rapidly as anticipated. Because new parole officers were not supposed to be added, experimental subjects were far fewer than control subjects. On August 1, 1963, nearly two years into the project, there were only 77 experimental subjects as compared to 167 control subjects. The situation was not much improved on January 21, 1964, when experimental subjects had increased only to 87.[65]

Efforts were therefore undertaken to increase the number of experimental subjects. Caseload sizes were expanded to a maximum of 12 offenders, and the number of Community Treatment Project parole officers was more than doubled to accomodate more experimental subjects.

By April 1966 the experimental and control groups were of roughly comparable size: 241 experimental subjects and 220 control subjects. More important, the two groups were equivalent in terms of their initial classification and their sex, socioeconomic status, type of commitment offense, age, and I.Q.[66] We thus can be relatively confident that any post-treatment differences between the experimental and control groups evident as of April 1966 were the result of treatment and not some other factor such as significant pretreatment differences.

Following April 1966, however, there is clear evidence that subjects were no longer being randomly assigned to the experimental and control groups. For "unknown reasons,"[67] the two groups were significantly different in terms of their initial classification, age, and sex. Additionally, the two groups were no longer of roughly comparable size. It therefore is necessary to be very cautious in interpreting either overall results or post-treatment differences following April 1966, because there is no reliable way of determining whether they are traceable to the experimental intervention or other factors, such as the pretreatment differences.

MEASURES OF RESULTS

Several aspects of the Community Treatment Project have turned out to be far different from what was planned. We examined what appeared to be an essentially benign mixture of community-based program elements only to discover that actual treatment was far more heavy-handed than originally intended. We also examined what appeared to be an experimental evaluative design only to learn that random assignment procedures were mysteriously absent after April 1966.

It should therefore come as no great surprise that the measures of results also are different from what they first appear to be. We will begin with California Youth Authority measures of results that appear to show that the project was a modestly successful delinquency control effort. We then will turn to Paul Lerman's measures of the results and to his conclusion that the only behavior the Community Treatment Project controlled was that of adult parole officers.

Youth Authority Measures of Results. The first three measures advanced by the Youth Authority appear to show that the Community Treatment Project was a modestly successful delinquency control effort (see Table 5.2). Experimental subjects experienced fewer parole revocations and recommitments than control subjects (among males, 42 percent versus 64 percent), had a higher rate of favorable discharge from parole (among females, 91 percent versus 78 percent), and a lower rate of unfavorable discharge from parole (among males, 8 percent versus 22 percent).

The other two measures provided by the Youth Authority suggest a somewhat different outcome. As shown in Table 5.2, parole suspensions among members of the experimental group were slightly more frequent than suspensions of members of the

Table 5.2 Community Treatment Project: California Youth Authority Measures of Results, 1961–1969

Measures of Results[a]	Males (n = 579)		Females (n = 122)	
	Experimental (n = 338)	Control (n = 241)	Experimental (n = 58)	Control (n = 64)
Percent parole revocations or recommitments	42	64	34	48
Percent favorably discharged from parole within 60 months	53	48	91	78
Percent *un*favorably discharged from parole within 60 months	8	22	0	17
Average number of parole suspensions per months on parole	1 suspension every 13.4 months	1 suspension every 15.8 months	1 suspension every 24.9 months	1 suspension every 38.8 months
Rate of arrest per dischargee (24-month follow-up)	.82	.81	.27	.00

[a]Measures limited to offenders from Sacramento and Stockton. San Francisco measures were incomplete at the time Dr. Palmer (see below) wrote the article from which these measures are constructed.

Source: Ted B. Palmer, "California's Community Treatment Project for Delinquent Adolescents." *Journal of Research in Crime and Delinquency* 8 (January 1971): 74–92. Constructed from table 3, p. 84 and footnotes 25 and 27, pp. 85–986. Copyright © 1971 by the National Council on Crime and Delinquency. Modified and reprinted by permission of Sage Publications, Inc.

control group (among females, one suspension every 24.9 months as compared to one suspension every 38.8 months). More important, there was virtually no difference in the rate of arrest once experimental and control subjects had been discharged from parole (among males, .82 arrests as compared to .81 arrests). Based on these measures, it would appear that the Community Treatment Project was no more or less effective than institutionalization followed by minimum parole supervision.[68]

According to the Youth Authority, however, the Community Treatment Project's overall record is one of modest success:

'"experimentals' who participated in the intensive, 1961–1969 community-based program . . . produced less delinquent behavior than . . . 'controls' who . . . participated in the traditional . . . program."[69]

Paul Lerman's Measures of Results. Working entirely with data published by the California Youth Authority, Paul Lerman assembled his own measures of the results of the Community Treatment Project[70] (see Table 5.3). Professor Lerman's data demonstrate that there were no important differences between experimental and control subjects in rates of parole suspensions traceable to arrests by police.[71] Experimental and control subjects were arrested in nearly equal numbers for crimes against persons, crimes against property, auto theft, petty theft, and such' other offenses as possession of marihuana. In the eyes of the police, experimental subjects were no less or more delinquent than control group subjects.

Table 5.3 Community Treatment Project: Professor Paul Lerman's Measures of Results as of April 1966

| | Suspensions[a] per 100 Parolees | |
Type of Offense	Experimental[b] (n = 241)	Control[c] (n = 220)
Crimes against persons	12	16
Crimes against property	35	33
Auto theft	29	32
Petty theft	12	11
Other offenses	12	9
Status/technical offenses	175	60

[a]Parole suspensions for alleged violations. In general, parole suspensions for crimes against persons, crimes against property, auto theft, petty theft, and other offenses are the result of arrests of parolees by police. Parole suspensions for status offenses also generally are the result of police arrests, although some are the result of actions by parole officers. Nearly all parole suspensions for technical offenses are the result of actions by parole officers.
[b]As of April 1966, the 241 experimental offenders had been in the community an average of 16.4 months.
[c]As of April 1966, the 220 control group offenders had been in the community an average of 17.9 months.

Source: Paul Lerman, *Community Treatment and Social Control: A Critical Analysis of Juvenile Correctional Policy* (Chicago: The University of Chicago Press, 1975), table 4, p. 60. Copyright © 1975 by The University of Chicago. Reprinted by permission.

At this point we seem to have encountered something of a paradox. According to the Youth Authority, experimental subjects were less delinquent as indicated by their lower rates of parole revocation and recommitment, higher rate of favorable discharge from parole, and lower rate of unfavorable discharge from parole. According to Professor Lerman, experimental subjects were no less or more delinquent as measured by police arrests. Is it possible for both the Youth Authority and Professor Lerman to be correct?

Table 5.4 provides the answer. When experimental group members were suspended from parole, they were much less likely to have their suspension result in parole revocation than members of the control group. This was the case for all of the offenses in Table 5.4. For example, for every 100 parole suspensions for auto theft among members of the experimental group, only 13 resulted in parole revocation as compared to 51 parole revocations per 100 auto thefts by members of the control group.

Professor Lerman's measures of the results of the Community Treatment Project undermine the image of modest success advanced by the California Youth Authority. Based on Professor Lerman's efforts, it is clear that the Community Treatment Project was not successful in controlling the delinquent behavior of its experimental subjects. Instead, the Community Treatment Project changed the frequency with which the parole officers recommended revocation and recommitment[72] once parole had

Table 5.4 Community Treatment Project: Professor Paul Lerman's Reanalysis of Parole Revocations by Type of Offense as of April 1966

	Revocations per 100 Offenses	
Type of Offense	Experimental ($n = 241$)	Control ($n = 220$)
Crimes against persons/property	35	42
Auto theft	13	51
Petty/other offenses	6	34
Status/technical offenses	2	17

Source: Paul Lerman, *Community Treatment and Social Control: A Critical Analysis of Juvenile Correctional Policy* (Chicago: The University of Chicago Press, 1975), table 4, p. 60. Copyright © 1975 by The University of Chicago. Reprinted by permission.

been suspended following arrest. The Community Treatment Project thus succeeded in changing the behavior of adult parole officers rather than adolescent parolees.

BRIEF REPLICATION: VIABLE OPTIONS

This chapter ends without the usual extended replicative analysis because the next three chapters focus primarily or exclusively on community-based efforts to alter or improve probation and parole services for juvenile offenders. Two of the three chapters that follow also compare community-based services with institutionalization, and therefore extend the findings presented in this chapter.

Presented in place of detailed analysis is a brief replication of the Community Treatment Project in Wayne County, Michigan, in the early 1980s. The goal is preliminary assessment of the generalizability of the Community Treatment Project's finding of no difference between intensive supervision and institutionalization.

In the early 1980s, Wayne County, Michigan, which includes Detroit, was experiencing a familiar problem. According to the state, the county was sending too many juveniles to already overcrowded juvenile correctional facilities. Wayne County would have to cap sentences to state facilities at 500 per year and find another way to deal with some of the juveniles the county was sending to state correctional facilities.

Viable Options[73] was the county's intensive probation supervision response to the state's juvenile correctional facility cap (see Table 5.5). Starting early in 1983, some adjudicated delinquents sentenced to the state from Wayne County were instead randomly assigned to either intensive probation caseloads with no more than ten offenders or to the state for placement. Juveniles randomly assigned to intensive supervision received special services for a full year, including 10 to 14 contacts per month with special emphasis on "strict behavioral supervision."[74] Intensive supervision subjects also experienced a variety of other less punitive interventions, including individual counseling, social skills training, youth groups, recreational activities, and parental counseling. Experimental subjects were then released to routine probation for a year. Most of the control subjects were institu-

Table 5.5 Description of Viable Options

Project Name:	Viable Options
Location:	Wayne County, Michigan
Dates:	February 1, 1983, to March 5, 1985
Subjects:	Males adjudicated delinquent—excluding the "very violent," the clearly psychotic, and those with no home to go to—and committed to the state Department of Social Services (DSS) for sentencing and placement. Offenders averaged 3.2 prior arrests, mostly for index crimes against property or nonindex crimes. More than two-thirds (69 percent) were African-American and a little more than three-quarters (76.3 percent) lived in Detroit. Nearly all came from disadvantaged social backgrounds and average age at sentencing was 15.4 years. Overall, the subjects were "relatively serious and chronic, though not highly violent, offenders."
Type of treatment:	Experimental treatment involved small probation caseloads (six to ten offenders per probation officer) and community-based services emphasizing frequent offender/probation officer contact. Most of the offenders sentenced to DSS (133 of 185, or 72 percent) spent their time locked up in a "large" public or private correctional facility followed by regular parole supervision.
Amount of treatment:	Experimental subjects assigned to "intensive probation supervision" received approximately 12 months of services followed by routine probation. Control subjects spent approximately one year locked up followed by one year of regular parole.
Evaluative design:	Experimental: Eligible offenders were randomly assigned to either intensive probation supervision or the Department of Social Services.
Measure of results:	New criminal charges in the two years following random assignment.

Source: William H. Barton and Jeffrey A. Butts, "Viable Options: Intensive Supervision Programs for Juvenile Delinquents," *Crime and Delinquency* 36 (April 1990): 238–56.

tionalized for about one year and then released back to the community where they experienced a year of routine parole supervision.

First impressions sometimes are misleading and such is the case with the results of Viable Options (see Table 5.6). As measured by new criminal charges in the two years following random assignment, the experimental subjects assigned to intensive supervision appear more delinquent than the juveniles in the control group. Experimental subjects averaged 1.85 new criminal

Table 5.6   Viable Options: New Charges for Experimental and Control
Subjects in the Two Years Following Random Assignment

New Charges	Experimental ($n = 326$)	Control ($n = 185$)
Average number of criminal charges	1.85	1.17
Average number of months at large	18.30	10.68
Average number of criminal charges per month at large[a]	.10	.11

[a]Average number of criminal charges divided by average number of months at large

Source: William H. Barton and Jeffrey A. Butts, "Viable Options: Intensive Supervision Programs for Juvenile Delinquents," *Crime and Delinquency* 36 (April 1990): 245. Copyright © 1990 by the National Council on Crime and Deliquency. Modified and reprinted by permission of Sage Publications, Inc.

charges while control subjects averaged 1.17 new criminal charges. However, there also were important differences in the amount of time experimental and control subjects were "at large" in the community. Experimental subjects were at large an average of 18.30 months while control subjects were at large an average of 10.68 months. Controlling for months at large, the misleading first impression difference between experimental and control subjects disappears. Experimental subjects averaged .10 new criminal charges per month at large while control subjects averaged .11 new criminal charges per month at large.

Viable Options' bottom line thus is precisely the same as that of the Community Treatment Project. Juveniles who otherwise would have been institutionalized were randomly assigned to community-based intensive supervision or a state correctional facility. There was no difference[75] between the two interventions.

SUMMARY AND CONCLUSIONS

This chapter began by examining probation and parole for juveniles, including intensive supervision programs. Sustained attention was then directed to the Community Treatment Project, with a careful ear for its lessons about intensive supervision programs. Examined next was brief replication of that early project to probe the generalizability of the "no difference" finding.

Old Lessons about "New" Intensive Supervision Programs

The Community Treatment Project of the 1960s teaches three important lessons about the intensive supervision programs of the 1990s. The Community Treatment Project started soft and ended tough. Contemporary intensive supervision programs start tough and require special attention lest they become impossible.[76] It is one thing when the probation and parole officers charged with intensive supervision speculate they could not comply with the conditions imposed on their youthful clients.[77] It is quite another when intensive supervision becomes impossible reality.

The Community Treatment Project reminds us how important it is that the results of delinquency control efforts be assessed using objective measures assembled by persons not connected with a project. Youth Authority data paint a portrait of modest success. Professor Lerman's independently assembled police arrest data demonstrate no difference between the two interventions during the time the design was clearly experimental.

Least obvious and most important is the finding of no difference between the two interventions. The experimental subjects involved in the Community Treatment Project had averaged 5.8 prior arrests and most would have spent 8 months in a Youth Authority correctional facility had it not been for the existence of the project. Yet, community-based intensive parole supervision was just as effective as institutionalization. Assuming the projects examined in the chapters that follow also show that community-based treatment is just as effective as incarceration, this is potentially a very important finding.

NOTES

1. Description of the origins of probation services for juveniles is based on Howard Abadinsky, *Probation and Parole: Theory and Practice*, 3rd ed. (Englewood Cliffs, N.J.: Prentice-Hall, 1987), pp. 17–24; Robert Bremner (ed.), *Children and Youth in America: A Documentary History, Volume I: 1600–1865* (Cambridge, Mass.: Harvard University Press, 1970), pp. 732–34; Robert Bremner (ed.), *Children and Youth in America: A Documentary History, Volume II: 1866–1932*, parts 1–6

(Cambridge, Mass.: Harvard University Press, 1970), pp. 492–501; United Nations, "The Origins of Probation in the United States," in Robert M. Carter and Leslie T. Wilkins (eds.), *Probation, Parole, and Community Corrections*, 2nd ed. (New York: John Wiley & Sons, 1976), pp. 89–92; Charles Lionel Chute and Marjorie Bell, *Crime, Courts, and Probation* (New York: Macmillan, 1956), pp. 31–88; David Dressler, *Practice and Theory of Probation and Parole*, 2nd ed. (New York: Columbia University Press, 1969), pp. 16–32; and David J. Rothman, *Conscience and Convenience: The Asylum and Its Alternatives in Progressive America* (Boston: Little, Brown, 1980), pp. 82–116 and pp. 205–35.

2. Dressler, *Practice and Theory of Probation and Parole*, p. 23.

3. Cited in Chute and Bell, *Crime, Courts, and Probation*, pp. 36–37. The original source for this description is John Augustus, *A Report of the Labors of John Augustus, in Aid of the Unfortunate* (Boston: Wright and Hasty, 1852), reprinted as *John Augustus, First Probation Officer* (New York: National Probation Association, 1939), pp. 4–5.

4. Dressler, *Practice and Theory of Probation and Parole*, pp. 27 and 44–45.

5. Chute and Bell, *Crime, Courts, and Probation*, pp. 40–41.

6. Bremner, *Children and Youth, Volume I: 1600–1865*, p. 733.

7. Cited in Chute and Bell, *Crime, Courts, and Probation*, p. 43.

8. Ibid., p. 59.

9. Dressler, *Practice and Theory of Probation and Parole*, p. 28.

10. Chute and Bell, *Crime, Courts, and Probation*, p. 65.

11. Dressler, *Practice and Theory of Probation and Parole*, p. 28.

12. Cited in Bremner, *Children and Youth, Volume II, 1866–1932*, parts 1–6, p. 508.

13. Chute and Bell, *Crime, Courts, and Probation*, p. 72; LaMar T. Empey and Mark C. Stafford, *American Delinquency: Its Meaning and Construction*, 3rd ed. (Belmont, Calif.: Wadsworth, 1991), p. 368.

14. Description of contemporary probation services for juveniles is based on Mark D. Jacobs, *Screwing the System and Making It Work: Juvenile Justice in the No-Fault Society* (Chicago: The University of Chicago Press, 1990); Abadinsky, *Probation and Parole*, pp. 83–133; and Empey and Stafford, *American Delinquency*, pp. 368–86.

15. Empey and Stafford, *American Delinquency*, pp. 328–31; Jacobs, *Screwing the System and Making It Work*, p. 161; Cheryl Chambers, Richard M. Grinnell, and Richard L. Gorsuch, "Factors Associated with Police and Probation/Court Dispositioning: A Research Note," *Journal of Sociology and Social Welfare* 7 (March 1980): 246–58; and Lawrence E. Cohen and James R. Kluegel, "Selecting Delinquents for Adjudication: An Analysis of Intake Screening in Two Metropolitan Juvenile Courts,"

Journal of Research in Crime and Delinquency 16 (January 1979): 143–63.

16. Lydia S. Rosner, "Juvenile Secure Detention," *Journal of Offender Counseling, Services, and Rehabilitation* 12 (Summer 1988): 57–76; Russell K. Schutt and Dale Dannefer, "Detention Decisions in Juvenile Cases: JINS, JDs, and Gender," *Law and Society Review* 22 (October 1988): 509–20; and Duran Bell, Jr., and Kevin Lang, "The Intake Dispositions of Juvenile Offenders," *Journal of Research in Crime and Delinquency* 22 (November 1985): 309–28.

17. Jacobs, *Screwing the System and Making It Work*, p. 121; Mordechai Frishtik, "The Probation Officer's Recommendation in His 'Investigation Report,'" *Journal of Offender Counseling, Services, and Rehabilitation* 13 (Spring 1988): 101–32; and Abadinsky, *Probation and Parole*, pp. 42–52.

18. Jacobs, *Screwing the System and Making It Work*, p. 151; J. William Spencer, "Conducting Presentence Investigations: From Discourse to Textual Summaries," *Urban Life* 13 (July–October 1984): 207–27.

19. Jacobs, *Screwing the System and Making It Work*, is the single best description and analysis of probation work I have encountered.

20. For a classic analysis of street cops and their encounters with the scared, hurt, and dangerous, see William Ker Muir, *Police: Streetcorner Politicians* (Chicago: The University of Chicago Press, 1977).

21. Jacobs, *Screwing the System and Making It Work*, pp. 112–13; William A. Reese II, Russell L. Curtis, Jr., and Albert Richard, Jr., "Juvenile Justice as People Modulating: A Case Study of Progressive Delinquent Dispositions," *Journal of Research in Crime and Delinquency* 26 (November 1989): 329–57; R. I. Mawby, "The State of Probation: Views from Within," *Social Policy and Administration* 15 (Autumn 1981): 268–85; Yeheskel Hasenfeld and Paul P. L. Cheung, "The Juvenile Court as a People-Processing Organization: A Political Economy Perspective," *American Journal of Sociology* 90 (January 1985): 801–24; and Paul W. Keve, "No Farewell to Arms," *Crime and Delinquency* 25 (October 1979): 425–35.

22. Reese, Curtis, and Richard, "Juvenile Justice as People Modulating."

23. Jacobs, *Screwing the System and Making It Work*, p. 108.

24. Empey and Stafford, *American Delinquency*, p. 374.

25. Description of the origins of parole services for juveniles is based on John R. Sutton, "The Political Economy of Madness: The Expansion of the Asylum in Progressive America," *American Sociological Review* 56 (October 1991): 665–66; Beverly A. Smith, "Female Admissions and Paroles of the Western House of Refuge During the 1880s: An

Historical Example of Community Corrections," *Journal of Research in Crime and Delinquency* 26 (February 1989): 36-66; Alexander W. Pisciotta, "Race, Sex, and Rehabilitation: A Case Study of Differential Treatment in the Juvenile Reformatory, 1825-1900," *Crime and Delinquency* 29 (April 1983): 254-69; John R. Sutton, "Social Structure, Institutions, and the Legal Status of Children in the United States," *American Journal of Sociology* 88 (March 1983): 915-47; and Bremner, *Children and Youth, Volume I: 1600-1865*, pp. 671-91.

26. Pisciotta, "Race, Sex, and Rehabilitation."

27. Ibid.

28. Ibid.

29. Smith, "Female Admissions and Paroles."

30. Cited in Bremner, *Children and Youth, Volume I: 1600-1865*, p. 688.

31. Pisciotta, "Race, Sex, and Rehabilitation," p. 261.

32. Ibid., p. 260.

33. Smith, "Female Admissions and Paroles."

34. Cited in Bremner, *Children and Youth, Volume I: 1600-1865*, pp. 684-85.

35. Ibid., pp. 696-99.

36. Ibid., p. 721.

37. Sutton, "Social Structure."

38. Rothman, *Conscience and Convenience*, pp. 261-89.

39. Cited in Bremner, *Children and Youth, Volume I: 1600-1865*, p. 698.

40. Cited in Bremner *Children and Youth in America, Volume II: 1866-1932*, parts 1-6, p. 492.

41. Ibid., p. 509.

42. LaMar T. Empey, *American Delinquency: Its Meaning and Construction* (Homewood, Ill.: Dorsey Press, 1978), p. 500.

43. Description of contemporary parole services for juveniles is based on Richard F. Catalono, Elizabeth A. Wells, Jeffrey M. Jenson, and David J. Hawkins, "Aftercare Services for Drug-Using Institutionalized Delinquents," *Social Service Review* 63 (December 1989): 553-77; Vanessa G. Hodges, Neil B. Guterman, Betty J. Blythe, and Denise E. Bronson, "Intensive Aftercare Services for Children," *Social Casework* 70 (September 1989): 397-404; and Abadinsky, *Probation and Parole*, pp. 135-227.

44. Hodges et al., "Intensive Aftercare Services for Children."

45. Norval Morris and Michael Tonry, *Between Prison and Probation: Intermediate Punishments in a Rational Sentencing System* (New York: Oxford University Press, 1990); William H. Barton and Jeffrey A. Butts, "Viable Options: Intensive Supervision Programs for Juvenile

Delinquents," *Crime and Delinquency* 36 (April 1990): 238-56; James M. Byrne, "The Future of Intensive Probation Supervision and New Intermediate Sanctions," *Crime and Delinquency* 36 (January 1990): 6-41; Todd R. Clear and Patricia L. Hardyman, "The New Intensive Supervision Movement," *Crime and Delinquency* 36 (January 1990): 42-60; Michael Tonry, "Stated and Latent Functions of ISP," *Crime and Delinquency* 36 (January 1990): 174-91; Joan K. Hall, Joseph H. Evans, and Linda G. Smith, "A Comparison of Program Administrator Attitudes about Florida Community Control: An Adult Intensive Probation Supervision Program," *Crime and Delinquency* 35 (April 1989): 303-08; Michael C. Musheno, Dennis P. Palumbo, Steven Maynard-Moody, and James P. Levine, "Community Corrections as an Innovation: What Works and Why," *Journal of Research in Crime and Delinquency* 26 (May 1989): 136-67; Judith Rumgay, "Talking Tough: Empty Threats in Probation Practice," *Howard Journal of Criminal Justice* 28 (August 1989): 177-86; Frank S. Pearson, "Evaluation of New Jersey's Intensive Supervision Program," *Crime and Delinquency* 34 (October 1988): 437-48; Howard Parker, Graham Jarvis, and Maggie Sumner, "Under New Orders: The Redefinition of Social Work with Young Offenders," *British Journal of Social Work* 17 (February 1987): 21-43; Joan Petersilia, Susan Turner, James Kahan, and Joyce Peterson, "Executive Summary of Rand's Study, 'Granting Felons Probation: Public Risks and Alternatives,'" *Crime and Delinquency* 31 (July 1985): 379-92; and James Austin and Barry Krisberg, "The Unmet Promise of Alternatives to Incarceration," *Crime and Delinquency* 28 (July 1982): 374-409.

46. Morris and Tonry, *Between Prison and Probation.*

47. Clear and Hardyman, "The New Intensive Supervision Movement."

48. Rumgay, "Talking Tough."

49. Tonry, "Stated and Latent Functions of ISP."

50. Description and analysis of the Community Treatment Project is based on Paul Lerman, "Evaluative Studies of Institutions for Delinquents: Implications for Research and Social Policy," *Social Work* 13 (July 1968): 55-64; Marquerite Q. Warren, "The Case for Differential Treatment of Delinquents," *The Annals of the American Academy of Political and Social Science* 381 (January 1969): 47-59; Ted B. Palmer, "California's Community Treatment for Delinquent Adolescents," *Journal of Research in Crime and Delinquency* 8 (January 1971): 74-92; Ted B. Palmer, "Matching Worker and Client in Corrections," *Social Work* 18 (March 1973): 95-103; Ted Palmer, "Youth Authority's Community Treatment Project," *Federal Probation* 38 (March 1974): 3-14; and Paul Lerman, *Community Treatment and Social Control: A Critical*

Analysis of Juvenile Correctional Policy (Chicago: The University of Chicago Press, 1975).

51. San Francisco was added in 1965. See Palmer, "California's Community Treatment," p. 76.

52. Palmer, "California's Community Treatment," p. 76.

53. For a discussion and analysis of this problem, see Walter B. Miller, "Inter-Institutional Conflict as a Major Impediment to Delinquency Prevention," *Human Organization* 17 (Fall 1958): 20-25.

54. Palmer, "California's Community Treatment," p. 81.

55. Ibid., note 15, p. 81.

56. Lerman, *Community Treatment*, p. 21.

57. Ibid.

58. Warren, "The Case for Differential Treatment," table 1, p. 54.

59. Lerman, *Community Treatment*, p. 36.

60. Warren, "The Case for Differential Treatment," table 1, p. 54.

61. Lerman, *Community Treatment*, p. 38. One method of illustrating just how frequent and lengthy detention became is to compare the amount of time parolees spent in detention facilities with the treatment services they received from parole officers. Lerman, *Community Treatment*, pp. 35-41, estimates that during a 16-month period ending in April 1966 the average experimental subject had spent 56 days in detention. During that same time the average experimental subject received the equivalent of five days of direct services from his or her parole officer.

62. Lerman, *Community Treatment*, p. 32.

63. Ibid.

64. The classification system used in the Community Treatment Project was developed by clinical psychologist Marquerite Q. Warren and is called the "Interpersonal Maturity Level Classification: Juvenile." Professor Warren's "I-level" system was used to match parole officers with parolees. As Professor Warren correctly notes, "long clinical experience . . . suggests that few, if any, workers relate equally well with all types of youth or are equally comfortable with the range of treatment styles and stances required by the full variety of offenders" ("The Case for Differential Treatment," p. 51). Parole officers were therefore assigned to work with only certain types of offenders, using I-level scores as the basis for the matching of officers and parolees. For example: parolees whose I-level indicated they would benefit most from individual and group therapy and loose supervision emphasizing trust rather than strict surveillance were matched with parole officers who emphasized and enjoyed the social work aspects of their job and disliked and avoided the law enforcement approach. Professor Warren's classification system also was used to identify juveniles in need of foster or group home placement and those who would benefit from detention. In addition to Warren,

"The Case for Differential Treatment," see Palmer, "Matching Worker and Client in Corrections."

65. Lerman, *Community Treatment*, p. 31.

66. Ibid., p. 32.

67. Ibid.

68. It should also be recognized that following April 1966, the experimental and control groups were significantly different in I-level, age, and gender. Because the Youth Authority's measures encompass the period 1961–1969, there is no way of determining whether the modest differences apparent in the first three measures in Table 5.2 are the result of the community-based program elements or the nonequivalency of the experimental and control groups.

69. Palmer, "Youth Authority's Community Treatment Project," p. 13.

70. Lerman, *Community Treatment*, pp. 58–67.

71. Table 5.3 also shows that experimental subjects experienced significantly more parole suspensions for status and technical offenses. This almost certainly does not represent a real behavioral difference, because there is no reason to believe that experimental subjects who committed no less or more delinquent acts than their control group counterparts committed three times as many minor offenses. Instead, it is an indicator of what parole officers with small caseloads do with their time.

72. Community Treatment Project parole officers also were reluctant to recommit their parolees. See Lerman, *Community Treatment*, table 4, p. 60.

73. For a description of Viable Options, see Barton and Butts, "Viable Options."

74. Ibid., p. 242.

75. Ibid., p. 251.

76. Andrew von Hirsch, "The Ethics of Community-Based Sanctions," *Crime and Delinquency* 36 (April 1990): 162–73.

77. Clear and Hardyman, "The New Intensive Supervision Movement," p. 53.

6

SCARED STRAIGHT

On November 2, 1978, an independent television station in Los Angeles presented a film documentary entitled *Scared Straight*.[1] This documentary was a partial record of an intensive confrontation session between adult inmates serving long or life sentences at New Jersey's Rahway State Prison and juveniles brought to the prison in an effort to control their involvement in delinquency. On March 5, 1979, *Scared Straight* was shown on national television, although some local stations initially refused to air it because of its frank language and graphic scenes.[2] In April 1979, *Scared Straight* won an Academy Award for best film documentary.

State legislators and prison administrators were quick to take notice of *Scared Straight*. California legislators introduced a bill requiring the busing of 15,000 juveniles to state prisons for Rahway-type confrontation sessions. Alabama juveniles attended confrontation sessions where one inmate told of being gang raped while in prison.[3] In New York City, children of 11 and 12 years of age were taken on tours of city jails.[4]

What attracted the attention of legislators and prison administrators were the phenomenal claims of success advanced in *Scared Straight*. All 17 of the juveniles appearing in the documentary were described as frequently and seriously delinquent. Three months later, according to the film, 16 had become law-abiding. This was said to be common. Of the nearly 8,000 juveniles attending intensive confrontation sessions at Rahway State

Prison through 1978, *Scared Straight* reported that approximately 90 percent had not experienced further trouble with the law, a success rate "unequalled by traditional rehabilitation methods."

This chapter examines prison-based efforts to scare juveniles straight. It begins by demonstrating that Rahway-type programs are grounded in the deterrence approach to the control of juvenile delinquency. Attention is then directed to Professor James O. Finckenauer's assessment of Rahway's Juvenile Awareness Project. Last, review of three replicative efforts to scare juveniles straight is undertaken.

DETERRENCE THEORY

Central to the deterrence argument[5] is the rational juvenile. Deterrence theorists assume that juveniles pause to calculate the possible consequences of delinquent actions. If their calculations suggest that perceived benefits will exceed possible costs, then rational juveniles commit delinquent acts in anticipation of enjoying rewards. However, if these calculations lead juveniles to conclude that costs will exceed rewards, then the rational course of action is to seek gratification in ways other than delinquency.

Deterrence theorists therefore argue that certain, swift, and severe punishment will stop juveniles from committing delinquent acts. Certainty of punishment refers to the probability of apprehension once a delinquent act has been committed. Swiftness of punishment refers to the amount of time between the commission of a delinquent act and punishment for that act. Severity of punishment refers to the harshness of the sanctions applied to offenders.

Certain, swift, and severe punishment is thought to deter youthful criminal offenders in at least two ways. Specific deterrence occurs when juveniles are punished by the state for their delinquent actions. The experience of being caught and punished alerts the offender to the painful consequences of continued involvement in delinquency and pushes the juvenile in the direction of law-abiding behavior. General deterrence occurs when others learn of the punishment of particular offenders and suppress involvement in delinquency out of fear that the same painful sanctions will be applied to them.

Efforts to scare juveniles straight were firmly grounded in the deterrence approach to juvenile delinquency,[6] especially the idea that fear of severe punishment suppresses delinquency. During intensive confrontation sessions, adults inmates worked very hard to alter juveniles' perceptions of the severity of punishment. They told vivid tales of sad men living dangerous lives inside the walls of shabby and overcrowded maximum-security prisons. Their message was that deprivation, assault, rape, and murder were routine parts of the prison experience. Their threat was that if the juveniles continued their seriously delinquent ways, they too would end up behind bars.

THE RAHWAY STATE PRISON JUVENILE AWARENESS PROJECT

The Juvenile Awareness Project at New Jersey's Rahway State Prison is easily the best known and most controversial of prison-based efforts to scare juveniles straight. In addition to the Academy Award–winning documentary, Rahway's program has been the subject of debate in the popular and social science literature[7] and the topic of two books,[8] including one by Rutgers University criminologist James O. Finckenauer. Table 6.1 summarizes the major features of Professor Finckenauer's assessment of the Juvenile Awareness Project and serves as a guide for the description and analysis that follow.

DESCRIPTION OF THE PROJECT

The Juvenile Awareness Project[9] began at Rahway State Prison in September 1976. It continues to operate, although controversy over its methods and effectiveness significantly decreased the number of juveniles attending and dramatically changed the nature of their experiences while at Rahway. As early as 1980, for example, Professor Finckenauer reported that "sessions declined from ten a week to about two per week; participation from two-hundred juveniles a week to about twenty-five."[10] By the early 1990s, the number of juveniles attending remained "dramatically down," and the youths brought to Rahway all met adult inmates in a "forum, discussion, seminar" setting as opposed to the intensive confrontations of the past.[11] This chapter, however,

Table 6.1   Description of the Juvenile Awareness Project During the Late 1970s

Project Name:	Juvenile Awareness Project
Location:	Rahway State Prison, Rahway, New Jersey
Dates:	September 1976 to present
Subjects:	By the end of the 1970s, over 13,000 juveniles had attended intensive confrontation sessions at Rahway. Very little is known about them.
Type of treatment:	During the late 1970s, juveniles were given a sense of prison life by taking a brief tour and attending an intensive confrontation session run by inmates serving long or life sentences. During the intensive confrontation sessions, the most negative aspects of prison life were emphasized. The primary methods of describing prison life were shouted taunts and threats of sexual assault.
Amount of treatment:	One three-hour visit, with two hours devoted to the intensive confrontation session.
Evaluative design:	Quasi-experimental: although efforts were made to randomly assign subjects to the experimental groups, assignment was "not purely random" for all subjects.
Measures of results:	The extent to which intensive confrontation sessions altered perceptions of the severity of punishment was collected using questionaires. Recidivism data were collected six months after the visit by the experimental subjects.
Replication:	Attention is first directed at the Michigan Reformatory Visitation Program, a project that began in the early 1960s. Examined next are two true replications of the Juvenile Awareness Project—Juvenile Offenders Learn Truth (JOLT) at the State Prison of Southern Michigan in Jackson and the Insiders Juvenile Crime Prevention Program at the old Virginia State Penitentiary in Richmond.

Source: James O. Finckenauer, *Scared Straight! and the Panacea Phenomenon* (Englewood Cliffs, N.J.: Prentice-Hall, 1982).

focuses on the Juvenile Awareness Project as it was conducted during the late 1970s.

Through May 1979 over 13,000 juveniles had attended intensive confrontation sessions run by adult inmates serving long or life sentences. According to the documentary *Scared Straight*, juveniles attending these sessions were "chronic . . . young offenders already desensitized and willing to continue their petty careers as muggers, rip-off artists, pickpockets, and so forth."[12] Actually, very little is known about the over 13,000 juveniles who attended intensive confrontation sessions at Rahway. Moreover, what little is known suggests that many were straight even before they were scared.

In June 1979, Jerome Miller, President of the National Center on Institutions and Alternatives, appeared before a United States House of Representatives subcommittee holding hearings on Rahway's Juvenile Awareness Project.[13] Dr. Miller testified that the young people who appeared in *Scared Straight* lived in a small, middle-class New Jersey suburb, one without a serious delinquency problem. The juveniles congregated in a local park and had agreed to participate when asked to do so by a local police sergeant. Dr. Miller also testified that he had visited the high school attended by the juveniles appearing in the documentary. He learned that of the 1,200 middle-class students, 450 had already attended sessions at Rahway and that the typical method of recruitment was to make an announcement over the school's loudspeaker. The apparent goal was to have all 1,200 students eventually attend sessions at Rahway.

Professor Finckenauer's data also challenge the image that juveniles attending Rahway sessions were seriously and frequently delinquent. As part of his assessment of the Juvenile Awareness Project, Professor Finckenauer found that 49 agencies had sent juveniles to Rahway in the three months ending in November 1977. He reported that most were counseling, educational, employment, and recreational organizations rather than agencies dealing exclusively with delinquent juveniles.[14] In addition, of the juveniles directly involved in his assessment of the project, 41.3 percent had no prior record of delinquency. Of those with a prior record, most had committed minor offenses.[15]

TYPE OF TREATMENT

The Juvenile Awareness Project was designed to control delinquency by altering juveniles' perceptions of the severity of punishment for criminal acts.[16] It was hypothesized that attending intensive confrontation sessions would cause juveniles to stay within the law out of fear that if they strayed they too could end up in a place like Rahway State Prison (see Figure 6.1).

The effort to alter juveniles' perceptions of the severity of punishment began with a brief tour of Rahway State Prison. The juveniles saw the crowded cells, heard the almost constant metal

FIGURE 6.1   The Juvenile Awareness Project's deterrence hypothesis
              in diagrammatic form

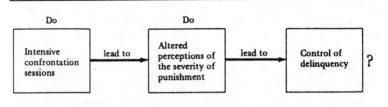

Source: The Juvenile Awareness Project's deterrence hypothesis is based upon
description in James O. Finckenauer, *Scared Straight! and the Panacea Phenomenon* (Englewood Cliffs, N.J.: Prentice-Hall, 1982), pp. 29-44.

on metal sound of a maximum security institution, and listened
to the verbal taunts of hardened prisoners. If the juveniles were
attractive, inmates undoubtedly indicated what would happen to
them in prison.

At the end of the brief tour, juveniles in groups of about 15
were taken to a room for an intensive confrontation session with
about 20 adult inmates serving long or life sentences. During
these sessions inmates attempted to "cover the full spectrum of
crime and its nonrewards, [explain] about prison, crime and its
ramifications, [show] young people that the stories about the big
house . . . being the place of bad men is in all reality the place of
sad men, [and] prove the fact of what crime and its involvement is
really all about."[17]

Explaining about crime and the reality of prison life involved
shouting, swearing, and threats of physical abuse. What follows
are some of the statements directed at the juveniles by the adult
inmates:

I'm gonna hurt you.
You take something from me and I'll kill you.
You see them pretty blue eyes of yours? I'll take one out of
    your face and squish it in front of you.
Do you know what we see when we look at you—we see
    ourselves.
If someone had done this to me I wouldn't be here.

> Who do you think we get? Young, tough motherfuckers like
> you. Get a pretty fat buck like you and stick a prick in your
> ass.[18]

Confrontation sessions sometimes even went beyond taunts
and threats. Jerome Miller testified that: "An earlier study of the
program sponsored by the New Jersey Department of Corrections
indicated that the Juvenile Awareness Program had two primary
techniques: (1) 'exaggeration,' and (2) 'manhandling.' This latter
technique has probably led to certain incidents which have
generally not been publicly known. We received allegations of
certain youngsters being culled about, lifted by the head and
shaken, 'goosed' or pinched on their behind. We are also aware of
more serious allegations which we would prefer to corroborate
more completely before specifying."[19] Professor Finckenauer reports much the same thing, noting that some of the adolescent
males attending sessions were "kissed and fondled"[20] by inmates.

EVALUATIVE DESIGN

Professor Finckenauer's goal was to evaluate the Juvenile Awareness Project experimentally.[21] He secured the names of the 49
community agencies that had sent juveniles to Rahway in the fall
of 1977. He then selected a random sample of these agencies ($n =$
28) and contacted them to determine whether they would be
willing to permit random assignment of juveniles to an experimental and a control group. Of the agencies contacted, 11 promised cooperation. However, only five of these agencies actually
abided by the random assignment procedures. Of the other six
agencies, "two . . . took both experimental and controls to Rahway . . . [t]wo other sponsors failed to take the experimentals . . .
as scheduled . . . [o]ne agency . . . twice failed to show up at
Rahway, [and] one other agency . . . backed out."[22]

These problems resulted in two important changes in Professor Finckenauer's evaluation procedures. The projected sizes of
the comparison groups were reduced from 50 each to 46 in the
Rahway-visit group and 35 in the control group. More important, initial refusals by agencies to cooperate along with mistakes
by cooperating agencies in sending or failing to send experimen-

tal juveniles to Rahway resulted in a quasi-experimental evaluative design.

MEASURES OF RESULTS

The extent to which attending intensive confrontation sessions altered juveniles' perceptions of the severity of punishment was assessed by Professor Finckenauer using questionnaires. These instruments were designed to probe attitudes toward prisons and punishment. Professor Finckenauer found that attending intensive confrontation sessions did not alter juveniles' perceptions of the severity of punishment.[23]

Attending intensive confrontation sessions also did not lead to control of juvenile delinquency (see Table 6.2). Among juveniles visiting Rahway, 41.3 percent committed a new offense during the six months following their visit. By comparison, only 11.4 percent of the juveniles in the control group committed a new offense during that same time period. The Juvenile Awareness Project not only failed to control delinquency, but it apparently made things worse.

REPLICATION: MICHIGAN REFORMATORY
VISITATION PROGRAM

Although the Juvenile Awareness Project at Rahway State Prison is easily the best-known effort to scare juveniles straight, it was not the first such attempt. Some 15 years earlier a nearly identical project took place at the Michigan Reformatory with results

Table 6.2 Juvenile Awareness Project: Percent Experimental and Control Group Subjects Committing New Recorded Offense in the Six Months Following an Intensive Confrontation Session at Rahway State Prison

Group	New Recorded Offense	No New Recorded Offense	Totals
Experimental	41.3	58.7	100 $(n = 46)$
Control	11.4	88.6	100 $(n = 35)$

Source: James O. Finckenauer, *Scared Straight! and the Panacea Phenomenon* p. 135. © 1982. Reprinted by permission of Prentice-Hall, Englewood Cliffs, New Jersey.

Table 6.3 Description of the Michigan Reformatory Visitation Program

Project Name:	Michigan Reformatory Visitation Program
Location:	Michigan Reformatory, Ionia, Michigan
Dates:	Early 1960s to May 1967
Subjects:	Males residing in Ingham County and sentenced to probation
Type of treatment:	Juveniles visited the Michigan Reformatory and met with young inmates serving long or life sentences.
Amount of treatment:	Likely a single-day field trip to the reformatory
Evaluative design:	Experimental: Juveniles about to visit the reformatory were randomly assigned either to make the trip or to a control group.
Measures of results:	Juvenile court records were checked for the six months following the visit to the reformatory.

Source: Michigan Department of Corrections. Research Report #4. "A Six-Month Follow-up of Juvenile Delinquents Visiting the Ionia Reformatory." Program Bureau, Michigan Department of Corrections, Stevens T. Mason Building, Lansing, Mich. 48913, May 22, 1967. This report is reprinted in James O. Finckenauer, *Scared Straight! and the Panacea Phenomenon* (Englewood Cliffs, N.J.: Prentice-Hall, 1982), pp. 59–61.

strikingly similar to those reported by Professor Finckenauer. This section therefore stretches the meaning of replication by examining the Michigan Reformatory Visitation Program.[24] Attention is then directed to two true replications of the Juvenile Awareness Project.

Table 6.3 summarizes the major features of the Michigan Reformatory Visitation Program. When the program began in the early 1960s at the Michigan Reformatory in Ionia, Michigan, the institution was already 100 years old and showing its age. Surrounded by walls over 18 feet high, the Michigan Reformatory was overcrowded and barely able to meet the needs of young male inmates who were serving "unusually long sentences, who [were] an escape risk or . . . who [had] been unresponsive to treatment programs in other facilities . . . "[25]

Very little is known about the juveniles who met with inmates at the Michigan Reformatory, other than the fact that they lived in Ingham County some 40 miles southeast of the reformatory, that they were male, and that they had been adjudicated delinquent. The age, race, and social class of the juveniles as well as the types of offenses they had committed are all unknown.

However, it is possible to infer two of these characteristics: their age and the severity of their offenses. The juveniles involved almost certainly were on probation because one purpose of the program was to act as a "catalyst to later counseling." Probationary status also seems likely because it would have made little sense to take youths out of one correctional facility and make them visit another. Given the fact that they apparently were on probation, it seems reasonable to infer that they were young offenders adjudicated delinquent for status or minor criminal offenses.

Little also is known about the nature of the treatment juveniles received at the Michigan Reformatory. The brief report describing the project indicates that they visited the reformatory and met with the young inmates serving long or life sentences. It is unlikely, however, that they were shouted at or physically threatened by the inmates. The report describing the program calls the trip to the reformatory a "visit," not an intensive confrontation session. Additionally, adults were not as worried about the delinquent actions of juveniles in the mid-1960s[26] and thus not as likely to permit inmates to verbally and physically threaten young offenders.

What does seem likely is that the juveniles toured the facility, talked with administrators and perhaps custodial personnel, and then met with the young adult inmates. They certainly saw the aged and imposing reformatory grounds, witnessed the regimentation of life in an overcrowded institution, and listened to inmates' descriptions of the "pains of imprisonment."[27] It appears most accurate to view the juveniles' visit as similar to an unusual school field trip.

Other aspects of the Michigan Reformatory Visitation Program are certain, with two of prime importance. First, the visitation program was one of the first-known attempts to scare juveniles straight by showing young offenders "the ultimate consequences of delinquency."[28] Second, the project was experimentally evaluated. Members of the Ingham County juvenile court staff furnished Michigan Department of Corrections research personnel with the names of juveniles about to visit the Michigan Reformatory. Using a table of random numbers, research personnel assigned juveniles to the experimental visitation group or to a control group that did not visit the reformatory.

The results of the visitation program were assessed using juvenile court records obtained six months after the experimental group visited the reformatory. Among juveniles who participated in the visitation program, 43 percent had a court petition or probation violation entered on their records as compared to only 17 percent of the juveniles in the control group (see Table 6.4). Clearly, visiting a reformatory did not control delinquency. On the contrary, visits to the Michigan Reformatory, as was true of intensive confrontation sessions at Rahway State Prison some 15 years later, apparently increased involvement in delinquency.

REPLICATION: JUVENILE OFFENDERS LEARN TRUTH

Prior to Professor Finckenauer's assessment of the effectiveness of Rahway's Juvenile Awareness Project, efforts to scare juveniles straight were fast becoming a major juvenile justice system fad.[29] Prompted by claims of success advanced in the film *Scared Straight* and elsewhere,[30] states created similar programs in their maximum security institutions involving thousands of juveniles. Attention is now directed to the results of two of these programs, starting with Michigan's Juvenile Offenders Learn Truth (JOLT).[31]

Table 6.5 summarizes the major features of JOLT, a true replication of the Juvenile Awareness Project. JOLT was one of many projects that emerged in the wake of initially positive reports of the effectiveness of Rahway's program. Its creators were members of the Jaycee chapter at the State Prison of Southern Michigan,

Table 6.4   Michigan Reformatory Visitation Program: Percent Experimental and Control Group Subjects with Probation Violations or Court Petitions in the Six Months Following a Visit to the Michigan Reformatory

Group	Probation Violation or Court Petition	No Probation Violation or Court Petition	Totals
Experimental	43	57	100 (n = 28)
Control	17	83	100 (n = 30)

Source: Michigan Department of Corrections, "A Six-Month Follow-up of Juvenile Delinquents Visiting the Ionia Reformatory," Program Bureau, Michigan Department of Corrections, Stevens T. Mason Building, Lansing, Mich. 48913, May 22, 1967. Research Report #4, p. 3. Reprinted by permission.

Table 6.5   Description of Juvenile Offenders Learn Truth (JOLT)

Project Name:	Juvenile Offenders Learn Truth
Location:	State Prison of Southern Michigan, Jackson, Michigan
Dates:	May 1978 to July 1979
Subjects:	Juveniles residing in three Michigan counties: Wayne, Washtenaw, and Jackson. To be considered eligible, juveniles had to be male, have a prior record as evidenced by an arrest or court petition for a criminal offense, and be accompanied to the prison by a parent or legal guardian. Juveniles attending sessions averaged 15½ years of age, and one-half were white.
Type of treatment:	The major part of the tour consisted of an "intensive confrontation session." Adult inmates used "street language" to describe prison life and to suggest what might happen to the juveniles if they continued their delinquent ways.
Amount of treatment:	The tour and confrontation session together lasted two and one-half hours.
Evaluative design:	Experimental: Juveniles were randomly assigned either to a group that visited the prison or to a control group.
Measures of results:	Criminal offenses charged in the six months following the visit to the prison by the juveniles in the experimental group were used to measure results.

Source: James C. Yarborough, "Evaluation of JOLT as a Deterrence Program," Program Bureau, Michigan Department of Corrections, Stevens T. Mason Building, Lansing, Mich. 48913, July 18, 1979. JOLT is briefly described in James O. Finckenauer, Scared Straight! and the Panacea Phenomenon (Englewood Cliffs, N.J.: Prentice-Hall, 1982), pp. 217–18.

the world's largest walled prison.[32] Unlike most "scared straight" regimens, JOLT was experimentally evaluated from its inception. JOLT therefore was suspended following initial assessment of its impact on adolescents.

JOLT sessions were limited to adolescent males living in three contiguous Michigan counties—Wayne (which encompasses metropolitan Detroit), Washtenaw, and Jackson. Sessions were also limited to juveniles with a record of delinquency, as evidenced by a prior arrest or petition to juvenile court, and a parent or legal guardian willing to accompany them to the prison. Juveniles meeting these criteria during the time JOLT was evaluated averaged 15½ years of age, and one-half were white.

JOLT's purpose was to "deter juvenile delinquents from further criminal offenses."[33] Juveniles and their parent or guardian began their two-and-one-half-hour visit with a brief tour of the prison. Juveniles were then separated from the accompanying adults, searched and fingerprinted, and locked in an empty cell for a few minutes. While locked in the cell, juveniles were taunted and harassed by real inmates in nearby cells. Following this brief introduction to prison life, juveniles were taken to a small room for an intensive confrontation session with selected inmates. James C. Yarborough, who was chief of research in the Michigan Department of Corrections' Program Bureau in the late 1970s, described a typical confrontation as "somewhat like the session depicted in the film documentary, *Scared Straight*, as far as format and structure are concerned. However, differences do exist which primarily involve language and tactics. For example, while 'street language' is used during JOLT sessions, it does not contain the extreme obscenities used in the New Jersey program. Gross verbal intimidation is also avoided. The message being delivered, however, is essentially the same: if you continue to engage in delinquent and criminal behavior, you may in time find youself a prisoner confined in an institution like Jackson, and that the 'pains of imprisonment' and their consequences will then become a reality of considerable duration rather than a momentary pretense."[34]

JOLT was experimentally evaluated from its inception. When a county JOLT coordinator had assembled a list of juveniles eligible to make the visit to prison, their identification numbers were reported to the Department of Corrections' research office for random assignment to the experimental and control groups. The JOLT coordinator was then informed of the results of the random assignment procedure and arranged for the experimental juveniles to visit the prison.

Meausres of involvement in delinquency were collected three and six months following the visit to the prison by the juveniles in the experimental group. Table 6.6 contains the six-month-follow-up data. Examination reveals virtually no differences between the two groups of juveniles in rates of recidivism: 30.8 percent of the juveniles who had visited the prison had one or more criminal charges filed against them as compared to 28.9 percent of the juveniles in the control group.

REPLICATION: THE INSIDERS CRIME PREVENTION PROGRAM

Table 6.7 summarizes the major features of the Insiders Juvenile Crime Prevention Program,[35] a project that also was inspired by

Table 6.6   Juvenile Offenders Learn Truth (JOLT): Percent Experimental and Control Group Subjects Charged with Criminal Offense(s) in the Six Months Following an Intensive Confrontation Session at the State Prison of Southern Michigan

Group	One or More Criminal Charges	No Criminal Charges	Totals
Experimental	30.8	69.2	100 ($n = 39$)
Control	28.9	71.1	100 ($n = 45$)

Source: James C. Yarborough, "Evaluation of JOLT as a Deterrence Program," Program Bureau, Michigan Department of Corrections, Stevens T. Mason Building, Lansing, Mich. 48913, July 18, 1979, table 26B. Reprinted by permission.

Table 6.7   Description of the Insiders Juvenile Crime Prevention Program

Project Name:	Insiders Juvenile Crime Prevention Program
Location:	Virginia State Penitentiary, Richmond, Virginia
Dates:	November 1978 to late 1984
Subjects:	At the time of the evaluation in June 1979, approximately 600 juvenile and young adult offenders had attended "shock-confrontation lectures" at the old penitentiary. All were between the ages of 13 and 20 and had been convicted of at least two criminal acts.
Type of treatment:	Offenders were given a taste of penitentiary life by being searched, stripped of their personal possessions, and briefly locked in one of the cramped cells of "The Walls." The major part of the experience was a "shock-confrontation lecture" during which perisoners used explicit language "to deter [young offenders] from a life of crime."
Amount of treatment:	One three-hour visit, with two hours devoted to the shock-confrontation lecture
Evaluative design:	Experimental: once court personnel had selected offenders to visit the penitentiary, subjects were randomly assigned to make the visit or to the control group.
Measures of results:	New court intakes for all subjects 6 months after the experimental group's visit to the penitentiary; new court intakes 9 and 12 months after the visit for some of the experimental and control subjects.

Source: Stan Orchowsky and Keith Taylor, "The Insiders Juvenile Crime Prevention Program: An Assessment of a Juvenile Awareness Program," Research and Reporting Unit, Division of Program Development and Evaluation, Virginia Department of Corrections, P.O. Box 26963, Richmond, Va. 23261, August 1981, report no. 79111.

the early reports of success at Rahway. It began in November 1978 at the Virginia State Penitentiary, also known as "The Walls" (see Box 6.1), then one of the nation's oldest continuously operating penitentiaries. Through June 1979, approximately 600 juvenile and young adult offenders had attended "shock-confrontation lectures" at the penitentiary. All of those attending were between the ages of 13 and 20 and had been convicted of at least two criminal offenses. The Insiders Program continued to operate until late 1984.

Box 6.1   The Virginia State Penitentiary

If ever there was a place that should have scared offenders straight, the Virginia State Penitentiary in Richmond was it. Conceived by Thomas Jefferson and designed by Benjamin Latrobe (who designed the U.S. Capitol), the penitentiary opened in 1800. It was then a model institution, offering each of its inmates a separate cell for solitude and reflective reformation.

By the late 1970s, "The Walls" was about as bad as a prison could get and still be in the business of housing inmates. Located in the middle of downtown Richmond and surrounded by imposing walls, the old penitentiary was Virginia's institutional anchor, housing the state's most troublesome offenders. Full of blind spots that invited stabbings and assaults, it was an overcrowded, dirty, and noisy facilitity with "cramped cells, failing plumbing, poor ventilation and exposed wiring."

On December 13, 1990, Buddy Earl Justus was executed at the Virginia State Penitentiary. Its population reduced to zero, the institution closed on December 14, 1990, with a ceremony attended by 100 people, including twelve of the institution's former wardens.

Sources: Telephone conversation with Dr. Patrick Gurney, assistant warden, Powahatan Reception and Classification Center, State Farm, Va., December 24, 1991; NAACP Legal Defense and Educational Fund, Inc., *Death Row USA* (New York: NAACP Legal Defense and Educational Fund, Inc., April 24, 1991), p. 8; John F. Harris, "After Serving 190 Years, Va. Penitentiary Is Closed," *The Washington Post*, December 15, 1990, p. E1; and Marjorie Hyer, "Va. Church Leaders Decry Richmond Prison Conditions," *The Washington Post*, August 1, 1989, p. A10.

The purpose of the Insiders Program was to "demonstrate the realities of prison life to hard-core youthful offenders in an effort to deter them from a life of crime and incarceration."[36] The young offenders visiting the penitentiary were searched, stripped of their personal possessions, and then briefly locked in one of the small cells. The major part of the three-hour visit was devoted to a shock-confrontation lecture "full of very explicit, descriptive, and loud street language. . . . Inmates tell juveniles of murder, drugs, prison gangs, and [rape] inside the prison, and are threatened that this will be part of their experience if they continue their life of crime."[37]

The Insiders Program was experimentally evaluated and complete court appearance measures were collected after 6 months for both experimental and control subjects (see Table 6.8). Follow-up measures of recidivism were collected for some of the subjects 9 and 12 months following the shock-confrontation session at the penitentiary. After 6 months, a point when the data were complete for all subjects, there was no difference between the two groups. After 9 and 12 months, points where data were complete for only some of the subjects, those attending shock-confrontation sessions were less criminal than their control counterparts.

However, there are two good reasons to question results based on the 9- and 12-month follow-up data. The data are seriously incomplete. After 12 months, the court records of less than half of the experimental (17 of 39, or 43.6 percent) and control (19 of 41, or 46.3 percent) subjects are part of the analysis (Table 6.8). Further, the data are from the summer of 1981. If there was an enduring positive story to be told, then we would have heard it by now. Instead, the data remain incomplete, apparently permanently so.[38]

In the end, the bottom line with respect to the Insiders Program must be based on the complete 6-month data. Using only those data, we are forced to conclude that the Insiders Program failed to deter.

SUMMARY AND CONCLUSIONS

This chapter examined prison-based efforts to scare juveniles straight. It began by demonstrating that Rahway-type programs

Table 6.8 The Insiders Program: Percent of Experimental and Control Subjects to Court and Average Number of Court Intakes in the 6, 9, and 12 Months Following an Intensive Confrontation Session at the Virginia State Penitentiary

Group	6 Months		9 Months		12 Months	
	Percent To Court	Average Number of Court Intakes[a]	Percent To Court	Average Number of Court Intakes[a]	Percent To Court	Average Number of Court Intakes[a]
Experimental	41 (16 of 39)	0.49	43 (10 of 28)[b]	0.48	47 (8 of 17)[d]	0.53
Control	39 (16 of 41)	0.61	67 (16 of 24)[c]	1.04	68 (13 of 19)[e]	1.27

[a]Adjusted mean to "control for the small amount of variability . . . that could be accounted for by pre-insiders scores."
[b]At the time the evaluation was undertaken only 23 experimental group subjects had been out of treatment for 9 months.
[c]At the time the evaluation was undertaken only 24 of the control group subjects were available for analysis.
[d]At the time the evaluation was undertaken only 17 experimental group subjects had been out of treatment for 12 months.
[e]At the time the evaluation was undertaken only 19 of the control group subjects were available for analysis.

Source: Stan Orchowsky and Keith Taylor, "The Insiders Juvenile Crime Prevention Program: An Assessment of a Juvenile Awareness Program," Research and Reporting Unit, Division of Program Development and Evaluation, Virginia Department of Corrections, P.O. Box 26963, Richmond, Va. 23261, August 1981; report no. 79111, pp. 23, 24, 27, 28, 31, and 32. Reprinted by permission.

Box 6.2   Prisons Have Gotten Out of the Business of Trying To Scare Kids Straight

Juveniles no longer are being threatened by scowling, angry-sounding adult inmates. The pains of imprisonment are no longer being physically demonstrated on juveniles who thought they were supposed to be viewing prison life, not participating in it.

However, adult inmates in most states continue to talk to juvenile offenders. Consider two examples. The Juvenile Awareness Project at New Jersey's Rahway State Prison is still operating, but it is very different from what it used to be. The number of juveniles going to Rahway is "dramatically down" and the sessions they attend involve a "forum, discussion, seminar" type of approach, not intimidation and threats.

Virginia's Mecklenburg Correctional Center currently offers a Youth Assistance Program for three audiences. Classes of children in fifth grade and above, along with their teachers, meet with small groups of inmates at the maximum security facility. Juveniles convicted of delinquent acts also meet with inmates as part of their "community diversion sentence." Last, young adults convicted of criminal acts attend sessions at Mecklenburg as part of their community diversion sentence. Only the young adults tour the prison and spend some time in a small cell. Virginia state law prohibits people under the age of 18 from touring the housing units of an adult prison.

The sessions at Mecklenburg take place in the prison's visiting room and are low-key. The goal is to provide information, not to incite fear. Inmates begin by explaining what being locked up in a place like Mecklenburg is like. Inmates then describe why they were sent to prison and how they might have stayed out of trouble. A question and answer session concludes the one and one-half hour meeting. On occasion, teachers arrange in advance for a youth they perceive as headed for trouble with the law to meet with an inmate in a corner of the visiting room during the general session.

Sources: Information on Rahway's Juvenile Awareness Project is based on a telephone conversation with Professor James O. Finckenauer, School of Criminal Justice, Rutgers University, New Brunswick, N.J., on December 16, 1991. Information on the Youth Assistance Program at the Mecklenburg Correctional Center is based on a telephone conversation with Pat O'Halloran, rehabilitation counselor, Mecklenburg Correctional Center,

Boydton, Va., on December 24, 1991. For a description of the Youth
Assistance Program at New York's Auburn Correctional Facility, a project
that anticipated this low-key approach, see Bruce L. Berg, "Inmates as
Clinical Sociologists: The Use of Sociodrama in a Nontraditional Delinquency Prevention Program," *International Journal of Offender Therapy
and Comparative Criminology* 28 (September 1984): 117–24.

are grounded in the deterrence approach to the control of juvenile delinquency. Attention was then directed to Professor
James O. Finckenauer's assessment of the Juvenile Awareness
Project at New Jersey's Rahway State Prison. Last, review of
three replicative efforts to scare juveniles straight was undertaken.

The projects examined and assessment of other prison-based
programs[39] indicate that intensive confrontation sessions do not
deter. At best, taking probationers and other juveniles to prisons
for intensive confrontation sessions has no measurable effect. At
worst, these programs increase involvement in delinquency. It
thus is fortunate that prisons have gotten out of the business of
trying to scare kids straight (see Box 6.2).

NOTES

1. Description of the film *Scared Straight* is based on notes I took
when it was shown in Columbus, Ohio, on May 16, 1979. Other sources
consulted include Aric Press and Donna Foote, "Does 'Scaring' Work?"
Newsweek, May 14, 1979, p. 131; James O. Finckenauer, *Scared Straight!
and the Panacea Phenomenon* (Englewood Cliffs, N.J.: Prentice-Hall,
1982), pp. 91–110; National Center on Institutions and Alternatives,
Scared Straight: A Second Look (1337 22nd Street, N.W., Washington,
D.C. 20037, undated); James O. Finckenauer, "Juvenile Awareness Project: Evaluation Report No. 2," unpublished paper, Rutgers University
School of Criminal Justice, April 18, 1979; and Testimony Before the
Subcommittee on Human Resources, United States House of Represen-
tatives, by Jerome G. Miller and Herbert H. Hoelter, Hearings on
Rahway State Prison "Juvenile Awareness Project" and the "Scared
Straight" Film, June 4, 1979. The last source will hereafter be identified
as Subcommittee, *Rahway State Prison*.

2. For example, *Scared Straight* was not shown in Columbus, Ohio, until May 16, 1979.

3. Press and Foote, "Does 'Scaring' Work?"

4. Subcommittee, *Rahway State Prison*, p. 3.

5. A classic analysis of deterrence theory can be found in Jack P. Gibbs, *Crime, Punishment, and Deterrence* (New York: Elsevier, 1975). A more recent analysis is Anne L. Schneider, *Deterrence and Juvenile Crime* (New York: Springer-Verlag, 1990).

6. Finckenauer, *Scared Straight*, pp. 29–63.

7. Press and Foote, "Does 'Scaring' Work?"; Eileen Keerdoja et al., "Prison Program Gets a New Boost," *Newsweek*, November 3, 1980, p. 16; Finckenauer, *Scared Straight*, pp. 190–208.

8. Finckenauer, *Scared Straight?* and Sidney Langer, *Scared Straight: Fear in the Deterrence of Delinquency* (Washington, D.C.: University Press of America, 1982).

9. Description of Professor Finckenauer's evaluation of the Juvenile Awareness Project is based on Finckenauer, "Juvenile Awareness Project"; and Finckenauer, *Scared Straight*.

10. Finckenauer, *Scared Straight*, p. 196.

11. Telephone conversation with Professor Finckenauer, December 16, 1991.

12. Notes taken during showing of *Scared Straight* in Columbus, Ohio, on May 16, 1979.

13. Subcommittee, *Rahway State Prison*.

14. Finckenauer, *Scared Straight*, p. 118. Also see National Center, *Scared Straight*, p. 7, where it is asserted that "40 to 60% of the juveniles who were visiting Rahway had never been inside an institution, gone to court, or even had a police record."

15. Finckenauer, "Juvenile Awareness Project," p. 7. Also see Finckenauer, *Scared Straight*, pp. 111–12.

16. Finckenauer, *Scared Straight*, pp. 29–44.

17. Cited in National Center, *Scared Straight*, p. 6.

18. From notes I took when *Scared Straight* was shown in Columbus, Ohio, on May 16, 1979.

19. Subcommittee, *Rahway, State Prison*, pp. 14–15.

20. Finckenauer, *Scared Straight*, p. 85.

21. Ibid., pp. 111–31.

22. Ibid., p. 121.

23. Ibid., pp. 156–70.

24. This section is based on Research Report #4, Michigan Department of Corrections, "A Six-Month Follow-up of Juvenile Delinquents Visiting the Ionia Reformatory," May 22, 1967. I thank James C. Yarborough, who in 1980 was chief of research, Program Bureau, Michigan

Department of Corrections, Stevens T. Mason Building, Lansing, Mich. 48913, for having the report retyped and sent to me. The report was reprinted in Finckenauer, *Scared Straight*, pp. 59-61. In 1992 Yarborough was warden at the Richard A. Handlon Michigan Training Unit, P.O. Box 492, Ionia, Mich. 48846 (telephone conversation December 24, 1991).

25. Michigan Department of Corrections, *Dimensions: A Report of the Michigan Department of Corrections*. Lansing, Mich.: Michigan Department of Corrections, Fall 1976, p. 44. I again thank James C. Yarborough for providing me with a copy of this report and for assuring me in a letter dated October 20, 1980, that "there has been little if any change" in the Michigan Reformatory since the mid-1960s, the time of the Michigan Reformatory Visitation Program.

26. Writing in 1973, Edwin M. Schur argued that the deterrence approach "does not at present exert a significant influence on delinquency policies." See Edwin M. Schur, *Radical Non-Intervention: Rethinking the Delinquency Problem* (Englewood Cliffs, N.J.: Prentice-Hall, 1973). p. 19.

27. The classic statement on the "pains of imprisonment" is Gresham M. Sykes, *The Society of Captives: A Study of a Maximum Security Prison* (Princton, N.J.: Princeton University Press, 1958).

28. Research Report, "A Six-Month Follow-up," p. 1.

29. For recent discussion of fads in juvenile justice, see Thomas J. Bernard, *The Cycle of Juvenile Justice* (New York: Oxford University Press, 1991).

30. Numerous newspaper articles also contained claims of success. See Finckenauer, *Scared Straight*, pp. 91-107 and 179-82.

31. This section is based on James C. Yarborough, "Evaluation of JOLT as a Deterrence Program," Program Bureau, Michigan Department of Corrections, July 18, 1979, Stevens T. Mason Building, Lansing, Mich. 48913. I thank James C. Yarborough for sending me a copy of this paper.

32. Michigan Department of Corrections, *Dimensions*, pp. 35-39. The "world's largest prison" in terms of total walled acreage.

33. Yarborough, "Evaluation of JOLT," p. 1.

34. Ibid., p. 3.

35. Description of the Insiders Program is based on Stan Orchowsky and Keith Taylor, "The Insiders Juvenile Crime Prevention Program: An Assessment of a Juvenile Awareness Program," Research and Reporting Unit, Division of Program Development and Evaluation, Virginia Department of Corrections, August 1981, report no. 79111. I thank Stan Orchowsky for sending me a copy of this report.

36. Orchowsky and Taylor. "The Insiders." p. 11.

37. Ibid.

38. When I called the Research and Reporting Unit at the Virginia Department of Corrections on March 10, 1983, I was then told that the data were still incomplete. I called again on December 23, 1991, and was told the same thing. This is unfortunate because Langer's *Scared Straight* also reports a "sleeper effect" not apparent after six months but present after 22 months. Professor Langer's design, however, was far less precise than any of those included in this book and very little confidence can therefore be placed in his report of a delayed effect.

39. Richard L. Berry, "SHAPE—UP: The Effects of a Prison Aversion Program on Recidivism and Family Dynamics" (Ph.D. diss., College of Education, Division of Professional Studies, University of Northern Colorado, Greeley, Colorado, August 1985), p. 91; Douglas G. Dean, "The Impact of a Juvenile Awareness Program on Select Personality Traits of Male Clients," *Journal of Offender Counseling, Services and Rehabilitation* 6 (Spring 1982), p. 84.

7

COMMUNITY TREATMENT

This chapter directs attention to three classic community-based treatment projects for delinquent juveniles: the Provo Experiment (1959–1965),[1] the Silverlake Experiment (mid 1960s),[2] and Jerome Miller's closing of all institutions for juvenile offenders in Massachusetts in the early 1970s (the Massachusetts "Experiment").[3] All three are classic projects because of their innovative contributions to contemporary delinquency control strategies. Additionally, all three projects teach classic lessons about opposition to community-based treatment.

Consider first the innovative contributions of the Provo, Silverlake, and Massachusetts experiments to contemporary delinquency-control strategies. It is now common to argue that intermediate interventions standing midway between existing responses to delinquent juveniles are needed.[4] In the early 1960s the Provo Experiment was furnishing delinquent juveniles with community-based intermediate interventions. Intensive supervision programs are currently a major delinquency-control strategy.[5] In the mid-1960s the Silverlake Experiment was providing for the intensive supervision of delinquent juveniles in Los Angeles. It is now common to urge that more state juvenile correctional dollars be devoted to community-based treatment.[6] In the early 1970s Massachusetts was spending 69 percent[7] of its juvenile corrections budget on community-based interventions. Provo, Silverlake, and Massachusetts were doing things decades ago that many people in the corrections field are still just talking about.

Also consider classic lessons about opposition to community-based treatment. The Provo Experiment fought a tough and protracted battle over funding with Utah County, one it ultimately lost. The Silverlake Experiment was forever at odds with the local public high school about the delinquent students the project was sending its way. In Massachusetts, Jerome Miller, who had been hired to humanize and democratize the state's training schools, was met with open resistance every step of the way. Fed up, Dr. Miller emptied out the state's juvenile correctional facilities and created a network of state-funded, privately run, community-based facilities. Neighborhood opposition to community treatment was so strong that some of the facilities had to be located "on the grounds of [the recently closed] state institutions,"[8] while others were hidden in "low-income industrial neighborhoods."[9]

This chapter examines these innovative projects, including their lessons about opposition to community-based treatment. We start with the Provo Experiment, continue with the Silverlake Experiment, and end with the Massachusetts "Experiment."

THE PROVO EXPERIMENT

The Provo Experiment[10] was one of the earliest projects to provide a community-based intermediate intervention midway between routine probation and institutionalization. Additionally, the Provo Experiment was one of the first to rigorously compare its intermediate intervention with probation and incarceration. Table 7.1 summarizes the major features of this classic project and serves as a guide for the description and analysis that follow.

DESCRIPTION OF THE PROJECT

The origins of the Provo Experiment can be traced to a small-scale project begun in the mid-1950s. The Utah County juvenile court judge formed a Citizens' Advisory Committee and with $10,000 from the Utah County Commission launched a nonresidential treatment program for serious juvenile offenders. These

Table 7.1 Description of the Provo Experiment

Project Name:	The Provo Experiment
Location:	Utah County, Utah
Dates:	1959–1965
Subjects:	Seriously delinquent juveniles, excluding those who were overtly psychotic, severely retarded, or convicted of a capital offense or sexually assaultive behavior. All of the juveniles were male, their average age was 16, and nearly all came from lower-middle-class or upper-lower-class family backgrounds.
Type of treatment:	The nonresidential program utilized "an intensive group program . . . work and the delinquent peer group as the principal instruments for change. During the winter, those boys who were still in school continued to attend. Those who were not in school were employed in a city program. On Saturdays, all boys worked. Later in the afternoon each day boys left school or work . . . and attended a group meeting. After the meetings were completed, they returned to their own homes. During the summer every boy attended an all-day program that involved work and group discussions. On rare occasions a boy might work apart from the others if he had a full-time job."
Amount of treatment:	Juveniles in the community-based program averaged between five and six months of treatment.
Evaluative design:	Experimental and quasi-experimental: The community program–probation comparison was experimentally designed, whereas the community program–institution comparison was quasi-experimentally evaluated.
Measures of results:	Average number of arrests of the juveniles in the community program, assigned to probation, and sentenced to the State Industrial School for four years following their respective treatment experiences was used to measure results.
Replication:	The Silverlake Experiment is the clearest replication of the Provo Experiment. Of equal replicative interest is the closing of training schools in Massachusetts by Jerome Miller in the early 1970s. Also see the community-based intensive supervision projects reviewed in Chapter 5 and the comparisons of community-based and institutional interventions in Chapter 8.

Source: LaMar T. Empey and Maynard L. Erickson, *The Provo Experiment: Evaluating Community Control of Delinquency* (Lexington, Mass.: Lexington Books, 1972).

initial efforts were not very successful. The largely volunteer staff was not prepared for the sometimes offensive behavior and language of repeat offenders. Program teachers, for instance, were "often reduced to tears"[11] by the deed and words of their delinquent students.

In 1959, a new project director was appointed and a six-year $182,000 grant from the Ford Foundation was obtained. The treatment program was considerably refined and provisions were made for an experimental evaluation of its effectiveness. When the Provo Experiment officially began in 1959, it was hoped that the project would be able to continue beyond the six years made possible by the Ford Foundation grant, especially if the initial experimental assessment proved positive.

However, a mistake by the project administrators and unrelenting opposition by the County Commission forced the project to close after six years, even though modest evidence of success was available. Utah was somewhat unique in the late 1950s because its juvenile court and correctional programs were both under state rather than local control. Ordinarily, a delinquency-control project such as the Provo Experiment would have been under state control.

The Provo Experiment's directors decided to operate the project on the county level and not seek state approval or funding. Because the county was already providing some funds to match the Ford Foundation grant, it was felt that state money would not be immediately needed. Furthermore, it was hoped that program or evaluative changes brought on by state involvement could be avoided by leaving the state out of the picture. Last, it was assumed that once the foundation money had been spent the project would have proven its effectiveness, and the state would then be willing to provide the money that would allow the Provo Experiment to continue.

The decision to stay clear of the state was a mistake, although this was not apparent when the experiment was first announced in June 1959. The project was met with considerable public and press support with one local newspaper observing: "With a six-year program cut out for them and $182,000 added to their regular funds with which to carry on the work, who knows but that The Provo Experiment will contribute something of great importance to the campaign against juvenile delinquency?"[12] Equally important, there was no reaction from the state.

A Classic Lesson in Opposition.   Local elections in November 1961 resulted in a dramatically different Utah County Commission. Prior to the election the commission had been somewhat liberal and largely supportive of the experiment. Its newly elected members were more conservative, and a former deputy sheriff became commission chairman. Additionally, a budget deficit was projected for 1962, and the commission announced that it would attempt to balance the county's budget by making a number of cuts. Funding for the Provo Experiment was among the announced expenditure reductions. The immediate consequence was that "the chickens of the project strategy [to secure county support and funding and avoid state involvement] had come home to roost."[13]

What followed the County Commission's decision to eliminate funding for the project was an "unbelievable series of events"[14] best described chronologically.[15]

DECEMBER 1961: The deputy sheriff who turned chairman of the County Commission declares that the experiment is illegal because it is being run on the county rather than the state level.

FEBRUARY 1962: Under pressure from a supportive public and press, the County Commission shifts responsibility to the Utah attorney general by asking for an opinion on whether county funds should be provided "for use by the juvenile court in connection with research being conducted by the Ford Foundation."[16] The attorney general rules that the Ford Foundation should fund its own research, and the County Commission then appropriates the experiment's funds for flood control.

MARCH 1962: After being provided with new information indicating that county funds would go to control delinquency and not to foster Ford Foundation research, the attorney general rules again. The essence of the new ruling is that county funds can be used to pay the staff hired by the experiment who were to be specially deputized as probation officers by the Utah County juvenile court judge.

APRIL 1962: The chairman of the County Commission declares that the experiment is still illegal because the specially deputized employees are not fully certified as state probation officers. Before the county would release its funds, the experiment's staff members would have to pass the State Merit System Exam. The employees take the exam and pass, with one achieving "the highest score among all applicants for that year."[17]

OCTOBER 1962: Confronted by fully certified state employees, the County Commission insists that the experiment is still illegal because it has not been approved by the state. The commission also indicates that it will not appropriate funds until a letter of endorsement is received from the state agency responsible for juvenile correctional programs.

NOVEMBER 1962: Experiment staff meet with state legislators and members of the state agency responsible for juvenile corrections. After accusing the experiment of "brainwashing" the juvenile offenders under its control, the agency writes the members of the County Commission and observes that while it would "not presume to tell you what you should do . . . we would be most pleased to see Utah County make a financial contribution to this project . . ."[18] Because the state did not presume to tell the county what to do, the county washes its hands of the experiment and declares that if money is needed to continue the project, the experiment staff should go talk to the state.

DECEMBER 1962–   The experiment staff talks to the state
NOVEMBER 1965:   about money but to no avail: No state
                   funds are ever provided the project. The
                   experiment continues to operate using
                   Ford Foundation money.

DECEMBER 1965:   Its pockets empty, the experiment closes
                   its doors.

Throughout all of this opposition to the experiment's community-based treatment, a total of 326 juveniles were assigned to the community treatment alternative the project made available, to probation, or to the State Training School. All of the juvenile subjects had extensive records of involvement in delinquency. Additionally, all were male, their average age was 16, and nearly all came from lower-middle-class or upper-lower-class family backgrounds. The only juveniles excluded were those who were overtly psychotic, severely retarded, or convicted of a capital offense or other acts of violence such as rape.

TYPE OF TREATMENT

The Provo Experiment's treatment program was grounded in a theory of delinquency familiar to us from our review of the ideas of Clifford Shaw and Henry McKay in Chapter 3.[19] Delinquency was conceptualized as the group behavior of lower-class juveniles who lacked easy access to legitimate means of reaching important goals. Delinquent groups formed as a result of this lack of access and represented "an alternative means of acquiring, or attempting to acquire, social and economic goals idealized by the social system which are acquired by other people through conventional means."[20]

Added to these ideas were two important assumptions that linked familiar theory with community-based treatment. The first was that members of delinquent groups were exposed to law-abiding values that made them ambivalent about their own involvement in delinquency. Second, although commitment to delinquency was less than total, delinquent groups rewarded words and deeds that signaled adherence to delinquent rather than conventional values.

FIGURE 7.1   The Provo Experiment's treatment hypothesis in diagrammatic form

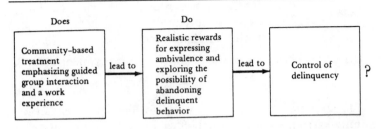

Source: The treatment hypothesis is based on description of the Provo Experiment in LaMar T. Empey and Maynard L. Erickson, *The Provo Experiment: Evaluating Community Control of Delinquency* (Lexington, Mass.: Lexington Books, 1976, pp. 1–21).

The experiment's initiators, LaMar T. Empey and Maynard L. Erickson, therefore developed the treatment hypothesis diagrammed in Figure 7.1. They reasoned that treatment had to be community based, because it was in the community that juveniles made their delinquent decisions. Professors Empey and Erickson also reasoned that treatment had to be group oriented, because it was the reward structure of delinquent groups that caused juveniles to mask ambivalence in favor of an appearance of delinquent commitment. Last, treatment had to provide realistic alternative rewards for expressing ambivalence and exploring the possibility of abandoning delinquent behavior.

Group treatment took the form of daily guided group interaction sessions. Guided group interaction is the "idea that only through a group and its processes can a boy work out his problems. From a peer point of view, it has three main goals: (1) to question the utility of a life devoted to delinquency; (2) to suggest alternative behavior; and (3) to provide recognition for a boy's personal reformation and his willingness to reform others."[21]

The primary goal of the daily guided group interaction sessions was to alert group members to the need to make an important choice. They could "continue to be delinquent and expect, in most cases, to end up in prison; or they [could] . . . learn to operate sufficiently within the law to avoid being locked up. Acceptance of the second alternative [did] . . . not mean that they would have to change their entire style of living, but it [did] . . . mean that most would have to find employment and be willing to disregard delinquent behavior in favor of the drudgery of everyday living."[22]

Several events early in the experiment helped establish the daily guided group interaction sessions as the major alternative to ending up behind bars. During the first few days of the experiment, a group member missed being picked up for a meeting and left a note indicating that he was visiting his sick sister in the hospital. He was arrested, spent the weekend in the juvenile detention center, and then was returned to the experiment.[23] Also early in the project, a juvenile resisted group involvement and asked for a new hearing before the judge. His request was immediately granted and in less than 24 hours he was doing time in the State Training School.[24] The messages were clear: become involved in the group sessions or risk being locked up.

To further emphasize the importance of the daily meetings the groups were given considerable power. When new juveniles were sent to the experiment, they understandably had many questions and were inclined to rely on adults for answers. The adults did not answer their questions and instead indicated that answers would be forthcoming in the group sessions. Additionally, it was the groups that punished members for their failure to participate in the daily meetings or for their lack of candor. Sometimes group members were ridiculed or ostracized. On other occasions members were sent to spend a weekend in the detention center to think again of the choice they had to make. Most important, it was the group that decided when a member was ready to be released from the experiment.

The adults who guided the daily group sessions initially played a very minor role. After assembling the group, they simply sat and waited for someone to say something. When the experiment began, few juveniles knew what to say and so they sat staring at each other and at the strangely silent adult. Only at the very end of each meeting did the group leader participate. At that time he provided a summary of the session's accomplishments. Because the initial sessions had no accomplishments, "he simply said that nothing had been accomplished. He did point out, however, that he would be back the next day . . . in fact, he would be there a year from that day. Where would they be? The problem was theirs."[25]

Eventually the juveniles grew tired of silence and asked the group leader what they should talk about. He suggested that it would be useful if a group member described the delinquent acts he had committed. Someone was usually willing to do this, although the person generally omitted acts that had escaped police attention. The group leader responded by noting that not all delinquent acts result in police intervention. He hoped that the next person would be more candid. Perhaps out of boredom or as a method of enhancing their delinquent reputations, group members slowly provided more complete descriptions of their delinquent careers. When this happened, juveniles learned that no action would be taken against them for their undetected delinquent acts. More important, they learned that the group meeting was a place where they could risk being open and honest.

As group members told their peers about their delinquent careers, the hypothesized ambivalence of delinquents' commitments to criminal acts became clear. They expressed doubts and fears about past involvement in delinquency and about the possibility of ending up behind bars in adult institutions. The expression of such feelings was encouraged by the adult guiding the group and, with time, by group members. As a result, group members gained another insight: Out on the street they seemed alone in their doubts and fears while everyone else appeared fully committed to their delinquent deeds. In the daily group sessions they learned that delinquent deeds frequently masked fear and a willingness to consider more conventional behaviors.

But the street was never very far away. Because the Provo Experiment was community based, juveniles returned home each night and on weekends. On the street they had to choose between delinquent and conforming behavior. Moreover, they were making visible choices. Group members generally knew one another directly or by reputation and were thus aware of what a member was doing apart from the group. As a result, street behavior also was a focus of discussion in the group meetings.

As the group meetings progressed, the adult leaders' summaries at the end of each meeting became more important. The adults used their summary statements to: "examine what had happened that day . . . examine to what ends various efforts were leading . . . suggest areas of discussion which had been neglected, ignored, or . . . hidden [and] describe the goals of the treatment system in such a way that boys could come to recognize the meaning of group discussions as a realistic source of problem resolution."[26]

The rewards for conforming behavior were several, but none were of great consequence save for the alternative of ending up behind bars. Group members who engaged in law-abiding behavior gained prestige and recognition. They also took responsibility for working with new members of the group, thus becoming actively involved in the process of treatment. Most important was freedom. Only with the approval of the group could a juvenile be released from the program.

One way to get a sense of the guided group interaction sessions is to consider the words of the juveniles involved in the various stages of group process:

RECITING ONE'S DELINQUENT CAREER

The first thing I done is steal a can full of pennies from my neighbor. There was about $10 in it. . . . I went down to the service station and put 'em in this peanut machine. . . . [W]hen I was going to the Franklin School, when I was in the sixth grade, me and _____ and _____ used to go over to this little store . . . and take candy bars and soda pop and ice cream and these big packages of candy. . . . I got caught stealing in there once. . . . I'm gonna talk . . . now . . . how I got [involved in] . . . bigger stuff. Me 'n _____, one Sunday night we went ridin' around . . . to siphon some gas. . . . I shot a cop car . . . with my pistol. We was goin' down the highway, and this cop care passed us. . . . And I pulled my .22 pistol and shot at it. I don't know if I hit it or not but it started chasin' us and I just took off . . . we lost 'em.[27]

AMBIVALENCE ABOUT DELINQUENT ACTIONS

I'll tell you . . . I was just scared all the time. I was always worried about the police and that, worried about 'em coming down. I'd go out and do something wrong then I'd always worry about it for a couple of days after that. A couple of days, or a week, I'd worry about every time somebody'd knock on the door, I'd wonder. Oh, God, is that the cops for what I done.[28]

STREET BEHAVIOR

Rog: Hersh, has Phil ever been with you when you have been stealing or drinking?

Hersh: I go with him, but when I get in trouble I always leave him and go with those other guys. I don't want to cause no trouble for him 'cause he's really tryin' in here.

Leader: I don't believe you.

Hersh: No. I never took him with me.

George: It don't look right to me. When the guys in the other group told me about that nonsquealers club, I began to get suspicious of you. You're bullshitting us.

Hersh: Fuck you.

Jack: Have you been getting in trouble with him, Phil?

Phil: Yep.

Joe: I was too.

George: Well, what in the hell has been goin' on in the group then?

Rog: We've been split right down the middle, that's what. I don't know how the fuck we're ever goin' to get out of here with this kind of shit going on.

George: Are you tellin' me that the reason you was always dragging your feet in here is because you had that thing goin' on on the outside . . . 'cause you were coverin' up for each other.[29]

ACTIVE INVOLVEMENT IN TREATMENT OF OTHERS

Marty: You know that new kid, Buster? Well we either got to help him with that new English teacher he has, or he'll fuck it up sure.

Phil: Which one is that?

Marty: You know. The teacher that gave Phil and George such a hard time. She's all right so long as you keep your mouth shut, but if you don't she'll get you in all kinds of trouble.

Rog: What can we do?

Ike: I think we got to stick close to him and keep him cool. Teach him to "cool it."

MARTY: If we can help him cool there, we'll have a better chance
to work on his problems here.[30]

REWARDS FOR CONFORMITY

. . . Now that I'm not actin' the hard-ass, my neighbors an' my
friends' parents are lookin' at me friendly, an' they're talkin' to me.
They never used to do that. An' I found out they're important to
me. I just like bein' friends with them, an' don't want them lookin'
down at me as a criminal, and let me run around with their sons
and daughters.[31]

In addition to the daily guided group interaction sessions, the
juveniles involved in the experiment worked in city work crews
initially supervised by adults. The purpose of the work groups
was to improve the juveniles' work habits and provide legitimate
opportunities for success. The juveniles worked at "the beautifi-
cation of vacant lots and parks, temporary repairs on city streets
or sidewalks, seasonal needs for special crews at the city cemetery
before and after Decoration Day, needed repairs or improvements
at the city golf course, the baseball park, or the city skating
rink."[32]

The work program was not without its problems. The juveniles were not accustomed to working at regular jobs while the
adults originally hired to supervise their work were not used "to
the dress, the language, and often the aggression"[33] of the juveniles. In addition, residents of Provo expressed fears about convicted delinquents roaming their city's streets and complained
that in addition to roaming loose, the juveniles were loafing
when they should have been working.

The problems and complaints forced change in the work component of the Provo Experiment. The adults hired to supervise
the juveniles were fired and group members assumed "foreman"
responsibilities on a rotating basis. When it was time for a break
or lunch at work, the juveniles were driven to places free of
public scrutiny so as to reduce accusations of loafing. Last, daily
guided group interaction sessions were devoted to problems between group members acting as foreman and their sometimes
recalcitrant fellow group members:

FOREMAN: You can have your foreman's job and, by god, you know
what you can do with it.

LEADER: Why? What happened?
FOREMAN: I thought all I'd have to do is go out there, sit on my ass,
         and tell these bastards what to do. But you know what
         they did? Everytime I told somebody . . . to do some-
         thing he'd tell me to go get fucked. . . .
    ROG: You know why don't you? You acted like you were king—
         like your ass weighed a ton.
   SKIP: Yeah, you pissed me off. . . .
FOREMAN: Bullshit! I never worked so fucking hard in my life—
         running around trying to keep those new kids in line,
         and tryin' to get that septic tank cleaned. Besides, I
         never saw so many guys wantin' to go get a drink or just
         goof off. You can keep your job, I quit!![34]

EVALUATIVE DESIGN

The Provo Experiment was intended to be experimentally evaluated[35] (see Figure 7.2). First, eligible offenders were identified. If
one of these offenders was adjudicated delinquent, then the judge
sentenced the offender either to probation or to the State Training School "as though the Experiment did not exist."[36] Once the
sentencing decision had been made, offenders in both the probation and State Training School groups were to be randomly
assigned to serve the sentences handed down by the judge or to
the Provo Experiment. Had the experimental evaluative design
been implemented as intended, it would have permitted examination of the effectiveness of: (a) routine probation as compared
to the Provo Experiment; and (b) the State Training School as
compared to the Provo Experiment.

However, one of the reasons the Utah County juvenile court
judge had been willing to work with the Provo Experiment was
that he "had always been disinclined to commit boys to the State
. . . School."[37] The judge's reluctance to sentence offenders to the
state school compromised the experimental evaluative design
because one of the planned comparisons shown in Figure 7.2—
State Training School and the Provo Experiment—was quickly
without sufficient numbers of offenders to permit meaningful
analysis.

Professors Empey and Erickson solved the problem of too few
State Training School sentences in two ways: (1) all eligible
offenders sentenced by the Utah County juvenile court judge to

FIGURE 7.2   The Provo Experiment's *intended* evaluative design

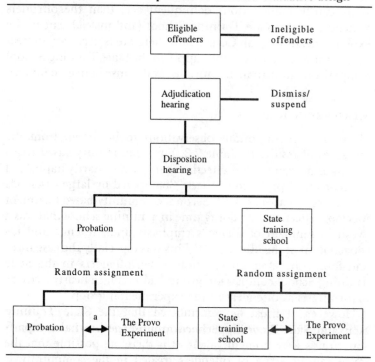

[a]Routine probation/Provo Experiment comparison.
[b]State Training School/Provo Experiment comparison.

Source: Reprinted with permission of Lexington Books, an imprint of Macmillan, Inc. from *The Provo Experiment: Evaluating Community Control of Delinquency* by LaMar T. Empey and Maynard L. Erickson. Copyright © 1972 by D. C. Heath and Company.

the State Training School were instead assigned to the Provo Experiment; and (2) offenders sentenced to the State Training School from all of Utah were used to create an incarcerated comparison group.[38] These two actions resulted in sufficient numbers of offenders to permit meaningful comparison.

   These two actions also moved portions of the Provo Experiment's evaluative design in a quasi-experimental direction and made the two groups nonequivalent in one very important respect. The offenders in the quasi-experimentally created incarceration comparison group had committed significantly more and significantly more serious delinquent acts than the offenders sentenced to the State Training School (and instead sent to the experiment) from Utah County.[39] It therefore is necessary to treat the measures of results as they apply to the State Training School comparison groups in a cautious and conservative manner.[40]

MEASURES OF RESULTS

There are two important observations to be drawn from the measures of results in Table 7.2. First, community-based treatment was no more or less effective than the necessarily haphazard supervision of probation officers "hampered by large caseloads and excessive paperwork."[41] Second, community-based treatment was more effective than doing time in a training school that was a "vestigal remnant of society's emphasis upon revenge and incapacitation of the offender."[42] This was especially the case three and four years after intervention, when offenders in the State Training School comparison group had averaged nearly twice as many arrests as offenders in the experimental group.

However, it must be remembered that the State Training School and the Provo Experiment quasi-experimental comparison groups were nonequivalent. It is therefore possible that the lower rate of arrest of offenders treated in the community is traceable to the important background difference between the

Table 7.2 The Provo Experiment: Average Number of Arrests of Juveniles in the Probation and State Training School Comparison Groups, First, Second, Third, and Fourth Year after Treatment

Average Number of Arrests Year after Treatment	Sentenced to Probation		Sentenced to State Training School	
	Probation ($n = 69$)	The Provo Experiment ($n = 62$)	State Training School ($n = 132$)	The Provo Experiment ($n = 37$)
First	0.70	0.55	1.71	1.11
Second	0.93	0.97	3.34	1.95
Third	1.01	1.24	4.54	2.24
Fourth	1.42	1.32	5.28	2.43

Source: Reprinted with permission of Lexington Books, an imprint of Macmillan, Inc., from *The Provo Experiment: Evaluating Community Control of Delinquency*, by LaMar T. Empey and Maynard L. Erickson. Copyright © 1972 by D. C. Heath and Company.

two groups. Because of this possibility, replication once again assumes extraordinary importance.

REPLICATION: THE SILVERLAKE EXPERIMENT

Table 7.3 summarizes the major features of the Silverlake Experiment,[43] a delinquency-control project that replicated the Provo Experiment in many of its important elements. The Silverlake Experiment began in Los Angeles in the mid-1960s and, like the Provo Experiment, its subjects all had previous records of delinquency. Additionally, the subjects in both projects were male and came from working-class backgrounds.

Table 7.3   Description of the Silverlake Experiment

Project Name:	The Silverlake Experiment
Location:	Los Angeles, California
Dates:	Mid-1960s
Subjects:	Juveniles adjudicated delinquent in Los Angeles County, generally for status or property offenses, excluding those who were serious sex offenders, narcotics addicts, seriously retarded, or psychotic. All of the juveniles were male; their average age was 16; 75 percent were white, 10 percent African-American, 10 percent Hispanic, and 5 percent were Asian-American; all came from working-class backgrounds and had previously been adjudicated delinquent; and 20 percent had previously been institutionalized.
Type of treatment:	Experimental juveniles lived in a group home in a middle-class residential neighborhood near downtown Los Angeles. While living at the home, the juveniles participated in daily guided group interaction sessions, attended the neighborhood public school, and performed routine housekeeping activities. On the weekends they went home.
Amount of treatment:	Juveniles in the community-based program averaged slightly less than six months of treatment.
Evaluative design:	Experimental: Juveniles sentenced to Boys Republic, "an open institution in which only moderate attention was paid to custody," were randomly assigned either to the experimental community-based program or to serve their sentence at Boys Republic.
Measures of results:	Recidivism rates were collected within 12 months following release from the community-based treatment program or Boys Republic

Source: LaMar T. Empey and Steven G. Lubeck, *The Silverlake Experiment: Testing Delinquency Theory and Community Intervention* (Chicago: Aldine, 1971).

There also are some important differences between the two projects. Unlike the subjects in the Provo Experiment, some of those in the Silverlake Experiment were African-American or Hispanic, and provide an opportunity to probe the utility of community-based treatment with other than white offenders. Further, the Silverlake Experiment was a residential program because of its location: "The . . . size of Los Angeles, and its lack of adequate transportation, made it impossible for boys both to live at home and to attend a daily program. Since the homes of experimental subjects were widely scattered throughout Los Angeles County, a non-residential program was not feasible. The program [had] . . . to be residential."[44]

The juveniles assigned to the residential program lived in a group home in a middle-class, white, residential neighborhood near downtown Los Angeles. While living at the group home the experimental juveniles participated in daily guided group interaction sessions, attended the local high school, performed routine maintenance and housekeeping tasks, and went home on weekends. The juveniles stayed at the group home an average of slightly less than six months.

The group home, as well as the daily group interaction sessions, were administered by a residence director who had been trained in criminology and had "considerable work experience in group programs with juveniles and adult offenders."[45] The remaining staff included an assistant residence director "with considerable group experience,"[46] a work supervisor, and an academic tutor. The intent of the group home and group meetings was to control delinquency, provide opportunities to express ideas and feelings, and link the juveniles with legitimate opportunities in the community, especially the school.

The juveniles randomly assigned to the control group were sent to Boys Republic, a somewhat progressive correctional institution for male delinquents. Boys Republic "stressed citizenship, education, work, and discipline and its program components included a boy government system, an accredited high school, vocational training, a farm and dairy, recreational facilities, and individual counseling. In most of its aspects, it conformed to the public notion of what a correctional organization should be."[47]

One distinctive element of the treatment program at Silverlake was "community linkage,"[48] the attempt to provide group home residents legitimate opportunities for success. One linkage with the community was location of the group home in a middle-class, white, residential neighborhood. The second was with the school. Both community strategies met with considerable opposition, especially the linkage between the group home and the local public high school.[49] It provides a classic lesson in opposition to community-based treatment.

The local high school served a middle-class, white area of Los Angeles. Its principal and staff, in insisting that the school could not absorb the working-class, racially mixed group of Silverlake residents, said that these adolescents were "not . . . part of their local constituency."[50] School officials also argued that Silverlake's residents would bring narcotics and violence to their school and exhaust limited counseling, teaching, and administrative resources. School officials suggested that Silverlake's residents instead be sent to a special adjustment school, an educational institution designed to handle the troublemaking kinds of students school officials assumed Silverlake's residents would prove to be.

The resistance of school officials was overcome after a "long series of negotiations" involving a number of compromises. It was ultimately agreed that Silverlake's residents could enter the local high school if their records were free of narcotics, sex, or violent offenses. Additionally, the project agreed to provide Silverlake residents with academic tutors and to devote some group sessions to counseling juveniles about school-based problems. Once this agreement was in place, school officials were still "uneasy and reluctant" and recurrent "relationship problems remained throughout the life of the experiment."[51]

When Silverlake's residents actually entered the school, the principal and other members of the staff made their school life miserable. School officials complained about time and money spent searching for records from previous schools, long hair, sloppy dress, and the smoking of cigarettes on or near school grounds. School officials also developed and applied a truancy rule "far more extreme than that imposed on students who were not in the experimental program."[52] If Silverlake's residents recorded one unexcused absence, they automatically were kicked out of the local high school.[53] They could, however, attend the special adjustment school, the educational institution to which school officials continued to insist Silverlake's residents should have been sent in the first place.

Relationship problems with the school caused serious compromises in the Silverlake Experiment. One was in the content of the daily group interaction sessions. The daily meetings were originally intended to change attitudes toward involvement in delinquency. As problems with the school recurred, group meetings were increasingly devoted to school problems and how they might be resolved. The residence director in charge of the daily group interaction sessions noted: "They [the group meetings] did help some. Some kids needed to learn to bathe; others needed either a full-time dermatologist or a change in diet. The mere analysis of different life styles and personal idiosyncrasies helped. It was good for the boys to recognize that such things as speech habits or dress could hinder adjustment. At the same time, the necessary accommodations between school and experiment was far too one-sided. . . . The boys got so they were spending a hell of a lot of time pressing shirts and trousers so they would look nice. . . . [M]any problems persisted not so much through a lasting unwillingness on the part of the delinquents to change as it did the school's arbitrariness and preoccupation with control."[54]

Compromises were not limited to the content of group meetings. The Silverlake Experiment was not intended to be heavily punitive in orientation or operation. Yet, the punitive posture of the school, especially its inflexibility regarding truancy, made living at Silverlake far more heavy handed than originally intended. Because of the school's truancy rule, Silverlake established a rule that if a juvenile ran away once, he would be dropped from Silverlake and recommended for incarceration. Silverlake was thus under intense pressure from the school, and that pressure resulted in a punitive group-home environment (see Box 7.1) that paradoxically mirrored the school's "preoccupation with control."

One culmination of the relationship problems with the school was a fistfight between several Silverlake residents and a vice principal of the school. Although no one was seriously injured, the vice principal was briefly hospitalized. Furthermore, two Silverlake residents were sent to Boys Republic as a result of their involvement in the fight.

Box 7.1 Community Treatment as Punishment

The names given to certain approaches to the control of juvenile delinquency sometimes are partially misleading. Community treatment is one example. Its name seems to imply a benign approach to the problem of delinquency that avoids the punitive aspects of institutionalization.

However, community treatment also involves punishment. The Community Treatment Project examined in Chapter 5 sent large numbers of experimental subjects to the local juvenile detention center for long periods of time. Community-based, intensive supervision programs, also examined in Chapter 5, deliberately start tough. The Provo Experiment was quick to resort to detention when experimental subjects refused to become involved in the daily guided group interaction sessions. Similarly, the Silverlake Experiment dropped truant group home residents from the community program and recommended their institutionalization.

There are at least three reasons why community-based programs are more punitive than their name would seem to imply. First, some of the offenders sentenced to a community-based program perceive their sentence as something of a lark. Strict rules and harsh sanctions represent one method of attracting the attention of such offenders. Second, community-based programs generally encounter considerable opposition, and a punitive operating philosophy is one method of attempting to reduce resistance. Third, social work has its limits and when those limits are reached, law enforcement actions are the only available alternative.

Community-based treatment thus is not characterized exclusively by such things as smaller probation or parole caseloads, guided group interaction, or residential group homes. Offender perceptions, community opposition, and the limits of social work make frequent recourse to punishment a central feature of this method of dealing with juvenile offenders.

Throughout all of the problems, including the fistfight, Silverlake's residents continued to attend a high school where they were not wanted. As might be expected, Silverlake's residents were frustrated and angered by their treatment in school and by the punitive nature of life at Silverlake. Some gave up and ran away,[55] while others responded violently (as in the incident with the vice principal). Most quietly endured the hassles and degradation associated with attending a school that did not want them as "part of their . . . constituency."[56]

In order to assess the effectiveness of the community-based treatment program, juveniles were randomly assigned to either Silverlake or Boys Republic. Among the measures of results collected are those in Table 7.4. Examination of the table reveals that there were no important differences between the experimental and control group subjects in rates of recidivism. For example, essentially equal percentages of juveniles in both groups had been arrested at least once in the 12 months following treatment. Unlike the Provo Experiment, then, the Silverlake Experiment's community-based treatment program was not more effective than institutionalization. It was, however, just as effective.

REPLICATION: THE MASSACHUSETTS "EXPERIMENT"

In the early 1960s, Massachusetts' Youth Service Board[57] operated a sizable juvenile correctional system responsible for 800 offenders. The young people it controlled were typical of institutionalized offenders nationwide. Most were male and their average age was a little over 15. Nearly all were poor. Most had committed crimes against property. Less than 5 percent were clearly violent.[58]

Table 7.4 The Silverlake Experiment: Percent of Experimental and Control Subjects Rearrested for New Offenses in the 12 Months Following Treatment at Silverlake or Incarceration at Boys Republic

Number of New Offenses	Silverlake ($n = 140$)	Boys Republic ($n = 121$)
0	60	56
1	25	24
2	6	13
3	4	3
4 or more	6	3
Totals	101[a]	99[a]

[a]Does not add up to 100 because of rounding.

Source: LaMar T. Empey and Steven G. Lubeck, *The Silverlake Experiment: Testing Delinquency Theory and Community Intervention* (Chicago: Aldine, 1971), p. 255. Copyright © 1971 by LaMar T. Empey and Steven G. Lubeck. Reprinted by permission.

Most of the training schools that were home to Massachusetts' institutionalized offenders were very old and all were tough places to do time. Deliberately so. John D. Coughlan was director of the Youth Service Board and an "articulate and vigorous advocate of the philosophy of youth training schools."[59] Included among the rules and procedures of the training schools was shaving the heads of new male inmates, "housedresses and granny caps"[60] for female inmates, silent marching to and from activities, and regular use of corporal punishment. At Boston's Roslindale facility bedtime meant "the boys were made to stand at attention outside their cell doors and were ordered to strip. Each was then inspected by a master, after which he could enter his locked cell for the night."[61] At the Lancaster facility for young women, inmates were locked in their rooms at night with buckets as their toilets.[62] It was estimated that the recidivism rate was between 40 and 70 percent, although no one really knew for sure.[63]

The Youth Service Board was understandably the target of frequent staff complaints and recurrent outside reports critical of its operations. In 1966, for example, the United States Department of Health, Education, and Welfare reported that Youth Service Board institutions were characterized by a "dominace of custodial goals over those of treatment, the lack of effective centralized supervision and direction of childcare, the absence of an adequate diagnostic and classification system, the failure to develop flexible and professional personnel practices, and the ineffectiveness of parole supervision."[64]

One result of frequent staff complaints and recurrent critical reports was Coughlan's resignation in 1969 after 17 years as director. Francis Sargent, governor of Massachusetts, appointed a "blue ribbon committee to undertake a national search"[65] for a commissioner of the reorganized and renamed Department of Youth Services. After the committee interviewed a large number of candidates, Jerome Miller, an associate professor of social work at Ohio State University, was selected.[66] Although Professor Miller lacked administrative experience, he won the approval of the committee with his commitment to making the state's training schools less brutal and more humane.[67]

Once appointed, Commissioner Miller began touring the facilities he was now responsible for. Many of his visits were at night and on weekends to talk with the children (see Box 7.2). Here is his description of some of what he saw during a visit to the Boys' Industrial School at Shirley: "the staff member ushered us into the 'tombs'—a series of cement cubicles not quite reaching the vaulted ceiling of the old building. The coffinlike rooms were aptly named. I asked to look inside one. The master unlocked the steel mesh door, and there, on the floor, nude in the darkness of his own tomb, sat a sixteen-year-old. He was being punished for having caused a scene in the cottage a few days earlier. I asked our

---

Box 7.2 To Talk with the Children

Jerome Miller regularly went to juvenile correctional facilities to talk with the children. Many of his conversations took place at night and on weekends. He knew the names and faces of the children inside the institutions. He knew where they came from. He knew what they had done. He knew what it was like for them inside the places he was hired to change.

Billy, "a grinning, hyperactive fourteen-year-old [who] had no family and no prospect of one," was doing his time at Lyman. Eddy escaped from a state facility to check on his father who was paralyzed from the neck down. He told Miller he had to run because his mother "died the year before" and there was no one else who would make sure his dad was OK. Joe Kerry was at the Boys' Industrial School at Shirley for "stealing some tires out of this guy's garage." Miller got to know Doug, a sixteen year-old heroin addict, during a late-night visit to the disciplinary cells ("tombs") at Shirley. Jimmy was "schackled to his bed" at Bridge-water when Miller met him.

Miller's actions in Massachusetts were strongly influenced by the visits he made to talk with the children. "Again and again," Miller writes, "I altered plans in response to the presence of some boy or girl."

Source: Jerome G. Miller, *Last One Over the Wall: The Massachusetts Experiment in Closing Reform Schools* (Columbus: Ohio State University Press, 1991), pp. 64, 65, 71, 85, 99, 102, and 126.

guide how long the boy would be kept in the tomb and was told it was usually a matter of days but could go on longer."[68]

Having seen what was happening inside the training schools and other facilities, Commissioner Miller worked hard to make the state's institutions less brutal and more humane. He issued a series of directives that halted the shaving of the heads of new male inmates, silent marching, and corporal punishment.[69] He solved the problem of isolation he had seen in the tombs at Shirley by requiring "that whoever ordered a youngster into isolation [sit in] isolation . . . with him until his release. . . . The rule effectively stopped use of isolation."[70] Miller also brought in experts to help staff learn new and better ways of responding to the adolescents placed in their care.

Most of Miller's actions and ideas were met with ridicule and open resistance. Youth Services' employees complained to friends in the state legislature that Miller was turning the training schools into "country clubs." Others labeled Miller the "hippy commissioner" because of his ban on shaving the heads of new male inmates. Still others posted escape maps on bulletin boards in an effort to foment trouble.[71] At first, efforts to humanize the institutions had little effect. Some six months after Miller took office a surprise visit to the disciplinary cottage at the Lyman School for Boys revealed "sixteen kids sitting in their underpants with their arms folded across their chests, sitting in steel chairs, at attention. They weren't saying a word and the supervisor was sitting in the back of the room with a loaded .38 . . . on the desk."[72]

Miller was relentless. He visited, cajoled, rewarded, and pleaded. He won a few allies, brought in some others, and together they made positive changes happen inside the institutions. Beatings were stopped. Inmates began to look and sound like kids. They were talking, sometimes even laughing. The young men wore their hair long, in keeping with the times, and the young women dressed in street clothes. Real efforts were made to rehabilitate, not just incapacitate. Staff-guided group interaction replaced staff-guided escape maps. Dr. Miller noted that when he "decided to close the institutions, they were among the more decent reform schools in the nation."[73] Researchers from Harvard agreed, reporting that significant positive change was clearly afoot inside Massachusetts' correctional facilities.[74]

So why close the places after working so hard—and success-fully—to effect positive changes?

Careful review of Miller's account[75] of his tenure as commis-sioner of Massachusetts' Department of Youth Services suggests several answers. The times were right. In the late 1960s, the idea of closing training schools and replacing them with community-based programs had attracted considerable attention and sup-port. In 1967, for example, the President's Commission on Law Enforcement and Administration of Justice recommended that juvenile correctional authorities "develop more extensive com-munity programs providing special, intensive treatment as an alternative to institutionalization [of] . . . juvenile offenders."[76] Additionally, a "growing chorus of politicians, liberal social scientists, and high-level managers of the social control appara-tus [argued] that . . . juvenile reformatories [were] 'decaying in-stitutions.' . . . Rather than trying to upgrade [them] we ought to get on with the work of emptying them."[77]

The improvements in the state's institutions were the work of Dr. Miller and a handful of others in the "central office." They had come from the top and had been rammed down the throats of the civil service employees who ran the state's training schools. The employees responded by following Miller's directives while at the same time waiting for him to get tired, get sick, get killed, or just get going—after which the repressive policies of the past would be reinstated. One of Miller's trusted colleagues told him: "They're just going to wait us out, Jerry."[78]

With but a handful of exceptions, all of the juveniles inside the training schools would be released, most very quickly. Then as now, juveniles sentenced to the state's institutions spent only a few months incarcerated.[79] Releasing the kids to the community was something that was going to happen anyway.

The juveniles were not simply going to be dumped. Although plans were hastily made, offenders were carefully screened, matched with newly created programs, and monitored once placed.[80] Unlike the deinstitutionalization of the mentally ill where patients nationwide were kicked loose with no community safety nets for those who had troubles,[81] the young people re-leased from Massachusetts' training schools had places to go and people who were expecting them.

Dr. Miller knew the juveniles inside the training schools. Offenders worked for him at the Department of Youth Services' central office in Boston. He knew they came from poverty. He knew about the property crimes that had gotten most of them institutionalized. He knew that only a handful of violent offenders really needed to be institutionalized.

In closing Massachusetts' correctional facilities for juvenile offenders, Miller started with the Institute for Correctional Guidance at Bridgewater. The Bridgewater facility had been the source of frequent complaints of brutality, which the staff did not take great pains to hide. During one of Dr. Miller's visits to Bridgewater, he watched staff members beat three juveniles who had tried to escape.[82] Bridgewater was closed in August 1970. Of the 60 juveniles at the facility, 48 were sent home and 12 were reassigned to secure cottages at the Lyman School. In the next two years three additional training schools were closed, and at the start of 1974 only the industrial school for female offenders at Lancaster remained open. By July 1974 this last training school also had closed its doors.

In place of the training schools, Miller and his staff hurriedly created a network of state-funded, privately run community-based facilities. By the end of 1973, juvenile offenders under state control were receiving services in "80 nonresidential programs . . . 120 residential programs, and . . . 200 foster homes."[83] A minority of "dangerous and disturbed youth"[84] were housed in secure facilities.

The effects of Dr. Miller's actions are apparent in Table 7.5. As compared to other states, Massachusetts institutionalized far fewer juvenile offenders. Additionally, Massachusetts placed many more offenders in community-based facilities and consequently spent most of its correctional budget on community-based residential programs.

One thing that had not changed was the recidivism rate: "the policy of the Massachusetts Department of Youth Services to close the training schools has not resulted in a substantial increase in recidivism, but neither has it resulted in a substantial decrease."[85] Much like the other projects examined in this and earlier chapters, community-based treatment was just as effective as institutionalization.

Table 7.5   Selected Characteristics of State Juvenile Corrections Programs

Characteristic	United States	Massachusetts
Rate of institutionalization of juvenile offenders per 100,000 total population (1974, based on 50 states)	17.8	2.1
Percent of all offenders in state correctional programs who are in community-based residential programs (1974, based on 48 states)	17.7	86.6
Percent of state juvenile corrections budget spent on community-based residential programs (1974, based on 42 states)	9.4	69.0

Source: Lloyd E. Ohlin, Alden D. Miller, and Robert B. Coates, *Juvenile Correctional Reform in Massachusetts: A Preliminary Report of the Center for Criminal Justice of the Harvard Law School* (Washington, D.C.: U.S. Government Printing Office, no date listed), stock no. 027-000-00483-1, p. 106.

Other things also may have remained the same. Keeping track of what happens inside five training schools is hard enough. Monitoring over 400 community-based programs is even more difficult. It therefore is unclear whether problems such as isolation and mistreatment were significantly reduced as a consequence of the shift to community-based programs. Like people elsewhere, Massachusetts' citizens opposed housing offenders in their community. Efforts to establish community-based programs in "stable residential communities often met with insurmountable community resistance. As a result, most were located in low-income industrial neighborhoods or, ironically, in empty buildings on the grounds of [the recently closed] state institutions."[86] A state-funded detention center for young women was visited by a journalist for *The Boston Globe*, who reported that the facility was located in the basement of a YMCA "close to the city center where the neighbors wouldn't complain."[87] The reporter also saw clear evidence of the potential for mistreatment: "[O]ne of the . . . rooms had only a metal bed in it; the bed has no mattress, but it does have . . . handcuffs for when the girls have been fighting or 'acting out' and the staff decides to shackle their arms and legs to the bed frame. This room is called the quiet room."[88] Miller himself encountered evidence of potential mistreatment at a group home, and was uncomfortable with it: "I glanced into the next room. A boy was sitting with a sign hung around his neck, something to the effect that he'd been unwilling to deal with his problems. . . . [The] response was uncomfortably reminiscent of my first encounter . . . in the tombs. . . . A week or two later, I got wind that youngsters were occasionally sent upstairs to sit in a closet as punishment for not 'getting with' the program."[89]

Despite these setbacks, Jerome G. Miller unquestionably brought significant change to juvenile corrections in Massachusetts. In shutting down Massachusetts' large, institutionally-based correctional program for juvenile offenders—the type of program that still exists in most states—Miller created a network of state funded, privately run, community-based programs that were at least as effective as the institutions they replaced. When Dr. Miller left Massachusetts in 1973 to accept a similar position in Illinois, he left behind a profoundly different way of responding to juveniles in trouble with the law.

It is important to note that as the Massachusetts "Experiment" approaches its third decade, Massachusetts has the lowest rate of juveniles in public facilities[90]: 32 per 100,000 juveniles as compared to the national average of 185 per 100,000 juveniles. Massachusetts spends most of its juvenile corrections money on private programs: 79 percent as compared to 39 percent nationally. Massachusetts places most of the juveniles sentenced to the Department of Youth Services in private, community-based programs: 63 percent as compared to 16 percent nationally. Massachusetts has one of the lowest overall rates of state control of juveniles: 183 in public and private facilities per 100,000 juveniles as compared to 313 per 100,000 nationally.

Professor Miller was in Massachusetts for only four years. He made a lasting difference (see Box 7.3).

SUMMARY AND CONCLUSIONS

This chapter examined three classic community-based treatment projects for delinquent juveniles. It began by describing and analyzing the Provo Experiment. Attention was then directed to the Silverlake Experiment, a delinquency-control project that replicated the Provo Experiment in most of its important elements. Examined last was Jerome Miller's closing of all training schools in Massachusetts, an "experiment" now approaching its third decade.

Box 7.3   A Lasting Difference

Jerome Miller made a lasting difference because he shifted state juvenile correctional money from institutions to community-based programs. Once the money was in the community, an entirely new set of linkages emerged between the private, nonprofit agencies that provide programming, the contractors and vendors that service the community-based programs, and the state's politicians. The people and organizations that compose these linkages understandably developed strong interests in maintaining a system that sends state correctional money to local communities. Miller's lasting difference is the direct result of the new relationships that were created when state money was placed in the community.

Source: Jerome G. Miller, *Last One Over the Wall: The Massachusetts Experiment in Closing Reform Schools* (Columbus: Ohio State University Press, 1991), pp. 216–17.

The community-based programs examined in this chapter, projects examined in previous chapters, and the evaluative efforts of others[91] combine to yield one firm conclusion. Intermediate, community-based interventions are just as effective as institutionalization.

NOTES

1. For description and analysis of the Provo Experiment, see LaMar T. Empey and Maynard L. Erickson, *The Provo Experiment: Evaluating Community Control of Delinquency* (Lexington, Mass.: Lexington Books, 1972).

2. For description and analysis of the Silverlake Experiment, see LaMar T. Empey and Steven G. Lubeck, *The Silverlake Experiment: Testing Delinquency Theory and Community Intervention* (Chicago: Aldine, 1971).

3. For description and analysis of the Massachusetts "Experiment," see Jerome G. Miller, *Last One Over the Wall: The Massachusetts*

Experiment in Closing Reform Schools (Columbus: Ohio State University Press, 1991); Robert B. Coates, Alden D. Miller, and Lloyd E. Ohlin, *Diversity in a Youth Correctional System: Handling Delinquents in Massachusetts* (Cambridge, Mass.: Ballinger, 1978); Lloyd E. Ohlin, Alden D. Miller, and Robert B. Coates, *Juvenile Correctional Reform in Massachusetts: A Preliminary Report of the Center for Criminal Justice of the Harvard Law School* (Washington, D.C.: U.S. Government Printing Office, no date listed), stock no. 027-000-00483-1; Richard Kwartler (ed.), *Behind Bars: Prisons in America* (New York: Vintage Books, 1977), pp. 100–23; Andrew T. Scull, *Decarceration: Community Treatment and the Deviant* (Englewood Cliffs, N.J.: Prentice-Hall, 1977); and Christina Robb, "Locking Up Children: Massachusetts's Juvenile Detention System," *The Boston Globe Magazine*, October 26, 1980, pp. 12–13, 20, 25, 27–28, 30, 32, and 36.

4. Norval Morris and Michael Tonry, *Between Prison and Probation: Intermediate Punishments in a Rational Sentencing System* (New York: Oxford University Press, 1990).

5. Todd R. Clear and Patricia L. Hardyman, "The New Intensive Supervision Movement," *Crime and Delinquency* 36 (January 1990): 42–60. All of volume 36 of *Crime and Delinquency* is devoted to intensive supervision programs.

6. Ira M. Schwartz, *(In) Justice for Juveniles: Rethinking the Best Interests of the Child* (Lexington, Mass.: D. C. Heath, 1989), p. 170.

7. Ohlin, Miller, and Coates, *Juvenile Correctional Reform*, p. 106.

8. Kwartler, *Behind Bars*, p. 112.

9. Ibid.

10. Empey and Erickson, *The Provo Experiment.*

11. Ibid., p. 156.

12. Ibid., pp. 158–159.

13. Ibid., p. 160.

14. Ibid.

15. Ibid., pp. 160–68.

16. Ibid., p. 163.

17. Ibid., p. 165.

18. Ibid., p. 166.

19. Based on Ibid., pp. 1–22 and pp. 95–136.

20. Ibid., p. 5.

21. Ibid., p. 10.

22. Ibid., p. 14.

23. Ibid., p. 15.

24. Ibid., p. 15.

25. Ibid., p. 16.

26. Ibid., p. 17.

27. Ibid., pp. 100–01.

28. Ibid., pp. 128–29.

29. Ibid., pp. 122–23.

30. Ibid., p. 127.

31. Ibid., p. 128.

32. Ibid., p. 139.

33. Ibid., p. 141.

34. Ibid., p. 126.

35. Ibid., pp. 23–31.

36. Ibid., p. 25.

37. Ibid., p. 27.

38. Ibid., p. 27. These juveniles also had to meet the experiment's admission criteria.

39. Ibid., pp. 28–30.

40. Ibid., p. 29.

41. Ibid., p. 177.

42. Ibid., p. 177.

43. Empey and Lubeck, *The Silverlake Experiment.*

44. Ibid., p. 83.

45. Ibid., p. 86.

46. Ibid., p. 87.

47. Ibid., p. 5.

48. Ibid., pp. 83–86.

49. Ibid., pp. 88–89 and 173–79.

50. Ibid., p. 89.

51. Ibid., p. 89.

52. Ibid., p. 176.

53. Ibid., p. 176.

54. Ibid., p. 176.

55. Ibid., pp. 211–39.

56. Ibid., p. 89.

57. Miller, *Last One Over the Wall*; Coates, Miller, and Ohlin, *Diversity in a Youth Correctional System*; Ohlin, Miller, and Coates, *Juvenile Correctional Reform*; Kwartler, *Behind Bars*; Scull, *Decarceration*; Robb, "Locking Up Children."

58. Miller, *Last One Over the Wall*, pp. 50–51.

59. Ohlin, Miller, and Coates, *Juvenile Correctional Reform*, p. 3.

60. Miller, *Last One Over the Wall*, p. 66.

61. Ibid., p. 56.

62. Coates, Miller, and Ohlin, *Diversity in a Youth Correctional System*, p. 22.

63. Ohlin, Miller, and Coates, *Juvenile Correctional Reform*, p. 3.

64. Ibid.

65. Ibid., p. 4.

66. Miller, *Last One Over the Wall*, pp. 32–42.

67. Ibid., p. 33.

68. Ibid., p. 65.

69. Ohlin, Miller, and Coates, *Juvenile Correctional Reform*, pp. 4–5.

70. Miller, *Last One Over the Wall*, p. 90.

71. Ibid., pp. 98–99.

72. Kwartler, *Behind Bars*, p. 107.

73. Miller, *Last One Over the Wall*, p. 137.

74. Coates, Miller, and Ohlin, *Diversity in a Youth Correctional System*; Ohlin, Miller, and Coates, *Juvenile Correctional Reform*.

75. Miller, *Last One Over the Wall*.

76. The President's Commission on Law Enforcement and Administration of Justice, *The Challenge of Crime in a Free Society* (Washington, D.C.: U.S. Government Printing Office, 1967), p. 171.

77. Scull, *Decarceration*, p. 41.

78. Miller, *Last One Over the Wall*, p. 150.

79. Ibid., p. 119.

80. Ibid., p. 157.

81. Scull, *Decarceration*; Miller, *Last One Over the Wall*, p. 153; "Broken Minds," *Frontline*, January 7, 1992, Public Broadcasting System.

82. Kwartler, *Behind Bars*, p. 108.

83. Ohlin, Miller, and Coates, *Juvenile Correctional Reform*, p. 16.

84. Ibid., p. 17.

85. Ibid., p. 107.

86. Kwartler, *Behind Bars*, p. 112.

87. Robb, "Locking Up Children," p. 13.

88. Ibid., p. 36.

89. Miller, *Last One Over the Wall*, pp. 179–80.

90. U.S. Department of Justice, Office of Justice Programs, Bureau of Justice Statistics, *Children in Custody, 1975–1985: Census of Public and Private Juvenile Detention, Correctional, and Shelter Facilities, 1975, 1977, 1979, and 1985* (Washington, D.C.: U.S. Department of Justice, Bureau of Justice Statistics, May 1989 [NCJ-114065]). In comparing the rates in this paragraph with those in Table 7.5, it is important to note that the data in row 1 of Table 7.5 are rates per 100,000 total population whereas the rates reported in this paragraph are those per 100,000 juveniles.

91. William S. Davidson II, Robin Redner, Richard L. Amdur, and Christina M. Mitchell, *Alternative Treatments for Troubled Youth: The Case of Diversion from the Juvenile Justice System* (New York: Plenum, 1990), pp. 17–37; John T. Whitehead and Steven P. Lab, "A Meta-

Analysis of Juvenile Correctional Treatment," *Journal of Research in Crime and Delinquency* 26 (August 1989): 276-95; Solomon Kobrin and Malcolm W. Klein, *National Evaluation of Deinstitutionalization of Status Offender Programs: Executive Summary* (Washington, D.C.: National Institute for Juvenile Justice and Delinquency Prevention, Office of Juvenile Justice and Delinquency Prevention, U.S Department of Justice, June 1982).

8

INSTITUTIONALIZATION

The juvenile corrections pendulum swings in wide and frequently repetitive arcs.[1] Just a short time ago, training schools and other correctional facilities for juveniles were seen by many as the problem rather than the solution.[2] Diversion was being advocated as the most effective method of dealing with juveniles in minor trouble with the law.[3] For those committing more serious offenses, community-based treatment was seen as the best response.[4] Institutionalization was a last and reluctant response reserved for serious offenders.

Currently, the use of training schools and other correctional facilities for juvenile offenders is again being advocated as an effective method of controlling delinquency.[5] Some of those urging more frequent use of training schools are incapacitation theorists.[6] They argue that, because a small group of repetitively delinquent offenders is responsible for a large amount of youth crime, the solution to the youth crime problem is to sentence repeat offenders to long terms in correctional facilities.

Deterrence theorists[7] also support more frequent use of institutionalization. They argue that serving time in a correctional facility alerts offenders to the painful consequences of continued involvement in delinquency. They also argue that punishment of particular offenders demonstrates to other juveniles what can and will happen to them if they persist in their delinquent ways. Deterrence theorists hypothesize that specific and general awareness of the pains of imprisonment causes juveniles to refrain from delinquency out of fear of punishment.

This chapter examines the incapacitation and deterrence hypotheses. It begins by using cohort studies to estimate the extent to which incapacitating sentences reduce delinquency. Attention is then directed to the deterrent effects of institutionalization.

INCAPACITATION

The incapacitation hypothesis[8] is straightforward (see Figure 8.1). Proponents of incapacitation argue that most juvenile crime is the work of a small group of frequently and seriously delinquent offenders. To control delinquency, it is necessary to identify these repeat offenders early in their careers and then incapacitate them in secure facilities. Incapacitation theorists hypothesize that once chronic offenders have been locked up, the juvenile crime rate will decline significantly.

The least expensive means of assessing the incapacitation hypothesis is to examine the results of cohort studies (see Box 8.1). The major advantage of cohort studies is that they easily yield estimates of the effects of long sentences on juvenile crime without actually spending the money to lock up large numbers of juveniles. Cohort studies tell us how many offenses were committed by cohort members and therefore how many offenses could have been prevented had offenders been institutionalized rather

FIGURE 8.1   The incapacitation hypothesis in diagrammatic form

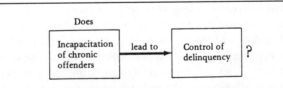

Source: The incapacitation hypothesis is based on Paul E. Tracy, Marvin E. Wolfgang, and Robert M. Figlio, *Delinquency Careers in Two Birth Cohorts* (New York: Plenum, 1990), pp. 295–98; and James Q. Wilson, *Thinking About Crime*, rev. ed. (New York: Vintage Books, 1985), pp. 145–61.

Box 8.1   Cohort Studies

Cohort studies focus descriptive and analytical attention on the delinquent behavior of a particular group of juveniles. In the typical cohort study, juveniles are identified by reference to birth in a specific year (or years) and residence in the same geographic location during their adolescent years. Once the cohort has been identified in terms of birth and residence, official records, such as arrests by police, are used to establish the delinquent acts committed by cohort members.

One of the best examples of a cohort study is *Delinquency in a Birth Cohort*, a project to be examined in detail in this chapter. Members of the cohort were identified by reference to their birth in 1945 and residence in Philadelphia between their tenth and eighteenth birthdays. Once the cohort had been identified, Philadelphia police records were used to establish the delinquent acts committed by the members of the birth cohort.

Sources: Marvin E. Wolfgang, Robert M. Figlio, and Thorsten Sellin, *Delinquency in a Birth Cohort* (Chicago: The University of Chicago Press, 1972); Donna M. Hamparian, Richard S. Schuster, Simon Dinitz, and John P. Conrad, *The Violent Few: A Study of Dangerous Juvenile Offenders* (Lexington, Mass.: Lexington Books, 1978); Lyle W. Shannon, *Criminal Career Continuity: Its Social Context* (New York: Human Sciences Press, 1988); and Paul E. Tracy, Marvin E. Wolfgang, and Robert M. Figlio, *Delinquency Careers in Two Birth Cohorts* (New York: Plenum, 1990).

---

than left alone to continue their delinquent ways. Instead of creating real and very expensive programs designed to incapacitate, we can use cohort studies to model what would have happened had such programs been in place.

This section uses cohort studies to probe the logic and accuracy of the incapacitation hypothesis. It begins with Marvin E. Wolfgang, Robert M. Figlio, and Thorsten Sellin's *Delinquency in a Birth Cohort*.[9] Replicative attention is then directed to Professor Wolfgang's 1958 birth cohort as reported in *Delinquency Careers in Two Birth Cohorts*.[10]

DELINQUENCY IN A BIRTH COHORT

Delinquency in a Birth Cohort examined the officially recorded delinquent acts committed by the 9,945 males born in 1945 who lived in Philadelphia between their tenth and eighteenth birthdays (see Table 8.1). Using reports written by Philadelphia police as evidence of involvement in delinquency. Professor Marvin E. Wolfgang and colleagues found that 35 percent of the cohort had experienced at least one contact with Philadelphia police that resulted in a written report. Juveniles with at least one contact had accumulated a total of 10,214 officially recorded offenses.

Study of the cohort revealed the presence of a small group of chronic offenders responsible for a disproportionate amount of officially recorded cohort delinquency (see Table 8.1). A total of 627 juveniles—only 6 percent of the entire cohort and 18 percent of the members of the cohort with at least one police contact—committed 5,305 officially recorded offenses, or almost 52 percent of the 10,214 offenses committed by the juveniles in the entire cohort.

Table 8.1 Description of *Delinquency in a Birth Cohort*

The cohort:	Males born in 1945 who lived in Philadelphia between their tenth and eighteenth birthdays.
Cohort size:	9,945
Measure of delinquency:	Police contact resulting in written record.
Percent of cohort delinquent:	35%—3,475 of the 9,945 members of the cohort had at least one police contact that resulted in a written report.
Total number of offenses:	10,214—the 3,475 juveniles with at least one contact had a total of 10,214 contacts resulting in written reports.
Number of offenses committed by one-time offenders:	1,613—15.8% of the 10,214 offenses were committed by the 1,613 juveniles committing only one offense.
Number of offenses committed by "recidivists" (juveniles with two to four offenses):	3,296—32.3% of the 10,214 offenses were committed by the 1,235 juveniles committing between two and four offenses.
Number of offenses committed by "chronic offenders" (juveniles with five or more offenses):	5,305—51.9% of the 10,214 offenses were committed by the 627 juveniles committing five or more offenses.

Source: Marvin E. Wolfgang, Robert M. Figlio, and Thorsten Sellin, *Delinquency in a Birth Cohort* (Chicago: The University of Chicago Press, 1972).

Table 8.2 Delinquency in a Birth Cohort: Number and Percent of Officially Recorded Cohort Offenses Prevented by Incapacitating Sentence after Offenses 1 to 8

Incapacitating Sentence after Offense Number	Number of Offenders Incapacitated	Officially Recorded Cohort Offenses Prevented	
		Number[a]	Percent[a]
1	3,475	6,739	66
2	1,862	4,877	48
3	1,212	3,665	36
4	868	2,797	27
5	627	2,170	21
6	456	1,714	17
7	368	1,346	13
8	282	1,064	10

[a]Of the 10,214 officially recorded offenses committed by the cohort.

Source: Marvin E. Wolfgang, Robert M. Figlio, and Thorsten Sellin, Delinquency in a Birth Cohort (Chicago: The University of Chicago Press, 1972). Reconstructed from matrices 11.1 to 11.8, pp. 176–78.

Incapacitation of cohort offenders through age 17 would have prevented[11] officially recorded cohort delinquency (see Table 8.2). The effect of incapacitating sentences would have been greatest had all first-time offenders been locked up until age 18: Two-thirds of the cohort's officially recorded offenses would have been avoided. Incapacitation of all two-time offenders would have reduced cohort delinquency by slightly less than half. After three offenses the number of delinquent acts prevented drops to a little over one-third and after five offenses to only 21 percent (see Box 8.2).

However, not all second- or even sixth-time offenders went on to commit an officially recorded next offense. Instead, many stopped of their own accord, making incapacitation unnecessary (see Figure 8.2). The problem is most apparent after offense number one because nearly half of the offenders did not go on to commit a second officially recorded offense. The incapacitation error rate declines thereafter, stabilizing at slightly above one-quarter after offenses three through five and at around 20 percent after offenses six through eight.

In order to avoid unnecessarily incapacitating large numbers of offenders, a reliable method of predicting further involvement in delinquency is needed. Unfortunately, the state of the predic-

---

Box 8.2   Cohort Offenders with Five or More Offenses

Cohort offenders with five or more offenses committed 5,305, or
51.9 percent, of the 10,214 officially recorded offenses committed
by the entire cohort. Yet, Table 8.2 shows that incapacitation after
five offenses would have prevented only 2,170, or 21 percent, of the
10,214 offenses committed by the entire cohort. If offenders with
five or more offenses committed 5,305 offenses, why wouldn't
incapacitation after five offenses have prevented all 5,305 offenses?

By the time of their fifth offense, the 627 five-time offenders had
committed a total of 3,135 offenses (627 × 5 = 3,135). Offenders
with more than five offenses went on to commit a total of 2,170
additonal offenses, thereby producing the 5,305 offenses committed by the 627 offenders with five or more offenses (3,135 + 2,170 =
5,305). By waiting until a fifth offense had been committed, it
obviously is impossible to have prevented the 3,135 offenses that
the five-time offenders had already committed. Only the additional 2,170 offenses could have been prevented.

---

tive art has not progressed since we last examined it in Chapter 3.
Despite collection of extensive background data on the members
of the cohort, Professor Wolfgang and colleagues report "that the
type [of] next offense . . . cannot well be predicted. . . . [I]n order
to prevent the occurrence of serious crimes in a delinquent boy's
future, efforts should be made to prevent all forms of recidivism."[12]

Incapacitation is one method of preventing recidivism, even in
the absence of reliable predictions of further involvement in
delinquency. But if it is not possible to identify offenders who
will continue their delinquent ways unless incapacitated, then a
search must be undertaken for other criteria to be used in establishing the point at which incapacitation should take place.

It is hard to find that point. It seems reasonable to assume that
an acceptable incapacitation intervention point would be one
that had a significant impact on cohort delinquency while avoiding the unnecessary incapacitation of large numbers of cohort
members. Based on the information in Table 8.2 and Figure 8.2,
incapacitation after offense number one is clearly unacceptable.

FIGURE 8.2 Delinquency in a Birth Cohort: percent of offenders unnecessarily incapacitated (incapacitation error rate)[a] after
offences one to eight.

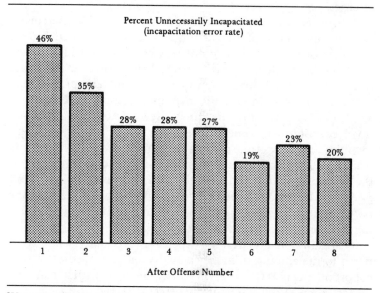

Percent Unnecessarily Incapacitated
(incapacitation error rate)

[a]Unnecessarily incapacited refers to the fact that the juvenile did not go on to
commit another officially recorded offense. For example, of the 3,475 juveniles
who committed at least one offense, 1,613, or 46 percent, did not commit a second
officially recorded offense.

Source: Marvin E. Wolfgang, Robert M. Figlio, and Thorsten Sellen, *Delinquency in a Birth Cohort* (Chicago: The University of Chicago Press, 1972).
Reconstructed from matrices 11.1 to 11.8, pp. 176–78.

Although such a policy would have reduced cohort delinquency
by two-thirds, nearly half of the first-time offenders would have
been unnecessarily incapacitated. Incapacitation after two offenses would have reduced cohort delinquency by slightly less
than half, but the incapacitation error rate would have been 35
percent. After three offenses, however, incapacitation would have
reduced cohort delinquency by a little over one-third. Additionally, the percent of juveniles unnecessarily incapacitated stabil-
izes at 28 percent after offense number three and remains firm

through offense number five. Application of these two criteria suggests that the most effective and least troubling incapacitation intervention point for this cohort would have been after three offenses.

Even after three offenses, however, other problems remain. One is that most of the delinquent acts committed by the members of the cohort were not very serious. Consider the cohort's chronic offenders who accumulated five or more police contacts and committed slightly more than half of the total cohort offenses. Using the distinctions developed in Chapter 1, 3,051, or 57.5 percent of the chronic few's 5,305 police contacts involved nonindex crimes. Fewer than one in ten (9.1 percent) involved an index crime against person.[13]

One indicator of just how minor most of these crimes were is the response of the Philadelphia cops in contact with cohort offenders. In 6,515 (64 percent) of the 10,214 cohort offenses, the police simply released the juvenile, usually with a verbal warning but sometimes not even that.[14]

Incapacitation also is very expensive, especially when compared to the amount of money actually spent to institutionalize cohort offenders.[15] Of the 3,475 cohort members with at least one police contact, only 381, or 11 percent, served any time in a training school. The average time served was nine months, the approximate cost per offender was $1,100, and the total cost of institutionalization for the cohort offenders was $419,100 (381 × $1,100). Incapacitation after three offenses would have been much more expensive. Assuming an average age of 13[16] after a third offense and a sentence until age 18, incapacitation would have cost slightly more than $7 million (1,212 offenders × $122 monthly cost × 48 months of incarceration = $7,097,472), a 1,593 percent increase in the amount of money spent to institutionalize cohort offenders.

Last, incapacitation requires radical change in the sequence of events surrounding punishment. Institutionalization currently follows conviction, meaning that punishment and the pains of imprisonment are directly related to what a juvenile *has* done. In the case of incapacitation, punishment follows prediction, not a specific crime, and the pains of imprisonment are for what a juvenile *might* do.

These problems, however, must not blind us to what appears to be the essential accuracy of the incapacitation crime-control hypothesis. *Delinquency in a Birth Cohort* demonstrates that there is a very small group of offenders responsible for a very large amount of crime. Incapacitation of the chronic few would result in significantly reduced cohort delinquency. Assuming replicative confirmation of these important findings, incapacitation clearly is a potentially effective method of controlling delinquency.

REPLICATION: PROFESSOR WOLFGANG'S 1958 BIRTH COHORT

Most social scientists teach and do research in a number of different areas. Most also use a variety of different data collection and analysis techniques.[17] Very few maintain a clear focus on a single substantive area and use one method of collecting data.

Marvin Wolfgang[18] is one of the few. Along with colleagues at the University of Pennsylvania, Professor Wolfgang has devoted most of his long and distinguished career to the study of juvenile delinquency using cohort studies.[19] Much of what is currently known about juvenile delinquency can be traced to Professor Wolfgang's exceptional focus and commitment.

Consider Professor Wolfgang's 1958 birth cohort (see Table 8.3), which replicates and extends his earlier work. Selected for attention were males born in 1958 who lived in Philadelphia between their tenth and eighteenth birthdays. These 13,160 juveniles accumulated a total of 15,248 contacts with Philadelphia police.

As can be seen in Table 8.3, Professor Wolfgang's 1958 birth cohort contained a small group of chronic offenders responsible for a large amount of cohort delinquency. The 982 juveniles with five or more police contacts made up only 7.5 percent of the cohort but accounted for 60.6 percent of total cohort contacts with police.

Incapacitation of this cohort's offenders would have prevented delinquency (see Table 8.4). The effect would have been greatest had all first-time offenders in the 1958 cohort been locked up until age 18: 72 percent of the cohort's total contacts would have been eliminated. Incapacitating all three-time offenders would

Table 8.3   Description of Professor Wolfgang's 1958 Birth Cohort

The cohort:	Males born in 1958 who lived in Philadelphia between their tenth and eighteenth birthdays.
Cohort size:	13,160
Measure of delinquency:	Police contact resulting in a written record.
Percent of cohort delinquent:	32.8%—4,315 of 13,160 members of the cohort had at least one police contact that resulted in a written report.
Total number of offenses:	15,248—the 4,315 juveniles with at least one contact had a total of 15,248 contacts resulting in written reports.
Number of offenses committed by one-time offenders:	1,804—11.8% of the 15,248 offenses were committed by the 1,804 juveniles committing only one offense.
Number of offenses committed by "recidivists" (juveniles with two to four offenses):	4,204—27.6% of the 15,248 offenses were committed by the 1,529 juveniles committing between two and four offenses.
Number of offenses commmitted by "chronic offenders" (juveniles with five or more offenses):	9,240—60.6% of the 15,248 offenses were committed by the 982 juveniles committing five or more offenses.

Source: Paul E. Tracy, Marvin E. Wolfgang, and Robert M. Figlio, *Delinquency Careers in Two Birth Cohorts* (New York: Plenum, 1990).

Table 8.4   Professor Wolfgang's 1958 Birth Cohort: Number and Percent of Officially Recorded Cohort Offenses Prevented by Incapacitating Sentence after Offenses 1 to 8

Incapacitating Sentence after Offense Number	Number of Offenders Incapacitated	Officially Recorded Cohort Offenses Prevented	
		Number[a]	Percent[a]
1	4,315	10,933	72
2	2,511	8,422	55
3	1,806	6,616	43
4	1,304	5,312	35
5	982	4,330	28
6	770	3,560	23
7	596	2,964	19
8	477	2,487	16

[a]   the 15,248 officially recorded offenses committed by the cohort.

Source: Paul E. Tracy, Marvin E. Wolfgang, and Robert M. Figlio, *Delinquency Careers in Two Birth Cohorts* (New York: Plenum, 1990). Reconstructed from table 9.1, pp. 119–20. Modified and reprinted by permission of Plenum Press.

have prevented 43 percent of contacts. Waiting until after five contacts would have eliminated 28 percent of the offenses.

Unfortunately, the problems that plagued the 1945 birth cohort also emerge when incapacitation is applied to Professor Wolfgang's 1958 birth cohort. The inability to accurately predict chronicity requires selection of an incapacitation intervention point. Because incapacitation error rates for the 1958 cohort (see Figure 8.3) are basically the same as those for the 1945 birth cohort (compare with Figure 8.2), incapacitation after three contacts seems the most effective and least troubling point of intervention.

Even after three offenses, however, only 8.7 percent of fourth contacts involved index crimes against persons[20] and Philadel-

FIGURE 8.3   Professor Wolfgang's 1958 Birth Cohort: percent of offenders unnecessarily incapacitated[a] (incapacitation error rate) after offenses one to eight.

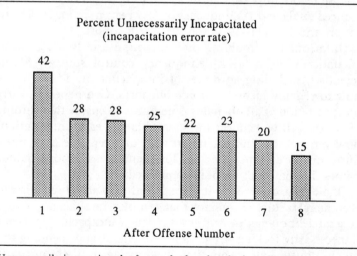

Percent Unnecessarily Incapacitated
(incapacitation error rate)

After Offense Number

[a]Unnecessarily incapacitated refers to the fact that the juvenile did not go on to commit another officially recorded offense. For example, of the 2,511 juveniles who committed a second offense, 705, or 28 percent, did not commit a third officially recorded offense.

Source: Paul E. Tracy, Marvin E. Wolfgang, and Robert M. Figlio, *Delinquency Careers in Two Birth Cohorts* (New York: Plenum, 1990). Reconstructed from table 9.1, pp. 119–20. Modified and reprinted by permission of Plenum Press.

phia police signaled recognition of the cohort's mostly minor-crime by disposing of 59 percent without a court referral.[21] In addition, incapacitation after three offenses would have significantly increased the amount of money spent to institutionalize members of the 1958 birth cohort.[22] Last, incapacitation after three offenses would have meant punishing all three-time offenders for what they *might* do.

INCAPACITATION: SUMMARY AND CONCLUSIONS

Use of Professor Wolfgang and colleague's birth cohorts to model the effects of incapacitation leaves no doubt that the logic of this approach to the control of delinquency is correct. There does exist a small group of chronic offenders responsible for a large amount of delinquency. Early and reliable identification and incapacitation of this chronic few among the delinquent many would have significantly reduced delinquency in both cohorts. Even waiting until the chronic few had committed a second offense before imposing an incapacitating sentence would have reduced total cohort delinquency by 39.7 percent in the 1945 birth cohort and 47.7 percent in the 1958 birth cohort.

Unfortunately, troubling problems significantly reduce incapacitation's utility as a delinquency control strategy. Social scientists, including advocates of incapacitation, do not know how to reliably identify chronic offenders. Consequently, early incapacitation of all offenders is necessary to ensure that chronic offenders will be kept off the street. Blanket early intervention, however, burdens incapacitation with unacceptable error rates, unreasonable cost increases, and long sentences for mostly minor crimes that have not yet been committed.

Of all these drawbacks, it is the inability of social scientists to accurately predict chronicity that cripples incapacitation as a general delinquency control strategy. Early incapacitation means unnecessarily locking up too many offenders and spending too much money. Late incapacitation—waiting until chronicity is an established fact rather than an early and accurate prediction—means controlling too little delinquency. Incapacitation is a potentially effective delinquency control strategy in search of reliable methods of predicting chronicity.

DETERRENCE: BEYOND PROBATION

In 1974 the late Robert Martinson observed: "We know almost nothing about the 'deterrent effect,' largely because 'treatment' theories have so dominated our research, and 'deterrence' theories have been relegated to the status of historical curiosity. Since we have almost no idea of the deterrent functions that our present system performs . . . it is possible that there is indeed something that works—that to some extent is working right now in front of our noses . . . something that deters rather than cures. . . . But whether that is the case . . . [is a] question we will not be able to answer until a new family of studies has been brought into existence."[23]

Beyond Probation by Charles A. Murray and Louis A. Cox, Jr.,[24] was precisely the type of study Professor Martinson had in mind. It examined the deterrent effects of institutionalization and concluded that deterrence was indeed working right in front of our noses. And as the first of a new group of studies to carefully examine the deterrent effects of institutionalization,[25] *Beyond Probation* also encouraged the search for neglected evidence of deterrence in previous delinquency control projects.[26] Table 8.5 summarizes the major features of this important study and serves as a guide for the description and analysis that follow.

DESCRIPTION OF THE PROJECT

In the early 1970s, the Illinois Law Enforcement Commission provided Chicago with funding for a new delinquency control organization: Unified Delinquency Intervention Services (UDIS). The purposes of this new agency were several. UDIS was to coordinate and integrate existing community-based treatment facilities for juvenile offenders. UDIS also was to determine whether chronic offenders could be treated in the community rather than in institutions. In one sense, UDIS was simply another example of the deinstitutionalization movement of the early 1970s.

Unlike Massachusetts, however, Illinois kept its training schools open and continued to institutionalize large numbers of juvenile offenders. Between October 1, 1974, when UDIS began

Table 8.5   Description of Beyond Probation

Project Name:	Unified Delinquency Intervention Services (UDIS)
Location:	Chicago, Illinois
Dates:	October 1, 1974, to July 31, 1976
Subjects:	Major analytical attention was directed at 317 juveniles sentenced to Illinois Department of Corrections facilities between October 1, 1974, and July 31, 1976. Prior to being sentenced to a training school these juveniles had averaged 13.6 arrests, with 8.2 arrests for *Uniform Crime Reports* index offenses and 5.4 arrests for nonindex crimes. Over three-quarters (78.2%) were African-American, 12.6 percent were white, and 8.5 percent were Hispanic. Added for purposes of quasi-experimental comparison were 266 juveniles sentenced to "less drastic" placement alternatives.
Type of treatment:	Most of the 317 offenders sentenced to a training school went to either St. Charles or Valley View, two "moderate-security, campus-type facilities near the town of Saint Charles, roughly a two hour's drive from downtown Chicago." Both facilities offer educational, recreational, and treatment services. But custody and fear of victimization dominate life in these and other moderate- and maximum-security correctional facilities for juveniles. For the juveniles receiving "less drastic" placements, nonresidential services included educational and vocational training, while the group-home placements emphasized group and family counseling.
Amount of treatment:	The juveniles sentenced to the training schools served an average of 10.86 months. Juveniles receiving alternative placements served an average of 8.1 months.
Evaluative design:	Quasi-experimental: The 266 juveniles sentenced to the less drastic placement alternatives were "reasonably comparable" to the 317 juveniles sentenced to the training schools.
Measure of results:	Suppression effect: Percent reduction in the number of arrests in the year following treatment was compared to the year preceding treatment.
Replication:	*Beyond Probation*'s finding that deterrence was indeed working stimulated two types of replicative efforts. The first was replicative reexamination of previous projects to determine whether evidence of deterrence had been overlooked. The second was direct replication with a specific focus on deterrence.

Source: Charles A. Murray and Louis A. Cox, Jr., *Beyond Probation: Juvenile Corrections and the Chronic Delinquent* (Beverly Hills, Calif.: Sage Publications, 1979).

operation, and July 31, 1976, Chicago sent 317 offenders to Illinois Department of Corrections facilities for juveniles. *Beyond Probation* takes a prolonged look at these 317 offenders. Prior to sentencing, these offenders had accumulated an average of 13.6

arrests with more than half for *Uniform Crime Reports* index
offenses, including "718 burglary charges . . . 317 battery, assault, or assault and battery charges . . . 305 charges of auto theft
and/or criminal trespass to vehicles . . . 183 armed robbery
charges . . . 23 rape charges . . . and 14 homicide charges. . . ."[27]
Most of these chronic offenders were from economically disadvantaged inner-city backgrounds.

Added to the Department of Corrections offenders were 266
UDIS offenders. The UDIS offenders also had long records of
arrest for serious crimes and lived in the same types of inner-city
neighborhoods as the Department of Corrections offenders. In
keeping with the UDIS mandate, however, these juveniles had
been sentenced to community-based treatment programs, such as
nonresidential services and group homes.

Type of Treatment

The purpose of *Beyond Probation* was to assess the deterrence
hypothesis diagrammed in Figure 8.4. Primary attention was
therefore directed toward the 317 Department of Corrections offenders sentenced to either the St. Charles Training School or the
Valley View Training School. Both institutions were "moderate-
security, campus-type facilities near the town of Saint Charles,
roughly a two hour's drive from downtown Chicago."[28]

There can be little doubt that doing time in a correctional
facility such as St. Charles is a painful experience. The State
Home for Delinquent Boys at St. Charles opened in July 1905

FIGURE 8.4   Beyond Probation's deterrence hypothesis in diagrammatic form

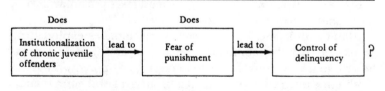

Source: Beyond Probation's deterrence hypothesis is based on Charles A. Murray and Louis A. Cox, Jr., *Beyond Probation: Juvenile Corrections and the
Chronic Delinquent* (Beverly Hills, Calif.: Sage Publications), 1979, pp. 173-84.

with an announced mission of training delinquents "to do commonplace work well."[29] In 1927 the facility was renamed the St. Charles School for Boys, and an official of the institution described its programs and one of its many rules: "The two outstanding features at the St. Charles School are order and obedience. Because it teaches obedience, military training is a necessity, being carried on to a high point of efficiency. With this training goes an appeal to all that is best in the future citizen. He is taught reverence and respect for the flag of his country so that his conduct may be in accord with its ideas. . . . In order to avoid unnecessary noise and confusion in a cottage, where as many as fifty or sixty boys are housed, conversation is prohibited. Also this restriction is a means of establishing habits of obedience and order in the boys who are so much in need of proper discipline and restraint."[30]

One of the juveniles sentenced to St. Charles in the late 1920s was "Stanley," author of the life history *The Jack-Roller* reviewed in Chapter 3. In his life history Stanley wrote about St. Charles and the pains of imprisonment. He described his fear when he was first sentenced to St. Charles and the institutional clothes he was issued: "At the receiving cottage I was directed to remove my clothes. . . . I was so scared that I couldn't remove my scant attire, but a little help from the rough hands of the . . . guard caused me to get them off in a hurry. After a bath, I received my prison suit of overalls, blouse, hard shoes, and white cap."[31]

Stanley went on to describe the institution's rules and their impact on the inmates, including the rule prohibiting conversation while in the cottages: "The boys were not allowed to talk in the cottage. . . . So they slipped around in their soft houseslippers, quietly and weirdly. They reminded me of dumb mutes. This ever-lasting quietness . . . gave me a creepy, clammy feeling and almost drove me crazy for a few weeks."[32]

Stanley also described the ways some inmates exploited the weak, the code that dominated inmate life, and the reluctance of guards to take action: "It was soon impressed upon my mind that life in this institution was a matter of survival of the fittest and it was hard enough for the fittest. . . .[33] [M]ost of the boys stuck together. . . . The boys had a code . . . 'To squawk on a fellow-prisoner is an unpardonable sin and only the lowest characters will squawk.[34] . . . The officers tell you to 'get used to it, it's too late now to sob about your crimes.'"[35]

Last, Stanley wrote of rape as a fact of life at St. Charles: "There were lots of . . . sodomy committed in . . . the cottages. The bullies would attack the younger boys . . . and force them to have relations. . . . I've seen lots of it. I know little boys who had sex relations with four or five older boys every night. It was easy to slip into another boy's bunk."[36]

What makes Stanley's description important is that contemporary training schools are only superficially different from St. Charles. All of what Stanley wrote about in 1930 would be entirely familiar to juveniles currently serving time in any large correctional facility for male offenders.[37] Most enter scared because they know these are tough places to do time. Inmates are issued color-coded coveralls that tell staff the juvenile's security status, "cottage," or escape potential. By day, life inside is structured and fairly well supervised by staff. Juveniles eat their meals,[38] attend school, go to "group" for alcohol and other substance-abuse problems, and exercise outside or in the gym. Those who know how to read go to the library for books and magazines and those with money buy candy and other items at the store. There are many rules, most of which are strictly enforced by the staff. At night and on weekends, however, fewer staff are present and social order is largely in the hands of the juvenile inmates. At these times, brutal and sadistic bullies take the clothes, sneakers, food, and cigarettes of the weak and fearful and those without allies. And rapists prey on their victims (see Box 8.3).

Not all of the juveniles studied by Murray and Cox were sentenced to St. Charles or Valley View. Added were 266 offenders sentenced to "less drastic" placement alternatives made available by UDIS (see Box 8.4). Because most of these UDIS offenders were sentenced to community-based programs, they experienced fewer of the pains of imprisonment. They therefore had less reason to abandon their delinquent ways.

EVALUATIVE DESIGN

Beyond Probation was quasi-experimentally evaluated. Selected first were the 317 Department of Corrections offenders sentenced either to St. Charles or Valley View between October 1, 1974, and

Box 8.3 Rapists and Their Victims

Rape is one of the more common and humiliating pains of imprisonment for male juveniles. In most large correctional facilities for males I have visited, offenders are locked into small rooms with large numbers of other juveniles for the night. A single staff member spends the night catching up on paperwork at a desk in an office located thirty or more feet from a long hallway that leads to the rooms where the juveniles are supposed to be sleeping. In such a situation, rape is easy and inevitable. Here is how one group of bullies took advantage of the tempting combination of darkness and minimal supervision:

Right after the light went out I saw . . . Cheyenne. . . . He went over and was talking to this kid and slapped him in the face with a belt. He was saying come on back with us and the kid kept saying I don't want to. . . . After being slapped with the belt he walked back . . . into E Dorm. They were telling him to put his hands down and stop crying so the guard will not know what is going on. They had the kid on the floor. About twelve fellows took turns with him. This went on for about two hours.

After this he came back to his bed and he was crying and he stated that "They all took turns on me." He laid there for about 20 minutes and Cheyenne came over to the kid's bed and pulled his pants down and got on top of him and raped him again. When he got done Horse did it again and then about four or five others got on him. Horse came over and said, "Open your mouth and suck on this and don't bite it." He then put his penis in his mouth and made him suck on it. The kid was hollering that he was gagging and Horse stated, "you better not bite it or I will kick your teeth out."

Sources: Alan J. Davis, "Sexual Assaults in the Philadelphia Prison System," in David M. Peterson and Charles W. Thomas (eds.), *Corrections: Problems and Prospects*, 2nd ed. (Englewood Cliffs, N.J.: Prentice-Hall, 1980), pp. 103–04; Clemens Bartollas, Stuart J. Miller, and Simon Dinitz, *Juvenile Victimization: The Institutional Paradox* (Beverly Hills, Calif.: Sage Publications, 1976); Clemens Bartollas and Christopher M. Sieverdes, "The Victimized White in a Juvenile Correctional Facility," *Crime and Delinquency* 29 (July 1981): 534–43; Alice Propper, *Prison Homosexuality: Myth and Reality* (Lexington, Mass.: Heath, 1981); Steven Learner, *Bodily Harm: The Pattern of Fear and Violence at the California Youth Authority* (Bolinas, Calif.: Common Knowledge Press, 1986); and Lydia S. Rosner, "Juvenile Secure Detention," *Journal of Offender Counseling, Services, and Rehabilitation* 12 (Spring 1988): 57–76.

Box 8.4 "Less Drastic" UDIS Placement Alternatives

In addition to information gathered by Murray and Cox on the 317 Department of Corrections offenders, data were collected on 266 Chicago youth sent to the "less drastic" placement alternatives made available by UDIS. These 266 offenders were placed into one of five general programs:

1. *Nonresidential Services*: 156 offenders received one of three general types of nonresidential services: (a) advocacy, where adults acted as representatives of their clients before the police and other agents of the juvenile justice system and as paid friends who took offenders on trips and athletic activities much like the adult counselors during the Cambridge-Somerville Youth Study; (b) counseling services similar to the Provo Experiment; and (c) academic and vocational training by tutors and placement in alternative schools.

2. *Residential Services*: 40 offenders were placed in group homes with counseling sessions and school attendance essentially similar to that provided offenders during the Silverlake Experiment.

3. *Wilderness Programs*: 14 offenders were placed in Outward Bound-type programs where they were "required to hike, climb, swim, canoe, and learn how to survive in the wild."

4. *Out-of-Town Residential Camps*: 45 offenders were placed either in a work camp that trained in "basic vocational activities such as painting, construction, and food preparation" or in a "rural and city exploration" camp that involved talks with farmers and "rap sessions with pimps."

5. *Intensive Care*: 11 offenders were placed either in the Intensive Care Unit of the Illinois State Psychiatric Institute, where they received the case- and group-work services of social workers, or in secure residential facilities offering intensive therapeutic programs.

Source: Charles A. Murray and Louis A. Cox, Jr., *Beyond Probation: Juvenile Corrections and the Chronic Delinquent* (Beverly Hills, Calif.: Sage Publications, 1979), pp. 95–136.

July 31, 1976. Added for purposes of quasi-experimental comparison were the 266 offenders placed by UDIS during the same time period as the Department of Corrections offenders. Examination of the background characteristics of the two groups of offenders showed that they "were comparable across socioeconomic and personal variables."[39] The two groups of offenders also averaged similar numbers of *Uniform Crime Reports* index offense arrests and total arrests. Because the two groups were "reasonably comparable"[40] on these important dimensions, nonequivalency does not appear to be a major problem.

MEASURES OF RESULTS

Murray and Cox used a measure of results they call the "suppression effect"[41] (see Box 8.5). This measure compares preintervention delinquency with postintervention delinquency. The search is for reductions in the volume of delinquency rather than for cessation of delinquent acts. And although Murray and Cox prefer not to attach a number to the suppression effect, it is very useful to do so. For example, as noted in Box 8.5, if a group of offenders averaged 6.3 arrests in the year preceding intervention and 2.0 arrests in the year following intervention, this can be expressed as a 68 percent reduction in the volume of delinquency. This percentage figure will be used to represent the suppression effect.

Several observations can be drawn from the suppression effect measures in Table 8.6. The first is an important caution that directs attention to the number of juveniles experiencing the various placements. With the exceptions of the UDIS nonresidential services and the Department of Corrections groups, the number of offenders experiencing other placements is really quite small. It therefore is a good idea to pay primary attention to the UDIS nonresidential services and Department of Corrections comparison, where group sizes are adequate.

With this caution taken into account, the data in Table 8.6 combine to yield a single conclusion: everything worked to suppress involvement in delinquency. All of the UDIS interventions suppressed delinquency and, in the UDIS nonresidential services group, where the sample size was large, the suppression effect was 53 percent. So too with Department of Corrections intervention: the suppression effect was 68 percent.

Box 8.5   The Suppression Effect

Most delinquency control projects use a "percent nondelinquent following intervention" measure of results. Examples of this traditional measure include percent of experimental and control subjects with no new arrests or no new court appearances following intervention. This traditional measure is actually a cessation of involvement measure because all it tells us is the percent of subjects that did not commit at least one delinquent act following intervention.

Murray and Cox correctly argue that cessation of delinquency is much too stiff a standard. They point out that it is unreasonable to expect a project to eliminate delinquency. More importantly, the traditional measure is insensitive to reductions in the volume of delinquency. Offenders arrested six times in the year preceding intervention and only twice in the year following intervention are profoundly different.

Murray and Cox therefore employed a measure of results they call the "suppression effect." This alternative measure is sensitive to reductions in the volume of delinquency and is easily calculated. For example, if a group of juveniles averaged 6.3 arrests in the year preceding intervention and 2.0 arrests in the year following intervention, then the effect of intervention was to suppress delinquency by 68 percent.

The suppression measure is a more reasonable and far more sensitive indicator of the effects of intervention. In addition to its use in *Beyond Probation*, it should supplement the traditional cessation measure in all future assessments of efforts to control delinquency.

Source: Charles A. Murray and Louis A. Cox, Jr., *Beyond Probation: Juvenile Corrections and the Chronic Delinquent* (Beverly Hills, Calif.: Sage Publications, 1979), pp. 31–43; and Michael D. Maltz, Andrew C. Gordon, Davis McDowall, and Richard McCleary, "An Artifact in Pretest-Posttest Designs: How It Can Mistakingly Make Delinquency Programs Look Effective," *Evaluation Review* 4 (April 1980): 225–40.

Murray and Cox argue that the major reason everything worked is that UDIS placements and Department of Corrections sentences credibly changed offenders' perceptions of the consequences of continued involvement in delinquency.[42] Prior to

Table 8.6 Beyond Probation: Suppression Effect of UDIS and Department of Corrections Placement

Placement	Number of Offenders	Mean Number of Arrests			Suppression Effect[a] (percent reduction in annual arrests)
		12 Months before Placement	12 Months after Placement	Difference	
UDIS[b]					
Nonresidential services	156	5.7	2.7	−3.0	−53
Residential services	40	5.5	2.2	−3.3	−60
Wilderness programs	14	7.6	4.0	−3.6	−47
Out-of-town camp	45	7.1	2.1	−5.0	−70
Intensive care	11	7.7	1.4	−6.3	−82
Department of Corrections	317	6.3	2.0	−4.3	−68
Totals	583	6.2	2.3	−3.9	−63

[a]See Box 8.5 for a discussion of the suppression effect.
[b]See Box 8.4 for a description of UDIS placements.

Source: Charles A. Murray and Louis A. Cox, Jr., *Beyond Probation: Juvenile Corrections and the Chronic Delinquent* (Beverly Hills, Calif.: Sage Publications, 1979), table 4.4, p. 118. Copyright © 1979 by Sage Publications, Inc. Reprinted by permission of Sage Publications, Inc.

their UDIS placement or Department of Corrections sentence, the offenders studied had averaged 13.6 arrests, with over half for *Uniform Crime Reports* index offenses. In addition, the typical offender had been to juvenile court six times.[43] Despite the juveniles' frequent brushes with the law, nothing had really happened to them. At least nothing serious. They had been placed under the informal or formal supervision of probation officers too busy to do much supervising. They had lost next to nothing, although they were repeatedly in trouble with the law. If the law had a bark, it certainly did not seem to know how to bite.

UDIS and Department of Corrections intervention changed offenders' perceptions of the law. UDIS was one step away from St. Charles and Valley View. Offenders knew if they experienced additional serious trouble with the law, they would almost certainly be sent to a Department of Corrections institution, where, unless they were strong, rapists would make them their next victims. Offenders sentenced to St. Charles and Valley View suffered the pains of imprisonment. These were distressing prospects and experiences, and they caused delinquents to fear the law's bite.

REPLICATIVE REEXAMINATION: THE PROVO AND
SILVERLAKE EXPERIMENTS

Beyond Probation's finding that deterrence did indeed work stimulated two types of replicative efforts. The first was replicative reexamination of previous projects to determine whether evidence of suppression had been overlooked.[44] The second was direct replication with a specific focus on the suppression effect.[45]

The Provo and Silverlake Experiments. The Provo and Silverlake experiments[46] compared institutionalization with community-based treatment. Both projects reported that institutionalization and community-based treatment were equally effective in controlling delinquency when measured by percent delinquent following intervention.

Table 8.7 shows that institutionalization and community treatment also were equally effective in controlling delinquency when reexamined using a suppression effect measure of results. In the

Table 8.7 The Provo and Silverlake Experiments: Suppression Effects of Community Treatment and Institutionalization

Experiment and Type of Intervention	Mean Number of Arrests		Difference	Suppression Effect (percent reduction in annual arrests)
	Year Before	Year After		
The Provo Experiment[a]				
Community treatment				
(n = 37)	3.57	1.11	−2.46	−69
State training school				
(n = 132)	4.43	1.71	−2.72	−61
The Silverlake Experiment[b]				
Community treatment				
(n = 140)	2.71	0.73	−1.98	−73
Boys Republic				
(n = 121)	2.66	0.74	−1.92	−72

[a]For description of the Provo Experiment, see Table 7.1.
[b]For description of the Silverlake Experiment, see Table 7.3.

Sources: Reprinted with the permission of Lexington Books, an imprint of Macmillan, Inc., from *The Provo Experiment: Evaluating Community Control of Delinquency*, by LaMar T. Empey and Maynard L. Erickson. Copyright © 1972 by D. C. Heath and Company; and LaMar T. Empey and Steven G. Lubeck, *The Silverlake Experiment: Testing Delinquency Theory and Community Intervention* (Chicago: Aldine, 19971), table 12.5, p. 259. Copyright © 1971 by Lamar T. Empey and Steven G. Lubeck. Reprinted by permission.

Provo Experiment, doing time in Utah's training school suppressed delinquency by 61 percent and community-based nonresidential services suppressed delinquency by 69 percent. In the Silverlake Experiment, community-based residential services and doing time in Boys Republic each suppressed delinquency by slightly more than 70 percent.

Replicative reexamination of the Provo Experiment and the Silverlake Experiment therefore provides considerable insight about the generalizability of the major findings of *Beyond Probation*. Two preliminary observations are particularly important: (1) The suppression effects observed among Chicago's seriously delinquent youth in the mid-1970s were not flukes traceable to factors such as regression toward the mean (Box 8.6) because these same effects are clearly present among less delinquent Utah and California youth during the 1960s; and (2) *Beyond Probation's* conclusion that institutionalization suppresses delin-

---

Box 8.6   Regression Toward the Mean

Regression toward the mean is a statistical phenomenon operative when a particular group has been selected on the basis of an unusually high mean (average) score. Simple probability dictates that the group's high mean score will eventually lower. For example, *Beyond Probation*'s 317 Department of Corrections offenders had averaged 13.6 arrests including 8.2 arrests for index offenses, a truly extraordinary record of delinquency. Probability dictates that the number of arrests would have declined even in the absence of Department of Corrections intervention. Put another way, their record of delinquency was so extraordinary that it had almost nowhere to go but down.

Regression toward the mean therefore is an alternative explanation for the suppression effect measures reported in *Beyond Probation*. Instead of linking the decline to fear of the law's bite, an alternative explanation is that sheer probability lowered mean arrests.

Replicative reexamination of the Provo and Silverlake experiments helps undermine this alternative explanation. In both Provo and Silverlake, offenders with extraordinary records of delinquency were excluded from the experiments. Exclusion of these offenders helps reduce the possibility that regression toward the mean explains the suppression effects reported in *Beyond Probation*, because these same declines occurred among the less extraordinarily delinquent juveniles involved in the Provo and Silverlake experiments.

Sources: Anne L. Schneider, *Deterrence and Juvenile Crime: Results from a National Policy Experiment* (New York: Springer-Verlag, 1990), pp. 82–89; and Michael D. Maltz, Andrew C. Gordon, Davis McDowall, and Richard McCleary, "An Artifact in Pretest-Posttest Designs: How It Can Mistakingly Make Delinquency Programs Look Effective," *Evaluation Review* 4 (April 1980): 225–40.

---

quency more than community-based treatment was opened to question because in the Provo Experiment community treatment was more effective, and because in the Silverlake Experiment there was no difference between the two interventions.

DIRECT REPLICATION: NATIONAL EVALUATION
OF JUVENILE RESTITUTION

In the early 1970s, restitution formally surfaced as another type of community-based intervention.[47] Juveniles sentenced to restitution were placed on probation, with monetary compensation to the victim or community service as added and specially monitored conditions of probation.

By the mid 1970s, the federal government's Office of Juvenile Justice and Delinquency Prevention was sufficiently interested in restitution to fund the National Evaluation of Juvenile Restitution Programs (see Table 8.8).[48] Six juvenile court jurisdictions were eventually chosen to participate in the national evaluation.

Anne L. Schneider quasi-experimentally evaluated the programs, comparing incarceration with monitored restitution, regular probation with monitored restitution, and restitution as an added but not specifically monitored condition of probation with monitored restitution. The suppression effect was the measure of results for all of the interventions, including incarceration.

Professor Schneider's National Evaluation of Juvenile Restitution Programs therefore replicates *Beyond Probation* in two important respects. As was the case with *Beyond Probation*, Professor Schneider compared incarceration with community-based interventions. And, Professor Schneider used a suppression effect measure of results.

Table 8.9 contains the suppression effect measures collected by Professor Schneider. Most important is the clear evidence of suppression traceable to incarceration (-32 percent). As was true of the other projects examined in this chapter, locking juveniles up yielded less delinquency in the year following intervention as compared to the year before.

However, institutionalization was not the only intervention that suppressed delinquency. Two of the community-based interventions, monitored restitution and restitution as an unmonitored condition of probation, suppressed delinquency as well. The only exception was regular probation, which yielded a very small increase in delinquency.

Professor Schneider's direct replication of *Beyond Probation* therefore substantiates the two observations previously described as preliminary: (1) direct replication confirms the suppressive

Table 8.8   Description of National Evaluation of Juvenile Restitution Programs

Project Name:	National Evaluation of Juvenile Restitution Programs
Locations:	Ada County (Boise), Idaho; Clayton County (Jonesboro), Georgia; Dane County (Madison), Wisconsin; Oklahoma County (Okalahoma City), Oklahoma; Ventura, California; and Washington, D.C.
Dates:	1977–1981
Subjects:	Juveniles adjudicated delinquent for index crimes against property (67 percent), nonindex crimes (24 percent), and index crimes against persons (7 percent). Most were male (87 percent), white (70 percent), and their average age was 15¾ years. Nearly two-thirds had committed one or more prior offenses.
Type of treatment:	Juveniles were assigned to one of four interventions. Restitution involved compensating victims for monetary losses or performing community service, with special monitoring to ensure compliance. Those incarcerated served time in a detention center or correctional facility. Probation required adherence to the conditions of probation including periodic meetings with probation officers. Ah hoc restitution had restitution as one of the conditions of probation, with no special monitoring to ensure compliance.
Amount of treatment:	Restitution, probation, and ad-hoc restitution all involved nine months of probation supervision. For restitution, the special monitoring to ensure compliance averaged two months. Most of the juveniles assigned to incarceration spent eight days across four successive weekends in a detention center followed by nine months of probation.
Evaluative design:	Quasi-experimental: Approximately 90 percent of the subjects were randomly assigned at the six locations. The other 10 percent were "crossovers" (juveniles randomly assigned to one intervention ended up crossing over to another intervention), rendering the overall evaluative design quasi-experimental.
Measure of results:	Suppression effect

Source: Anne L. Schneider, *Deterrence and Juvenile Crime: Results from a National Policy Experiment* (New York: Springer-Verlag, 1990); and Anne L. Schneider, "Restitution and Recidivism Rates of Juvenile Offenders: Results from Four Experimental Studies," *Criminology* 24 (April 1986): 533–52.

Table 8.9 National Evaluation of Juvenile Restitution Programs: Suppression Effects of Incarceration and Restitution ("Comparison One"), Probation and Restitution ("Comparison Two"), and Ad Hoc Restitution and Restitution ("Comparison Three")

Comparison[a] and Type of Intervention	Mean Number of Arrests			Suppression Effect (percent reduction in annual arrests)
	Year Before	Year After	Difference	
Comparison One				
Incarceration				
(*n* = 79)	1.20	.81	−.39	−32
Restitution				
(*n* = 97)	1.20	.88	−.32	−27
Comparison Two				
Probation				
(*n* = 140)	.75	.82	(+.07)	(+09)[b]
Restitution				
(*n* = 269)	.65	.58	−.07	−11
Comparison Three				
Ad hoc restitution				
(*n* = 65)	1.19	.76	−.43	−36
Restitution				
(*n* = 203)	.87	.59	−.28	−32

[a]Cases for comparison one were eligible for incarceration in Boise, Ventura, and Washington, D.C., and were assigned to incarceration or restitution. Cases for comparison two were eligible for probation in Jonesboro, Washington, D.C., and Oklahoma City and were assigned to probation or restitution. Cases for comparison three were eligible for restitution in Madison and Ventura and were assigned to ad hoc restitution or restitution.
[b]Probation was associated with a modest *increase* in postintervention delinquency.

Sources: Anne L. Schneider, *Deterrence and Juvenile Crime: Results from a National Policy Experiment* (New York: Springer-Verlag, 1990), constructed from table 6.1, p. 79. Copyright © 1990 by Springer-Verlag New York, Inc. Reprinted by permission.

effects of institutionalization; and (2) direct replication confirms that community-based interventions also suppress delinquency.

DETERRENCE: SUMMARY AND CONCLUSIONS

The projects examined combine to suggest that deterrence may well be working right in front of our noses. Looking only at institutionalization, the most punitive of our responses to delinquent juveniles, the suppression effects during the first year following intervention were 68 percent in *Beyond Probation*, 61 percent in the Provo Experiment, and 72 percent in the Silverlake

Experiment. Even in the National Evaluation of Juvenile Restitution Programs, where most of the incarcerated juveniles spent only eight days in detention across four successive weekends, the suppression effect was 32 percent.

Community-based interventions also suppressed delinquency. All of *Beyond Probation*'s community-based services reduced delinquency. So too with the Provo Experiment and the Silverlake Experiment, and two out of three of the community-based efforts that were part of the National Evaluation of Juvenile Restitution Programs. The only exception was regular probation in the National Evaluation of Juvenile Restitution Programs. It produced a modest increased in delinquency. Because these community-based interventions reduced delinquency, it is important to remember that institutionalization is not the only intervention that suppresses delinquency.

Additionally, deterrence is not the only explanation for suppression. All of the interventions involved treatment. Even at St. Charles, Valley View, and other correctional facilities for juvenile offenders where custody and fear of victimization dominate inmate life, offenders are routinely exposed to educational and vocational services and help is available for alcohol and other drug problems.

Still, deterrence seems the most likely explanation for suppression when the intervention is institutionalization. Doing time in a juvenile correctional facility is painful and it almost certainly is the pain, rather than the treatment all institutions provide, that makes the lasting impression. One offender put the issue this way: "No one needs to go to DOC [the Department of Corrections]. They put dog food in the spaghetti. *That place is awful.*"[49]

Three firm conclusions can be advanced. First, institutionalization and community-based treatment both suppress delinquency.[50] Second, when the intervention is institutionalization, deterrence is the likely explanation for suppression. Third, when the intervention is community-based, treatment and deterrence are among the reasons offenders suppress delinquency. Deterrence, in short, is not the definitive answer to the problem of controlling juvenile delinquency. Based on the available research, however, deterrence is part of the answer (see Box 8.7).

Box 8.7   Boot Camps

There is a new juvenile corrections fad—boot camps—and they are another example of the deterrence approach to the control of delinquency. Boot camps are very tough places to do time. Offenders get up early to exercise and drill, they march from meals to class to work, and they are shouted at and threatened by adult "drill instructors." Offenders who abide by the rules—including the regulations prohibiting conversation—are given positions of authority over other inmates.

Although boot camps for adolescents appear new, it is important to recognize that they are grounded in old ideas and pose old problems. Military-style discipline, no talking, and putting some offenders in charge of others all were commonplace when Stanley (see Chapter 3) served his time at St. Charles in the early 1900s. Angry-sounding and -acting adults also are not new. They were a central feature of efforts to scare juveniles straight just a short time ago (see Chapter 6). Last, judges and correctional officials almost certainly will skim good risks from probation and community-based treatment and place them in boot camps instead.

Once careful research catches up with the boot-camp trend, it will be interesting to learn whether boot camps suppress delinquency or make things worse.

Sources: Elizabeth Ross, "Boot Camps," *The Christian Science Monitor,* July 24, 1990, p. 7; Merry Morash and Lila Rucker, "A Critical Look at the Idea of Boot Camps as a Correctional Reform," *Crime and Delinquency* 36 (April 1990): 204–22; and Edward I. Koch, "For Anti-drug Boot Camps," *The New York Times,* May 24, 1989, p. A23.

NOTES

1. Thomas Bernard, *The Cycle of Juvenile Justice* (New York: Oxford University Press, 1991); James O. Finckenauer, *Scared Straight! and the Panacea Phenomenon* (Englewood Cliffs, N.J.: Prentice-Hall, 1982), pp. 3–28; Ira M. Schwartz, "Getting Tough with Juveniles: Is It Working?" *Public Welfare* 42 (Summer 1984): 40–41; and Ira M. Schwartz, "New Moves in Juvenile Justice: Alternatives to Getting Tough Are More Humane and Less Expensive," *Public Welfare* 42 (Fall 1984): 28–31.

2. For a classic statement of this position, see Edwin M. Schur, *Radical Non-Intervention: Rethinking the Delinquency Problem* (Englewood Cliffs, N.J.: Prentice-Hall, 1972).

3. For a book collected when diversion emerged in the 1970s, see Robert M. Carter and Malcolm Klein (eds.), *Back on the Street: The Diversion of Juvenile Offenders* (Englewood Cliffs, N.J.: Prentice-Hall, 1976).

4. For description of two important community-based treatment projects, see LaMar T. Empey and Steven G. Lubeck, *The Silverlake Experiment: Testing Delinquency Theory and Community Intervention* (Chicago: Aldine, 1971); and LaMar T. Empey and Maynard L. Erickson, *The Provo Experiment: Evaluating Community Control of Delinquency* (Lexington, Mass.: Lexington Books, 1972).

5. For an early and especially angry expression of this position, see Robert Fishman, *Criminal Recidivism in New York City* (New York: Praeger, 1977). For analysis of this position, see Anne L. Schneider, *Deterrence and Juvenile Crime: Results from a National Policy Experiment* (New York: Springer-Verlag, 1990). For the consequences of the renewed use of correctional facilities for juveniles, including overcrowding, see Bureau of Justice Statistics, *Children in Custody, 1975-85: Census of Public and Private Juvenile Detention, Correctional, and Shelter Facilities, 1975, 1977, 1979, 1983, and 1985* (Washington, D.C.: U.S. Department of Justice, Bureau of Justice Statistics, 1989).

6. For a general discussion of the incapacitation hypothesis, see James Q. Wilson, *Thinking About Crime*, rev. ed. (New York: Vintage Books, 1985), pp. 145-65. For brief discussion grounded in cohort studies, see Paul E. Tracy, Marvin E. Wolfgang, and Robert M. Figlio, *Delinquency Careers in Two Birth Cohorts* (New York: Plenum, 1990), pp. 295-98.

7. For a classic exposition and analysis of deterrence theory, see Jack P. Gibbs, *Crime, Punishment, and Deterrence* (New York: Elsevier, 1975).

8. Wilson, *Thinking About Crime*, pp. 145-65; Tracy et al., *Delinquency Careers in Two Birth Cohorts*, pp. 295-98.

9. Marvin E. Wolfgang, Robert M. Figlio, and Thorsten Sellin, *Delinquency in a Birth Cohort* (Chicago: The University of Chicago Press, 1972).

10. Tracy et al., *Delinquency Careers in Two Birth Cohorts.*

11. To estimate the effects of incapacitating sentences, I assume that all of the cohort offenders were guilty of the delinquent acts that brought them into contact with Philadelphia police. Because Wolfgang et al., *Delinquency in a Birth Cohort*, pp. 218-43, report that 6,515, or 64 percent of the 10,214 contacts, resulted in outright release of the juvenile

by police, the effect of this assumption is to overestimate the impact of incapacitating sentences.

12. Wolfgang et al., *Delinquency in a Birth Cohort*, p. 254. Tracy et al., *Delinquency Careers in Two Birth Cohorts*, p. 297, make the same point in the context of the 1958 birth cohort.

13. Wolfgang et al., *Delinquency in a Birth Cohort*, p. 101. Tracy et al., *Delinquency Careers in Two Birth Cohorts*, p. 90, report different offense compositions for the 5,305 contacts accumulated by the 627 chronic offenders in the 1945 cohort, with 3,579, or 67.5 percent, for nonindex crimes and 454, or 8.6 percent, for index crimes against persons. The difference is a result of dropping the "combination" offense category (e.g., a combination of burglary and assault in the same criminal event) that was originally used to report the 1945 birth cohort data (Wolfgang et al., *Delinquency in a Birth Cohort*, p. 101) from the recapitulation of the offenses by the 1945 birth cohort in the more recent book devoted primarily to the 1958 birth cohort (Tracy et al., *Delinquency Careers in Two Birth Cohorts*, p. 90).

14. Wolfgang et al., *Delinquency in a Birth Cohort*, p. 219. For rich description of Philadelphia police at work during the late 1960s, see Jonathan Rubinstein, *City Police* (New York: Farrar, Straus and Giroux, 1973).

15. Stevens H. Clarke, "Getting 'Em Out of Circulation: Does Incarceration of Juvenile Offenders Reduce Crime?" *Journal of Criminal Law and Criminology* 65 (December 1974): 530–31.

16. Wolfgang et al., *Delinquency in a Birth Cohort*, p. 315.

17. For evidence of multiple interests and methods, see the faculty listings in the American Sociological Association's *Guide to Graduate Departments 1990* (Washington, D.C.: American Sociological Association, 1991).

18. Tracy et al., *Delinquency Careers in Two Birth Cohorts.*

19. Wolfgang et al., *Delinquency in a Birth Cohort*; Tracy et al., *Delinquency Careers in Two Birth Cohorts*; Marvin E. Wolfgang, Terence P. Thornberry, and Robert M. Figlio, *From Boy to Man, From Delinquency to Crime* (Chicago: The University of Chicago Press, 1987). In Tracy et al., *Delinquency Careers in Two Birth Cohorts*, p. v, Professor Wolfgang indicates he is "convinced that a third birth cohort should be examined, perhaps one born in 1973, or thereabouts."

20. Tracy et al., *Delinquency Careers in Two Birth Cohorts*, p. 119.

21. Ibid., p. 246.

22. Ibid., p. 247, report that only 384, or 8.9 percent, of the 4,315 cohort members with at least one police contact spent any time in an institution. Because incapacitation after three contacts would have involved 1,806 juveniles, or 41.8 percent, of the 4,315 juveniles with at least

one police contact, the amount of money spent on institutionalization would have increased significantly.

23. Robert Martinson, "What Works? Questions and Answers About Prison Reform," *The Public Interest* 35 (Spring 1974): 50.

24. Charles A. Murray and Louis A. Cox, Jr., *Beyond Probation: Juvenile Corrections and the Chronic Delinquent* (Beverly Hills, Calif.: Sage Publications, 1979).

25. Anne L. Schneider, *Deterrence and Juvenile Crime: Results from a National Policy Experiment* (New York: Springer-Verlag, 1990); and Mark Fraser and Michael Normal, "Chronic Juvenile Delinquency and the 'Suppression Effect': An Exploratory Study," *Journal of Offender Counseling, Services, and Rehabilitation* 13 (Summer 1988): 55–73.

26. Richard J. Lundman, "Beyond Probation: Assessing the Generalizability of the Suppression Effect Measures Reported by Murray and Cox," *Crime and Delinquency* 32 (January 1986): 134–47.

27. Murray and Cox, *Beyond Probation*, pp. 34–35.

28. Ibid., p. 34.

29. Anthony M. Platt, *The Child Savers: The Invention of Delinquency*, 2nd ed. (Chicago: The University of Chicago Press, 1977), p. 149.

30. Cited in Clifford R. Shaw, *The Jack-Roller: A Delinquent Boy's Own Story* (1930; reprint, Chicago: The University of Chicago Press, 1966), notes 2 and 3, p. 66.

31. Ibid., p. 65.

32. Ibid., p. 66.

33. Ibid., p. 66.

34. Ibid., pp. 66–67.

35. Ibid., p. 70.

36. Ibid., p. 69.

37. Alan J. Davis, "Sexual Assaults in the Philadelphia Prison System," in David M. Peterson and Charles W. Thomas (eds.), *Corrections: Problems and Prospects*, 2nd ed. (Englewood Cliffs, N.J.: Prentice-Hall, 1980), pp. 103–04; Clemens Bartollas, Stuart J. Miller, and Simon Dinitz, *Juvenile Victimization: The Institutional Paradox* (Beverly Hills, Calif.: Sage Publications, 1976); Clemens Bartollas and Christopher M. Sieverdes, "The Victimized White in a Juvenile Correctional Facility," *Crime and Delinquency* 29 (July 1981): 534–43; Alice Propper, *Prison Homosexuality: Myth and Reality* (Lexington, Mass.: Heath, 1981); Alexander W. Pisciotta, "Race, Sex, and Rehabilitation: A Study of Differential Treatment in the Juvenile Reformatory, 1825–1900," *Crime and Delinquency* 29 (April 1983): 254–69; Steven Lerner, *Bodily Harm: The Pattern of Fear and Violence at the California Youth Authority* (Bolinas, Calif.: Common Knowledge Press, 1986); Lydia S. Rosner,

"Juvenile Secure Detention," *Journal of Offender Counseling, Services, and Rehabilitation* 12 (Spring 1988): 57–76; John R. Sutton, "The Political Economy of Madness: The Expansion of the Asylum in Progressive America," *American Sociological Review* 56 (October 1991): 665–78. For description of life inside institutions for female juveniles, see Barbara Carter, "Race, Sex, and Gangs: Reform School Families," *Trans-Action* 11 (November–December 1973): 36–43; Beverly A. Smith, "Female Admissions and Paroles of the Western House of Refuge in the 1880s: An Historical Example of Community Corrections," *Journal of Research in Crime and Delinquency* 26 (February 1989): 36–66; Joachim Kersten, "A Gender Specific Look at Patterns of Violence in Juvenile Institutions: Or, Are Girls Really More Difficult to Manage?" *International Journal of the Sociology of Law* 18 (November 1990): 473–93.

38. Because many institutions for juveniles are currently well above capacity, simply getting residents fed takes a great deal of time. They eat in groups whose size is determined by cafeteria space. As soon as the last group has had breakfast, the first group appears for lunch. As the last group finishes lunch, the first group arrives for dinner.

39. Murray and Cox, *Beyond Probation*, p. 112.

40. Ibid., p. 114.

41. Ibid., pp. 31–43.

42. Ibid., pp. 173–94.

43. Ibid., p. 181.

44. Lundman, "Beyond Probation."

45. Schneider, *Deterrence and Juvenile Crime.*

46. In addition to Chapter 7, see Empey and Erickson, *The Provo Experiment*; Empey and Lubeck, *The Silverlake Experiment*; and Lundman, "Beyond Probation."

47. For description of the formal surfacing of restitution as a community-based intervention, see Anne L. Schneider, "Restitution and Recidivism Rates of Juvenile Offenders: Results from Four Experimental Studies," *Criminology* 24 (April 1986): 533–52.

48. Schneider, *Deterrence and Juvenile Crime.*

49. Murray and Cox, *Beyond Probation*, p. 179, emphasis added.

50. For additional evidence of the effectiveness of community-based interventions, see John D. Wooldrege, "Differentiating the Effects of Juvenile Court Sentences on Eliminating Recidivism," *Journal of Research in Crime and Delinquency* 25 (August 1988): 264–300.

PART FOUR

CONCLUSION

9

RECOMMENDATIONS FOR THE FUTURE

Earlier chapters described and analyzed many of the best-known and most important delinquency prevention and control projects of the past six decades. The prevention efforts ranged from identification and treatment of individual juveniles to neighborhood-based area projects. The control efforts examined were considerably more diverse, starting with diversion of status and other minor offenders and ending with the use of correctional facilities to incapacitate and deter chronic offenders.

This final chapter uses the information and insights of these major projects as the foundation for a series of recommendations for the future. It begins by briefly reviewing evidence descriptive of the frequency and seriousness of juvenile delinquency. Attention is then directed to six recommendations for the future.

JUVENILE DELINQUENCY

Juvenile delinquency is frequent.[1] Police arrest nearly 2 million juveniles each year. These arrests only hint at the frequency of delinquency. Self-report studies indicate that if citizens and police detected and apprehended all adolescents committing delinquent acts, very few juveniles—probably less than 10 percent—would escape being labeled delinquent.

Most juveniles are not seriously delinquent. The majority of adolescents arrested each year are charged with nonindex offenses, such as liquor law violations, vandalism, and running away. Arrests of juveniles for index offenses are much more likely to involve crimes against property, such as larceny-theft, than index crimes against persons, such as murder. Self-report studies confirm that most juveniles are not seriously delinquent. Adolescents self-report nonindex offenses and index crimes against property much more frequently than index crimes against persons.

A minority of juveniles are frequently and seriously delinquent. *Delinquency in a Birth Cohort*'s 627 chronic offenders accounted for slightly more than half of the 10,214 officially recorded offenses committed by the 9,945 members of the birth cohort.[2] *Beyond Probation*'s 317 chronic offenders had each accumulated an average of nearly 14 arrests with more than half for index offenses including "317 . . . assault charges . . . 183 armed robbery charges . . . 23 rape charges . . . and 14 homicide charges."[3]

Future prevention and control efforts must therefore accommodate a range of offenders. Although an oversimplification, it is useful to conceive of three general types of offenders: (1) a large group of offenders accused of status and minor property offenses; (2) a smaller group of moderately to chronically delinquent offenders accused of nonindex offenses, such as vandalism, and index crimes against property, such a larceny-theft; and (3) a violent few adjudicated delinquent for index crimes against persons.

RECOMMENDATIONS FOR THE FUTURE

The information presented in earlier chapters tells us a great deal about what works and what does not work in preventing and controlling delinquent behavior. And although it is true that additional research would be very useful (see Box 9.1), it is now necessary to use what is known as a foundation for recommending what should be done in the future.[4] A total of six policy-sensitive recommendations will be advanced, starting with a call for the abandonment of traditional delinquency-prevention efforts.

Box 9.1   Additional Research

Social scientists frequently conclude their written work with a call for additional research, apparently for good reason. Additional research helps clarify contradictory findings and therefore contributes to less ambiguous recommendations. Equally important, suggesting more research is the only sure method of avoiding the embarrassment associated with advancing recommendations that are later challenged by new research.

However, concluding written work with a call for more research also raises serious problems. Because there always is more to be learned, development of policy-sensitive recommendations can logically be postponed indefinitely. Further, if social scientists backed by careful research and the best available evidence fail to advance recommendations, then others with less information and more vested interests to protect and promote will take their place. Last, failure to make good use of existing research invites endless replication of previous projects.

This book concludes with recommendations for the future. Additional research is welcome because many issues are in need of clarification. It is recognized that at least some of the recommendations will be challenged by additional research. But it remains necessary for social scientists at some point to use the data and insights of the past as the foundation for recommending what should be done in the future. This is that point.

ABANDONMENT OF TRADITIONAL DELINQUENCY-PREVENTION EFFORTS

It Is Recommended That Traditional Delinquency-Prevention Efforts Be Abandoned.

Delinquency-prevention efforts[5] have traditionally been of two general types. The usual procedure is to identify and treat juveniles believed headed for trouble with the law. An alternative prevention strategy is to identify high-delinquency neighborhoods and then alter some of the social forces thought supportive of illegal behavior.

Rationale.   Social scientists do not know how to reliably identify juveniles headed for trouble with the law. Despite extensive effort, Sheldon and Eleanor Glueck and Starke Hathaway and Elio D. Monachesi failed to develop instruments that accurately predict delinquency. More recent research, including studies of birth cohorts, indicates accurate prediction remains a stubbornly elusive goal.

Prevention of delinquency also remains a stubbornly elusive goal. The Cambridge-Somerville Youth Study's adult counselors were "no more effective than the usual forces in the community in preventing boys from committing delinquent acts." Youth Consultation Service's social workers "failed to prevent delinquency." The Chicago Area Project almost certainly failed to prevent delinquency, given Midcity and other similar neighborhood-based efforts. More recently, *The National Evaluation of Delinquency Prevention* concluded that "there is little positive evidence [projects] are effective in preventing delinquency."

Prevention projects are typically very expensive. As part of *The National Evaluation of Delinquency Prevention* the Justice Department spent over \$20 million to provide services to 20,000 juveniles in 68 cities. Leaving these juveniles alone almost certainly would have been just as effective and far less expensive.

Prevention efforts needlessly compromise the rights of juveniles (and their families) by forcing involvement in ineffective and expensive projects. During the Cambridge-Somerville Youth Study, for example, some of the adult counselors "feared . . . they might 'lose the case' . . . if they gave the family a free choice . . . to accept or reject services." The solution was to strip children and their parents of the right to resist treatment. Counselors succeeded in this effort, as only 1 of the 325 experimental subjects successfully resisted treatment.

The continued quest for effective prevention strategies has inspired bizarre recommendations and programs. In the early 1970s, Georgetown University psychologist Juan B. Cortes suggested a search for 7-year-old mesomorphs[6]—children with muscular body types. Once found, they would be screened to determine whether their families were capable of controlling the delinquent impulsivity and aggressiveness that Professor Cortes believed mesomorphy signals. In the mid 1970s, the YMCA and big business combined to provide 14,000 city children with motorized minibikes,[7] perhaps on the assumption that if the pleasure and responsibility of owning a minibike did not prevent delinquency, the accident rate would. In the late 1970s and early 1980s, the initially positive reports of the effects of scaring juveniles straight prompted nationwide emulation, including a bill in the California legislature requiring the busing of 15,000 nondelinquent children to state prisons for intensive confrontation sessions.[8] In the late 1980s, some juveniles were back on minibikes, this time with adults claiming to be doing "social work at 30 m.p.h."[9] At the same time, adolescents were being taught Tae Kwon Doe and other martial arts to reduce "delinquent tendencies."[10]

Prevention projects rarely affect the known correlates of urban delinquency. For over half a century the contours of inner-city delinquency have been well established. In any large city, delinquency rates are highest where infant mortality rates also are high, life expectancies short, jobs hard to find, education poor, and hope scarce. Despite this knowledge, prevention projects regularly provide only piecemeal solutions. Where babies and adults need health care, adolescents are assigned adult counselors trained in talk therapy. Where people need jobs, detached gang workers and recreational programs are provided. Where children need education, academics suggest a search for mesomorphs. Where people seek hope, children are given minibikes, taken to prisons for intensive confrontation sessions, and taught martial arts.

It therefore is recommended that traditional delinquency prevention efforts be abandoned. Prevention projects don't work and they waste money, violate the rights of juveniles and their families, inspire bizarre suggestions and programs, and fail to affect the known correlates of urban delinquency. Based on the best available evidence, it is time to get out of the business of attempting to prevent delinquency.

Diversion as the Standard Response to Juveniles Accused of Status and Minor Property Offenses

It Is Recommended That Diversion Be The Standard Juvenile Justice Response to Infrequently Delinquent Juveniles Accused of Status and Minor Property Offenses.

Supporters of diversion[11] argue that the best treatment for many alleged offenders is little or no treatment. This is especially thought to be the case when the juvenile is young and charged with nothing more serious than a status or minor property offense. For these types of alleged offenders and perhaps others, diversion away from the juvenile justice system is believed to be the most effective method of controlling delinquency.

Rationale. Release without services or diversion into short-term treatment are at least as effective as further penetration of the juvenile justice system. Working exclusively with status offenders, the Sacramento County Diversion Project was slightly more effective than regular intake processing, perhaps because the short-term treatment left diverted juveniles pretty much alone. Evaluation of Juvenile Diversion Projects revealed that expansion of diversion services to minor property offenders also was modestly effective, probably because of the inclusion of a large number of good risks. Working with minor property offenders, the National Evaluation of Diversion Projects reported that release without services and diversion into services were just as effective as further penetration of the juvenile justice system. Well over half of the juveniles involved in the Adolescent Diversion Project were accused of minor property crimes, yet diversion was just as effective as return to juvenile court.

Release without services is, of course, significantly less expensive than either diversion into services or further penetration. It costs very little to send juveniles out the back door of intake soon after they are ushered in the front door. Diversion into services is probably just as expensive as further penetration of the juvenile justice system. However, to the extent diversion into services replaces overnight detention and petition to juvenile court, it is possible that modest savings occur.

Despite the fact that diversion into services is just as effective as further penetration, there is no escaping the fact that juveniles diverted into services receive treatment without trial. Juveniles eligible for diversion intake typically are told that they (and their parents) have to make a choice. They can take advantage of the diversion unit's services or take their chances in court. If they choose to accept diversion, they are expected to present themselves for services on a more or less regular basis for a short period of time.

There also is no escaping the fact that diversion widens the net of social control. Although the estimates vary, a reasonable guess is that about half of diverted juveniles would have been left alone were it not for the existence of a diversion project. Diversion means more juveniles under the short-term control of the juvenile justice system.

But treatment without trial and net-widening seem justifiable when other factors are taken into account. Diversion is just as effective as further penetration of the juvenile justice system and no more expensive. Intervention is mostly benign and it is brief. And diversion reduces the frequency with which status and minor property offenders are exposed to the pains of detention and the chaos of juvenile court (see Box 9.2).

It is therefore recommended that diversion be the standard juvenile justice response to infrequently delinquent juveniles accused of status and minor property offenses. Diversion is clearly just as effective as further penetration of the juvenile justice system, no more expensive, and reduces the frequency with which juveniles are exposed to the pains of detention and the chaos of juvenile court. Based on the best available evidence, diversion is an effective and appropriate response to the deeds and words of infrequently delinquent juveniles in minor trouble with the law.

ROUTINE PROBATION AS THE FIRST AND MOST FREQUENT SENTENCING OPTION

It Is Recommended That Routine Probation Be the First and Most Frequent Sentencing Option for Moderately Delinquent Juveniles Convicted of Index Crimes Against Property.

Probation is the most frequently employed sentencing option.[12] Each year approximately 70 percent of the juveniles adjudicated delinquent serve their sentence in the community under the supervision of probation officers employed by the juvenile court. Because probation is so frequent, most probation officers have large caseloads and too little time to do more than meet infrequently with most of the juvenile clients.

Rationale. Despite the heavy workload of probation officers, routine probation is a moderately effective (see Box 9.3) method

Box 9.2   The Pains of Detention and the Chaos of Juvenile Court

Spending time in a juvenile detention center is a painful experience. Offenders are searched upon entrance and rules are numerous. Because most detention centers are overcrowded and understaffed, violent bullies among the detainees intimidate and take what they want from the weak and fearful. Rape consequently is one of the pains of detention. "[Group] assaults are common among the older boys. Younger boys are simply taken sexually; sometimes they offer themselves. . . . The [kid] who is not streetwise and is physically weak . . . gets it in every way and learns fast."

The chaos of juvenile court is traceable to two factors. The first is confusion over the proper role of the court. Historically, the juvenile court has been a place where juveniles had few rights, and treatment rather than punishment was said to be the primary goal. Recently due process protections, such as the right to counsel, have been granted juveniles, and the court is increasingly expected to punish rather than treat its youthful defendants. The second factor is an overwhelming number of cases and too few court personnel. After attempting to hear 32 cases on a single day in June, a juvenile court judge completed the afternoon by throwing the court's papers and records to the floor and announcing: "Go outside and adjourn every case until September. Everybody's remanded [sent back to detention] until September. All their motions are denied. All the other judges do it this way, why shouldn't I? Maybe the other judges are right: don't give a shit. The lawyers shout at me. What am I going to do? I give up. I don't know what to do."

Sources: Susan M. Fisher, "Life in a Children's Detention Center: Strategies for Survival," *American Journal of Orthopsychiatry* 42 (April 1972): 370; Lydia S. Rosner, "Juvenile Secure Detention," *Journal of Offender Counseling, Services and Rehabilitation* (12 (Winter 1988): 57–76; Peter Prescott, *The Child Savers: Juvenile Justice Observed* (New York: Knopf, 1981), p. 50; and Mark D. Jacobs, *Screwing the System and Making It Work: Juvenile Justice in the No-Fault Society* (Chicago: The University of Chicago Press, 1990), pp. 174 and 274.

Box 9.3   Explaining the Effectiveness of Routine Probation

The effectiveness of routine probation cannot easily be explained in terms of the supervisory and treatment efforts of probation officers. Because most probation officers have large caseloads and too much paperwork to do much supervising, probationers are by and large left pretty much on their own.

A much more likely explanation is the presentence investigation conducted by probation officers. During this investigation, probation officers pay close attention to such factors as the legal seriousness of the offense, the adolescent's prior record and attitude, and family stability. Offenders sentenced to probation are perceived to be "good risks," and many probationers do manage to stay out of formal trouble with the law.

Also important is the warning associated with a probationary sentence. Probationers are told that they must abide by special conditions including staying out of trouble with the law. If they fail, return to court is a very real possibility.

Last, probation officers find time to work intensively with at least some of their probationers. Consider just a few of the things caring probation officers have given needy probationers: "rides to a job or school . . . a place to 'hang out' at the probation office . . . initial meetings with an acutely withdrawn child under the child's bed, since the child refused to come out under any circumstance . . . medical care for a pregnant teenager . . . evenings to serve as the girl's partner in childbirth classes . . . coach[ing] the girl through labor and witness[ing] the birth. . . ."

The effectiveness of routine probation thus is not so much what is done once offenders are sentenced to the community. There is simply too much paperwork and too many clients for probation officers to do much of anything for most probationers. Instead, the effectiveness of probation can be traced to the presentence investigation, the warning associated with a probationary sentence, and the extraordinary effort on behalf of a few clients badly in need of heroic assistance.

Source: Mark D. Jacobs, *Screwing the System and Making It Work: Juvenile Justice in the No-Fault Society* (Chicago: The University of Chicago Press, 1990), pp. 35, 116 (quote), and 151.

of controlling the illegal behavior of moderately delinquent offenders. During the Provo Experiment, offenders sentenced to probation from Utah County were randomly assigned to routine probation or to the intensive, community-based services made available by the experiment. Although the juveniles assigned to probation received haphazard supervision by officers with "large caseloads and excessive paperwork," routine probation was just as effective as the community-based services.

However, probation is not uniformly just as effective. Professor Anne L. Schneider's assessment of the National Evaluation of Juvenile Restitution Programs reported that routine probation was slightly less effective than intensive, community-based probation supervision emphasizing restitution.

The differences, though, were very small. When routine probation was compared with intensive probation supervision, for example, there was a .07 offense per offender increase in a year, as compared to a .07 offense per offender decrease during the same time period. Further, the site-specific comparisons showed mixed results. At one site (Oklahoma County) routine probation was associated with a decrease in delinquency while intensive supervision probation emphasizing restitution increased delinquency. And the more intensive intervention was more expensive.

Just how much more expensive is suggested by the Provo Experiment. During the Provo Experiment, the average cost of services for offenders randomly assigned to probation was $200 as compared to $600 for offenders randomly assigned to the experiment's community-based treatment program.

Finally, probation is a conditional sentence to the community and its wisdom and consequences for particular offenders can easily be reassessed. Juveniles committing new offenses and crossing the line between moderation and chronicity can be quickly hauled back into court for reassignment to more intensive interventions.

It therefore is recommended that routine probation be the first and most frequent sentencing option. Routine probation is a moderately effective method of controlling moderately delinquent offenders. In addition, routine probation is less expensive than more intensive interventions and is easily changed in the wake of new offenses. Using what is known as a foundation for what should be done in the future means retention of routine probation as the first response of the juvenile court to moderately delinquent offenders.

PERMANENT ABANDONMENT OF EFFORTS TO SCARE AND INFORM JUVENILES STRAIGHT

It Is Recommended That Efforts to Scare Juveniles Straight— Including the Visitation and "Forum, Discussion, Seminar" Programs That Currently Operate in Many Prisons—Be Permanently Abandoned.

Starting in the mid 1970s, groups of juveniles, including some young offenders sentenced to probation, were taken to state prisons for intensive confrontation sessions with adult inmates serving long or life sentences. Inmates told juveniles of the pains of imprisonment using their own experiences as examples. The purpose of the sessions was to scare juveniles straight by showing the kinds of places they could end up if they persisted in their delinquent ways.[13]

Although prisons have gotten out of the business of trying to scare kids straight, many still offer visits and "forum, discussion, seminar" sessions intended to provide information about prison life.

Rationale. The record of efforts to scare juveniles straight is at best mixed and at worst alarming. One of the first attempts to scare juveniles straight occurred at the Michigan Reformatory in the mid-1960s. Analysis revealed that visiting a reformatory and meeting with young adult inmates serving long or life sentences increased rather than decreased involvement in delinquency. The best-known effort to scare juveniles straight took place at New Jersey's Rahway State Prison, and it too produced more rather than less delinquency. Michigan's Juvenile Offenders Learn Truth (JOLT) had no impact on rates of delinquency. Only the Insiders Juvenile Crime Prevention Program at the old Virginia State Penitentiary, with its longer follow-up and seriously incomplete data, claims to have controlled delinquency. Efforts to scare juveniles straight did not guarantee control of delinquency, and in some cases they produced more rather than less delinquency.

Given their mixed record, intensive confrontation sessions needlessly demeaned adolescent offenders. In addition to shouts and verbal abuse, juveniles attending sessions were menaced physically and threatened with rape by angry-appearing adult inmates. On occasion, sessions escaped the boundaries of mere words and gestures to include demonstrations of at least some of the pains of imprisonment.

Even simple visits and low-key sessions providing information, such as those operating at New Jersey's Rahway State Prison and Virginia's Mecklenburg Correctional Facility in the early 1990s, pose serious risks in exchange for no measurable rewards. The Michigan Reformatory Visitation Program consisted of a visit and low-key information session. It increased delinquency. JOLT involved a tour and a less intensive informational session. It had no effect on delinquency.

It therefore is recommended that efforts to scare and inform juveniles straight be permanently abandoned. Intensive confrontation sessions sometimes increase delinquency and they needlessly demean the adolescents who attend them. Informational visits risk increasing delinquency as well. As much as well intentioned inmates welcome the opportunity to help kids, it is time to permanently abandon attempts to scare and inform juveniles straight.

EXPANSION OF COMMUNITY TREATMENT

It Is Recommended That Community-Based Treatment, Including Intensive Supervision Programs, Be Permanently Expanded to Accommodate Nearly All Chronic Property Offenders Currently Sentenced to Juvenile Correctional Facilities.

Community-based treatments,[14] including intensive supervision programs, stand midway between the loose supervision and infrequent assistance of routine probation and the secure custody of correctional facilities for juvenile offenders. They are intermediate interventions for offenders who require something more than routine probation, something less than institutionalization.

Rationale. It has been repeatedly demonstrated that chronic offenders convicted of property crimes and sentenced to correctional facilities can be just as effectively treated in the community without compromising community safety (see Box 9.4). Intensive parole supervision during California's Community Treatment

---

Box 9.4 Community Safety

The recommended expansion of community-based treatment is limited to chronic property offenders safely treated in the community in the past. Review of the eligibility requirements of three community-based projects clarifies the limits of the recommendation:

1. The Community Treatment Project's subjects had averaged 5.8 arrests and would have been institutionalized had it not been for the existence of the community-based intensive parole supervision. *Offenders were excluded if they had been adjudicated delinquent for index crimes against persons of if local officials objected to their return. Overall, 35 percent were declared ineligible.*

2. The Provo Experiment's subjects averaged about seven previous arrests and would have served time in the State Training School had it not been for the existence of the community-based services. *Offenders were excluded if convicted of index crimes against persons or if they were clearly psychotic or severely retarded. Less then 5 percent were ineligible.*

3. Viable Options' subjects were "relatively serious and chronic, though not highly violent offenders" who would have been sent to a state facility had it not been for the existence of intensive probation supervision services. *Excluded were the very violent, the psychotic, and those with no suitable home to return to. Overall, 60 percent were declared ineligible and most of them simply lacked a place to go home to.*

Project (1961–1969) was just as effective as a year in a correctional facility followed by routine parole. Chronic property offenders treated in the community during Utah's Provo Experiment (1959–1965) and Los Angeles's Silverlake Experiment (mid 1960s) were no more or less delinquent than offenders who had been locked up. Jerome Miller's substitution of community treatment for confinement in Massachusetts in the early 1970s neither increased or decreased recidivism. *Beyond Probation*'s "less drastic" community-based interventions (1974–1976) for some of Chicago's chronic offenders clearly suppressed delinquent behavior. And Wayne County, Michigan's discovery of "Viable Options" (1983–1985) revealed that community-based intensive probation supervision of chronic property offenders was just as effective as institutionalization.

Additionally, community treatment programs sometimes are less expensive than institutionalization and they are usually not more expensive.[15] Services provided offenders during the Provo Experiment were significantly less expensive because community treatment averaged six months while institutionalization averaged ten months. The Silverlake Experiment's community efforts also were significantly less expensive because residence in the group home lasted about 6 months while institutionalization averaged nearly 13 months. Substitution of community programs in Massachusetts was just as expensive as institutionalization.

Community treatment also is more humane than incarceration. Offenders treated in the community escape most of the pains of imprisonment. Additionally, community treatment programs usually are of lesser duration than sentences served in correctional facilities and thus reduce the amount of time offenders spend under the control of the state. And offenders who do their time in the community experience fewer reintegration problems associated with release from a correctional facility.

Last, community-based treatment of chronic property offenders simply hastens the inevitable. Even without community-based treatment, chronic property offenders committed to long-term public facilities are quickly released to the community, with nearly all having served no more than seven months and many far less.[16]

It therefore is recommended that community-based treatment including intensive supervision programs be permanently expanded to accommodate nearly all[17] chronic property offenders currently sentenced to juvenile correctional facilities. Community treatment of chronic property offenders is just as effective as institutionalization and every bit as safe for the community. Community-based treatment also is less expensive, more humane, and simply hastens the inevitable. Given the available evidence, chronic property offenders should be treated in the community rather than forced to serve time in a correctional facility.

INSTITUTIONALIZATION RESERVED FOR JUVENILES ADJUDICATED DELINQUENT FOR INDEX CRIMES AGAINST PERSONS

It Is Recommended That Institutionalization Be Reserved for Juveniles Adjudicated Delinquent for Index Crimes Against Persons.

The traditional reason for sentencing juvenile offenders to state correctional facilities has been rehabilitation. Correctional facilities routinely offer academic and vocational training. Most institutions also supplement these routine services with special programs, such as alcohol and other drug counseling.

However, alternative reasons for institutionalization have recently gained legitimacy. Incapacitation theorists assert that sentencing chronic offenders to long terms in correctional facilities will significantly reduce juvenile crime. Deterrence theorists argue that incarceration alerts offenders and other juveniles to the pains of imprisonment and pushes them in the direction of law-abiding behavior out of fear of punishment by the state.[18]

Rationale. Research leaves little doubt that incarceration suppresses delinquency. *Beyond Probation*'s chronic offenders were 68 percent less delinquent in the year following institutionalization as compared to the year before. Replicative reexamination of the Provo and Silverlake experiments also revealed that spending time in a correctional facility suppressed delinquency (61 percent in the Provo Experiment and 72 percent in the Silverlake Experiment). Direct replication during the National Evaluation of Juvenile Restitution Programs, where most incarcerated juveniles spent only eight days across four successive weekends in detention, yielded a 32 percent suppression effect.

What is in doubt is the relative strength and long-term stability of the suppressive effects of institutionalization. Although most of *Beyond Probation*'s UDIS community placements were slightly less effective than a year at St. Charles or Valley View in suppressing delinquency, in both the Provo and Silverlake experiments the reverse was true: community treatment suppressed delinquency more than institutionalization. Equally important, the Provo Experiment's community-based efforts suppressed delinquency far more stably than institutionalization.[19]

Also troublesome is the cost of institutionalization. Although figures vary considerably, a solid guess is that sending an adolescent to a long-term correctional facility for a full year costs around $25,000,[20] about the same as sending an adolescent to a prestigious college or university for the same time period.[21]

Further, there is no sure way of knowing whether the suppressive effects of incarceration are the result of deterrence or the services all institutions provide. Even the biggest, meanest, and toughest juvenile correctional facilities offer educational opportunities and recovery programs for the chemically dependent. Correctional facilities are rich in trained adults who care and want to help juveniles.

Last, institutionalization exposes offenders to the pains of imprisonment. Some of these pains are deliberate, including restrictions on mobility, living space, eating, sleeping, and even going to the bathroom. Other pains of imprisonment are less a matter of intent, more the result of putting large numbers of juveniles under the precarious control of a few adults. In such an environment, violent bullies inevitably—and cruelly—take advantage of those too weak and fearful to resist.

Still, there is a place for institutionalization within the juvenile justice system. The pains of imprisonment apparently cause offenders to think again of the wisdom and consequences of continued involvement in delinquency. Having seen firsthand that the state means business when people commit index crimes against persons—murder, rape, robbery, and aggravated assault—offenders clearly suppress delinquent behavior, perhaps out of fear of again experiencing the pains of imprisonment.

It therefore is recommended that institutionalization be reserved for juveniles adjudicated delinquent for index crimes against persons. Institutionalization suppresses delinquent behavior, but its relative strength and long-term stability are open to question. Additionally, institutionalization is expensive and there is no sure way of knowing whether deterrence or treatment explains the suppression effect. Institutionalization exposes offenders to the pains of imprisonment, but in the case of violent offenders, institutionalization is an effective and appropriate response.

SUMMARY AND CONCLUSIONS

This final chapter used the information of earlier chapters as the foundation for a series of recommendations for future prevention and control effects. It began by reviewing evidence descriptive of the frequency and seriousness of delinquent behavior. Attention was then directed to six recommendations for the future.

The recommendations advanced outline an approach to the problem of delinquency that is obviously familiar in some respects, while at the same time making significant departures from established policies. It is familiar in that diversion and probation would remain as first responses to minor and moderately delinquent offenders. It is significantly different in that traditional prevention programs and efforts to scare and inform juveniles straight would be abandoned, community treatment permanently expanded to accommodate nearly all chronic property offenders, and institutionalization reserved for the violent few[22] among the delinquent many.

NOTES

1. This section is based on FBI, *Crime in the United States: Uniform Crime Reports, 1990* (Washington, D.C.: U.S. Government Printing Office, 1991), pp. 8-42; and Lloyd D. Johnston, Jerald G. Bachman, and Patrick M. O'Malley, *Monitoring the Future* (Ann Arbor, Mich.: Institute for Social Research, University of Michigan, 1990). Also see Chapter 1.

2. Marvin E. Wolfgang, Robert M. Figlio, and Thorsten Sellin, *Delinquency in a Birth Cohort* (Chicago: The University of Chicago Press, 1972).

3. Charles A. Murray and Louis A. Cox, Jr., *Beyond Probation: Juvenile Corrections and the Chronic Delinquent* (Beverly Hills, Calif.: Sage Publications, 1979), pp. 34–35.

4. Ronald A. Feldman, Timothy E. Caplinger, and John S. Wodarski, *The St. Louis Conundrum: The Effective Treatment of Antisocial Youths* (Englewood Cliffs, N.J.: Prentice-Hall, 1983), pp. 3–6.

5. This section is based on Starke R. Hathaway and Elio D. Monachesi, *Adolescent Personality and Behavior: MMPI Patterns of Normal, Delinquent, Dropout, and Other Outcomes* (Minneapolis, Minn.: The University of Minnesota Press, 1963); Sheldon Glueck and Eleanor Glueck, *Unraveling Juvenile Delinquency* (New York: The Commonwealth Fund, 1950); Wolfgang, Figlio, and Sellin, *Delinquency in a Birth Cohort*; Donna Martin Hamparian, Richard Schuster, Simon Dinitz, and John P. Conrad, *The Violent Few: A Study of Dangerous Juvenile Offenders* (Lexington, Mass.: Lexington Books, 1978); Paul E. Tracy, Marvin E. Wolfgang, and Robert M. Figlio, *Delinquency Careers in Two Birth Cohorts* (New York: Plenum, 1990); Edwin Powers and Helen Witmer, *An Experiment in the Prevention of Juvenile Delinquency: The Cambridge-Somerville Youth Study* (New York: Columbia University Press, 1951); Henry J. Meyer, Edgar F. Borgatta, Wyatt C. Jones, in collaboration with Elizabeth P. Anderson, Hanna Grunwald, and Dorothy Headley, *Girls at Vocational High: An Experiment in Social Work Intervention* (New York: Russell Sage Foundation, 1965); Solomon Kobrin, "The Chicago Area Project—a 25 Year Assessment," *The Annals of the American Academy of Political and Social Science* 322 (March 1959): 19–29; Walter B. Miller, "The Impact of a 'Total Community' Delinquency Control Project," *Social Problems* 10 (Fall 1962): 168–91; and Barry Krisberg, *The National Evaluation of Delinquency Prevention: Final Report* (San Francisco: National Council on Crime and Delinquency, Research Center, September 1981). Also see Chapters 2, 3, and 8.

6. Juan B. Cortes, *Delinquency and Crime: A Biophysical Approach* (New York: Seminar Press, 1972).

7. William E. Wright and Michael C. Dixon, "Community Prevention and Treatment of Juvenile Delinquency: A Review of Evaluation Studies," *Journal of Research in Crime and Delinquency* 14 (January 1977): 53.

8. Aric Press and Donna Foote, "Does 'Scaring' Work?" *Newsweek*, May 14, 1979, p. 131. Also see Chapter 6.

9. Gary A. Fashimpar and Larry T. Harris, "Social Work at 30

MPH: Mini-Bike Rehabilitation Groups for Juvenile Delinquents," *Social Work with Groups* 10 (Spring 1987): 33–48.

10. Michael E. Trulson, "Martial Arts Training: A Novel Cure for Delinquency," *Human Relations* 39 (December 1986): 1131–40.

11. This section is based on Roger Baron, Floyd Feeney, and Warren Thornton, "Preventing Delinquency Through Diversion," *Federal Probation* 31 (March 1973): 13–18; Roger Baron and Floyd Feeney, *Juvenile Diversion Through Family Counseling: A Program for the Diversion of Status Offenders in Sacramento County, California* (Washington, D.C.: U.S. Government Printing Office, 1976); Ted Palmer, Marvin Bohnstedt, and Roy Lewis, *The Evaluation of Juvenile Diversion Projects: Final Report* (Sacramento, Calif.: Division of Research, California Youth Authority, Winter 1978); Franklyn W. Dunford, D. Wayne Osgood, and Hart F. Weichselbaum, *National Evaluation of Juvenile Diversion Projects: Final Report* (Washington, D.C.: The National Institute of Juvenile Justice and Delinquency Prevention, Office of Juvenile Justice and Delinquency Prevention, U.S. Department of Justice, May 1981); William S. Davidson II, Robin Redner, Richard L. Admur, and Christina M. Mitchell, *Alternative Treatments for Troubled Youth: The Case of Diversion from the Justice System* (New York: Plemun, 1990); Paul Tappan, "Treatment Without Trial," *Social Forces* 24 (March 1946): 306–11; and Charles E. Frazier, Pamela Richards, and Robert H. Potter, "Juvenile Diversion and Net Widening: Toward a Clarification of Assessment Strategies," *Human Organization* 42 (Summer 1983): 115–22. Also see Chapter 4.

12. This section is based on Ralph England, "What Is Responsible for Satisfactory Probation and Post-Probation Outcome?" *Journal of Criminal Law, Criminology and Police Science* 47 (March–April 1957): 667–77; Frank R. Scarpitti and Richard M. Stephenson, "Juvenile Court Dispositions: Factors in the Decision-Making Process," *Crime and Delinquency* 17 (April 1971): 142–51; LaMar T. Empey and Maynard L. Erickson, *The Provo Experiment: Evaluating Community Control of Delinquency* (Lexington, Mass.: Lexington Books, 1972); Anne L. Schneider, *Deterrence and Juvenile Crime: Results from a National Policy Experiment* (New York: Springer-Verlag, 1990); and Mark D. Jacobs, *Screwing the System and Making It Work* (Chicago: The University of Chicago Press, 1990). Also see Chapter 5.

13. This section is based on Research Report #4, Michigan Department of Corrections, "A Six Month Follow-up of Juvenile Delinquents Visiting the Ionia Reformatory," May 22, 1967; James O. Finckenauer, *Scared Straight! and the Panacea Phenomenon* (Englewood Cliffs, N.J.: Prentice-Hall, 1982); James C. Yarborough, "Evaluation of JOLT as a Deterrence Program," Program Bureau, Michigan Department of Cor-

rections, July 18, 1979; Stan Orchowsky and Keith Taylor, "The Insiders Juvenile Crime Prevention Program: An Assessment of a Juvenile Awareness Program," Research and Reporting Unit, Division of Program Development and Evaluation, Virginia Department of Corrections, August 1981; Douglas G. Dean, "The Impact of a Juvenile Awareness Program on Select Personality Traits of Male Clients," *Journal of Offender Counseling, Services and Rehabilitation* 6 (Spring 1982): 73–85; Bruce L. Berg, "Inmates as Clinical Sociologists: The Use of Sociodrama in a Nontraditional Delinquency Prevention Program," *International Journal of Offender Therapy and Comparative Criminology* 28 (September 1984): 117–24; and Richard L. Berry, "SHAPE-UP: The Effects of a Prison Aversion Program on Recidivism and Family Dynamics" (Ph.D. diss., College of Education, Diversion of Professional Studies, University of Northern Colorado, Greeley, Colorado, August 1985). Also see Chapter 6.

14. This section is based on Paul Lerman, *Community Treatment and Social Control: A Critical Analysis of Juvenile Correctional Policy* (Chicago: The University of Chicago Press, 1975); Empey and Erickson, *The Provo Experiment*; LaMar T. Empey and Steven Lubeck, *The Silverlake Experiment: Testing Delinquency Theory and Community Intervention* (Chicago: Aldine, 1971); Lloyd E. Ohlin, Alden D. Miller, and Robert B. Coates, *Juvenile Correctional Reform in Massachusetts: A Preliminary Report of the Center for Criminal Justice of the Harvard Law School* (Washington, D.C.: U.S. Government Printing Office, no date listed); Robert B. Coates, Alden D. Miller, and Lloyd E. Ohlin, *Diversity in a Youth Correctional System: Handling Delinquents in Massachusetts* (Cambridge, Mass.: Ballinger, 1978); Charles A. Murray and Louis A. Cox, Jr., *Beyond Probation: Juvenile Corrections and the Chronic Delinquent* (Beverly Hills, Calif.: Sage Publications, 1979); Solomon Kobrin and Malcolm W. Klein, *National Evaluation of Deinstitutionalization of Status Offenders Programs: Executive Summary* (Washington, D.C.: National Institute for Juvenile Justice and Delinquency Prevention, Office of Juvenile Justice and Delinquency Prevention, U.S. Department of Justice, June 1982); William H. Barton and Jeffrey A. Butts, "Viable Options: Intensive Supervision Programs for Juvenile Delinquents," *Crime and Delinquency* 36 (April 1990): 238–56; Todd R. Clear and Patricia L. Hardyman, "The New Intensive Supervision Movement," *Crime and Delinquency* 36 (January 1990): 42–60; Jerome G. Miller, *Last One Over the Wall: The Massachusetts Experiment in Closing Reform Schools* (Columbus: Ohio State University Press, 1990); and Norval Morris and Michael Tonry, *Between Prison and Probation: Intermediate Punishments in a Rational Sentencing System* (New York: Oxford University Press, 1990). Also see Chapters 5, 7, and 8.

15. The exception is the Community Treatment Project and the reason for the greater cost of community treatment is that experimental subjects received intensive supervision and assistance for the full course of their parole. See Lerman, *Community Treatment*, pp. 98–101.

16. U.S. Department of Justice, Office of Justice Programs, Bureau of Justice Statistics, *Children in Custody, 1975–1985: Census of Public and Private Juvenile Detention, Correctional, and Shelter Facilities, 1975, 1977, 1979, 1983, and 1985 (Washington, D.C.: U.S. Department of Justice, Office of Justice Programs, Bureau of Justice Statistics, 1989)*, p. 59.

17. Two exceptions are the clearly psychotic who need psychiatric care and the severely retarded who need special education. Offenders who are otherwise eligible for community treatment but lack homes to go back to should be placed in community-based programs providing residential services. For an example of psychiatric care, see Murray and Cox, *Beyond Probation*. For an example of community-based residential services, see Empey and Lubeck, *The Silverlake Experiment*. Also see Chapters 7 and 8.

18. This section is based on Murray and Cox, *Beyond Probation*; Empey and Erickson, *The Provo Experiment*; Empey and Lubeck, *The Silverlake Experiment*; and Schneider, *Deterrence and Juvenile Crime*. Also see Chapter 8.

19. Richard J. Lundman, "Beyond Probation: Assessing the Generalizability of the Delinquency Suppression Effect Measures Reported by Murray and Cox," *Crime and Delinquency* 32 (January 1986): 134–47.

20. U.S. Department of Justice, *Children in Custody*, p. 58, reports that in 1984, the average cost per day was $69 × 366 days = $25,254 per year.

21. *U.S. News and World Report*, "America's Best Colleges," September 30, 1991, pp. 93 and 97, ranked Williams College as the nation's top liberal arts college and Harvard University as the nation's top university. *MONEY Magazine*, "MONEY'S Guide to 1,011 Colleges," October 19, 1991, pp. 76 and 125, reports that tuition and room and board at Williams in 1991 was $21,995 while tuition and room and board at Harvard was $22,080. Add telephone, textbooks, toothpaste, and transportation to the Williams and Harvard bills and total costs are clearly "about the same."

22. Hamparian et al., *The Violent Few*.

SELECTED BIBLIOGRAPHY

Abidinsky, Howard. *Probation and Parole: Theory and Practice.* 4th ed., Englewood Cliffs, N.J.: Prentice-Hall, 1991.

Augustus, John. *A Report of the Labors of John Augustus, in Aid of the Unfortunate.* Boston: Wright and Hasty, 1852.

Baron, Roger, and Floyd Feeney. *Juvenile Diversion Through Family Counseling.* Washington, D.C.: U.S. Government Printing Office, 1976.

Baron, Roger, Floyd Feeney, and Warren Thornton. "Preventing Delinquency Through Diversion." *Federal Probation* 37 (March 1973): 13–18.

Bartollas, Clemens, Stuart J. Miller, and Simon Dinitz. *Juvenile Victimization: The Institutional Paradox.* Beverly Hills, Calif.: Sage Publications, 1976.

Barton, William H., and Jeffrey A. Butts, "Viable Options: Intensive Supervision Programs for Juvenile Delinquents." *Crime and Delinquency* 36 (April 1990): 238–56.

Becker, Howard S. *Outsiders: Studies in the Sociology of Deviance.* New York: The Free Press of Glencoe, 1963.

Benda, Brent. "Predicting Juvenile Recidivism: New Method, Old Problem." *Adolescence* 32 (Fall 1987): 691–704.

Berleman, William C., James R. Seaburg, and Thomas W. Steinburn, "The Delinquency Prevention Project of the Seattle Atlantic Street Center." *Social Service Review* 46 (September 1972): 323–46.

Bernard, Thomas J. *The Cycle of Juvenile Justice.* New York: Oxford University Press, 1991.

Berry, Richard L. "SHAPE-UP: The Effects of a Prison Aversion Program on Recidivism and Family Dynamics" Ph.D. diss., College of

Education, Division of Professional Studies, University of Northern Colorado, Greeley, Colorado, 1985.

Black, Donald, and Albert J. Reiss, Jr. "Police Control of Juveniles." *American Sociological Review* 35 (February 1970): 63–77.

Brager, George A., and Francis P. Purcell (eds.). *Community Action Against Poverty: Readings From the Mobilization Experience.* New Haven, Conn.: College and University Press, 1967.

Bremmer, Robert (ed.). *Children and Youth in America: A Documentary History, Volume I: 1600–1865.* Cambridge, Mass.: Harvard University Press, 1970.

—— (ed.). *Children and Youth in America: A Documentary History, Volume II: 1866–1932.* Cambridge, Mass: Harvard University Press, 1970.

Burchard, John D., and Sara N. Burchard (eds.). *Prevention of Delinquent Behavior.* Newbury Park, Calif.: Sage, 1987.

Bureau of Justice Statistics, *Children in Custody, 1975–85: Census of Public and Private Juvenile Detention, Correctional, and Shelter Facilities, 1975, 1977, 1979, 1983, and 1985.* Washington, D.C.: U.S. Department of Justice, Office of Justice Programs, Bureau of Justice Statistics, 1989.

Byrne, James. "The Future of Intensive Probation Supervision and New Intermediate Sanctions." *Crime and Delinquency* 36 (January 1990): 6–41.

Campbell, Donald T., and Julian C. Stanley. *Experimental and Quasi-Experimental Designs for Research.* Chicago: Rand McNally, 1963.

Carter, Robert M., and Malcolm W. Klein (eds.). *Back on the Street: The Diversion of Juvenile Offenders.* Englewood Cliffs, N.J.: Prentice-Hall, 1976.

Clark, Kenneth B. *Dark Ghetto: Dilemmas of Social Power.* New York: Harper & Row, 1965.

Clarke, Stevens H. "Getting 'Em' Out of Circulation: Does Incarceration of Juvenile Offenders Reduce Crime?" *Journal of Criminal Law and Criminology* 65 (December 1974): 530–38.

Clear, Todd R., and Patricia L. Hardyman, "The New Intensive Supervision Movement." *Crime and Delinquency* 36 (January 1990): 42–60.

Coates, Robert B., Alden D. Miller, and Lloyd E. Ohlin. *Diversity in a Youth Correctional System: Handling Delinquents in Massachusetts.* Cambridge, Mass.: Ballinger, 1978.

Cortes, Juan B. *Delinquency and Crime: A Biophysical Approach.* New York: Seminar Press, 1972.

Craig, Maude M., and Selma Glick. "Ten Years Experience with the Glueck Prediction Table." *Crime and Delinquency* 9 (July 1963): 249–61.

Davidson, William S., II, Robin Redner, Richard L. Amdur, and Christina M. Mitchell. *Alternative Treatments for Troubled Youth: The Case of Diversion from the Justice System.* New York: Plenum, 1990.

Dean, Douglas G. "The Impact of a Juvenile Awareness Program on Select Personality Traits of Male Clients." *Journal of Offender Counseling, Services and Rehabilitation* 6 (Spring 1982): 73–85.

Dixon, Michael C., and William E. Wright. *Juvenile Delinquency Prevention Programs: An Evaluation of Policy Related Research on the Effectiveness of Prevention Programs.* Washington, D.C.: National Science Foundation, 1975.

Dunford, Franklyn, D. Wayne Osgood, and Hart F. Weichselbaum. *National Evaluation of Juvenile Diversion Projects.* Washington, D.C.: The National Institute of Juvenile Justice and Delinquency Prevention, Office of Juvenile Justice and Delinquency Prevention, U.S. Department of Justice, 1981.

Elliot, Delbert, and Suzanne S. Ageton. "Reconciling Race and Class Differences in Self-Reported and Official Estimates of Delinquency." *American Sociological Review* 45 (February 1980): 95–110.

Empey, LaMar T., and Maynard L. Erickson. *The Provo Experiment: Evaluating Community Control of Delinquency.* Lexington, Mass.: Lexington Books, 1972.

Empey, LaMar T., and Steven G. Lubeck. *The Silverlake Experiment: Testing Delinquency Theory and Community Intervention.* Chicago: Aldine, 1971.

Empey, LaMar T., and Mark C. Stafford. *American Delinquency: Its Meaning and Construction,* 3rd ed. Belmont, Calif.: Wadsworth, 1991.

England, Ralph. "What is Responsible for Satisfactory Probation and Post-Probation Outcome?" *Journal of Criminal Law, Criminology and Police Science* 47 (March–April 1957): 667–77.

Faris, Robert E. L. *Chicago Sociology: 1920–1932.* Chicago: The University of Chicago Press, 1970.

Feldman, Ronald A., Timothy E. Caplinger, and John S. Wodarski. *The St. Louis Conundrum: The Effective Treatment of Antisocial Youths.* Englewood Cliffs, N.J.: Prentice-Hall, 1983.

Finckenauer, James O. *Scared Straight! and the Panacea Phenomenon.* Englewood Cliffs, N.J.: Prentice-Hall, 1982.

Finestone, Harold. *Victims of Change: Juvenile Delinquents in American Society.* Westport, Conn.: Greenwood Press, 1976.

Fisher, Susan M. "Life in a Children's Detention Center." *American Journal of Orthopsychiatry* 42 (April 1972): 368–77.

Fishman, Robert. *Criminal Recidivism in New York City.* New York: Praeger, 1977.

Fraser, Mark, and Michael Norman. "Chronic Juvenile Delinquency and the 'Suppression Effect': An Exploratory Study." *Journal of Offender Counseling, Services, and Rehabilitation* 13 (Summer 1988): 55–73.

Gibbs, Jack. *Crime, Punishment, and Deterrence.* New York: Elsevier, 1975.

Glueck, Sheldon, and Eleanor Glueck. *Predicting Delinquency and Crime.* Cambridge, Mass.: Harvard University Press, 1959.

———. *Unraveling Juveniule Delinquency.* New York: The Commonwealth Fund, 1950.

Greenwood, Peter W. (ed.). *Intervention Strategies for Chronic Juvenile Offenders: Some New Perspectives.* New York: Greenwood Press, 1986.

Hamparian, Donna Martin, Richard Schuster, Simon Dinitz, and John P. Conrad. *The Violent Few: A Study of Dangerous Juvenile Offenders.* Lexington, Mass.: Lexington Books, 1978.

Hathaway, Starke R., and Elio D. Monachesi. *Adolescent Personality and Behavior: MMPI Patterns of Normal, Delinquent, Dropout, and Other Outcomes.* Minneapolis: The University of Minnesota Press, 1963.

———. "The Personalities of Predelinquent Boys." *Journal of Criminal Law, Criminology and Police Science* 48 (July–August 1957): 149–63.

Healy, William. *The Individual Delinquent: A Text-Book of Diagnosis and Prognosis for All Concerned in Understanding Offenders.* Boston: Little Brown, 1925.

Hirschi, Travis, and Joseph Weis. "Correlates of Delinquency: The Illusion of Discrepancy Between Self-Report and Official Measures." *American Sociological Review* 44 (December 1979): 995–1014.

Jack-Roller (The) and Jon Snodgrass, with Gilbert Geis, James F. Short, Jr., and Solomon Kobrin. *The Jack-Roller at Seventy.* Lexington, Mass.: Lexington Books, 1982.

Jacobs, Mark D. *Screwing the System and Making It Work: Juvenile Justice in the No-Fault Society.* Chicago: The University of Chicago Press, 1990.

Kersten, Joachim. "A Gender Specific Look at Patterns of Violence in Juvenile Institutions: Or, Are Girls Really More Difficult to Manage?" *International Journal of the Sociology of Law* 18 (November 1990): 473–93.

Killinger, George G., and Paul F. Cromwell (eds.). *Corrections in the Community: Alternatives to Imprisonment.* St. Paul, Minn.: West, 1978.

Klein, Malcolm W. "Issues and Realities in Police Diversion Programs." *Crime and Delinquency* 22 (October 1976): 421-27.

Klockars, Carl B., Jr. "A Theory of Probation Supervision." *Journal of Criminal Law, Criminology and Police Science* 63 (December 1972): 550-57.

Knapp, Daniel, and Kenneth Polk. *Scouting the War on Poverty: Social Reform Politics in the Kennedy Administration.* Lexinston, Mass.: Heath Lexington Books, 1971.

Kobrin, Solomon. "The Chicago Area Project—a 25-Year Assessment." *The Annals of the American Academy of Political and Social Science* 322 (March 1959): 19-29.

Kobrin, Solomon, and Malcolm W. Klein. *Community Treatment of Juvenile Offenders: The DSO Experiments.* Beverly Hills, Calif.: Sage Publications, 1983.

———. *National Evaluation of Deinstitutionalization of Status Offender Programs.* Washington, D.C.: National Institute for Juvenile Justice and Delinquency Prevention, Office of Juvenile Justice and Delinquency Prevention, U.S. Department of Justice, 1982.

Koch, J. Randy. "Community Service and Outright Release as Alternatives to Juvenile Court: An Experimental Evaluation." Ph.D. diss., Michigan State University, 1985.

Krisberg, Barry. *The National Evaluation of Delinquency Prevention: Final Report.* San Francisco: Research Center, National Council on Crime and Delinquency, 1981.

Kwartler, Richard (ed.). *Behind Bars: Prisons in America.* New York: Vintage Books, 1977.

Langer, Sidney. *Scared Straight? Fear in the Deterrence of Delinquency.* Washington, D.C.: University Press of America, 1982.

Lemert, Edwin M., and Forrest Dill. *Offenders in the Community: The Probation Subsidy in California.* Lexington, Mass.: Lexington Books, 1978.

Lerman, Paul. *Community Treatment and Social Control: A Critical Analysis of Juvenile Correctional Policy.* Chicago: The University of Chicago Press, 1975.

———. "Evaluative Studies of Institutions for Delinquents: Implications for Research and Social Policy." *Social Work* 13 (July 1968): 55-64.

Lichtman, Carol, and Sue M. Smock. "The Effects of Social Services on Probation: A Field Experiment." *Journal of Research in Crime and Delinquency* 18 (January 1981): 81-100.

Lipton, Douglas, Robert Martinson, and Judith Wilks. *The Effectiveness of Correctional Treatment: A Survey of Treatment Evaluation Studies.* New York: Praeger, 1975.

Lundman, Richard J., "Beyond Probation: Assessing the Generalizability of the Suppression Effect Measures Reported by Murray and Cox." *Crime and Delinquency* 32 (January 1986): 134-47.

———. "Will Diversion Reduce Recidivism?" *Crime and Delinquency* 22 (October 1976): 428-37.

Lundman, Richard J., Richard E. Sykes, and John P. Clark. "Police Control of Juveniles: A Replication." *Journal of Research in Crime and Delinquency* 15 (January 1978): 74-91.

Marris, Peter, and Martin Rein. *Dilemmas of Social Reform: Poverty and Community Action in the United States.* New York: Atherton Press, 1969.

Martinson, Robert. "What Works? Questions and Answers About Prison Reform." *The Public Interest* 35 (Spring 1974): 22-54.

McCord, Joan. "A Thirty-Year Follow-Up of Treatment Effects." *American Psychologist* 33 (March 1978): 284-89.

McCord, Joan, William McCord, and Emily Thurber. "The Effects of Foster-Home Placement in the Prevention of Adult Antisocial Behavior." *Social Service Review* 34 (December 1960): 415-20.

McCord, William, and Joan McCord, with Irving Kenneth Zola. *Origins of Crime: A New Evaluation of the Cambridge-Somerville Youth Study.* New York: Columbia University Press, 1959.

McKelvy, Blake. *American Prisons: A History of Good Intentions.* Montclair, N.J.: Patterson Smith, 1977.

Merton, Robert K. "Social Structure and Anomie." *American Sociological Review* 3 (October 1938): 672-82.

Meyer, Henry J., Edgar F. Borgatta, and Wyatt C. Jones, in collaboration with Elizabeth P. Anderson, Hanna Grunwald, and Dorothy Headley. *Girls at Vocational High: An Experiment in Social Work Intervention.* New York: Russell Sage Foundation, 1965.

Michigan Department of Corrections. "A Six-Month Follow-up of Juvenile Delinquents Visiting the Ionia Reformatory." Michigan Department of Corrections. Lansing, Mich., May 22, 1967.

Miller, Jerome G. *Last One Over the Wall: The Massachusetts Experiment in Closing Reform Schools.* Columbus: Ohio State University Press, 1991.

Miller, Walter B. "The Impact of a 'Total Community' Delinquency Control Project." *Social Problems* 10 (Fall 1962): 168-91.

———. "Inter-Institutional Conflict as a Major Impediment to Delinquency Prevention." *Human Organization* 17 (Fall 1958): 20-23.

Morris, Norval, and Michael Tonry. *Between Prison and Probation: Intermediate Punishments in a Rational Sentencing System.* New York: Oxford University Press, 1990.

Moynihan, Daniel P. *Maximum Feasible Misunderstanding: Community Action in the War on Poverty.* New York: Free Press, 1969.

Murray, Charles A., and Louis A. Cox, Jr. *Beyond Probation: Juvenile Corrections and the Chronic Delinquent*. Beverly Hills, Calif.: Sage Publications, 1979.

Needleman, Carolyn. "Discrepant Assumptions in Empirical Research." *Social Problems* 28 (February 1981): 247–62.

Neigher, Alan. "The Gault Decision: Due Process and the Juvenile Courts." *Federal Probation* 31 (December 1967): 421–27.

Ohlin, Lloyd, Alden D. Miller, and Robert B. Coates. *Juvenile Correctional Reform in Massachusetts: A Preliminary Report of the Center for Criminal Justice of the Harvard Law School*. Washington, D.C.: U.S. Government Printing Office, n.d.

Orchowsky, Stan, and Keith Taylor. "The Insiders Juvenile Crime Prevention Program: An Assessment of a Juvenile Awareness Program." Virginia Department of Corrections, Richmond, Va., August 1981.

Pacyga, Dominic A. "The Russell Square Community Committee: An Ethnic Response to Urban Problems." *Journal of Urban History* 15 (February 1989): 159–84.

Palmer, Ted B. "California's Community Treatment Project for Delinquent Adolescents." *Journal of Research in Crime and Delinquency* 8 (January 1971): 74–92.

———. "Matching Worker and Client in Corrections." *Social Work* 18 (March 1973): 95–103.

———. "Youth Authority's Community Treatment Project." *Federal Probation* 38 (March 1974): 3–14.

Palmer, Ted B., Marvin Bohnstedt, and Roy Lewis. *The Evaluation of Juvenile Diversion Projects: Final Report*. Sacramento, Calif.: Division of Research, California Youth Authority, 1978.

Piliavin, Irving, and Scott Briar. "Police Encounters with Juveniles." *American Journal of Sociology* 70 (September 1964): 206–14.

Pisciotta, Alexander. "Race, Sex, and Rehabilitation: A Case Study of Differential Treatment in the Juvenile Reformatory, 1825–1900." *Crime and Delinquency* 29 (April 1983): 254–69.

Platt, Anthony. *The Child Savers: The Invention of Delinquency*, 2nd ed. Chicago: The University of Chicago Press, 1977.

Polk, Kenneth, and Solomon Kobrin. *Delinquency Prevention Through Youth Development*. Washington, D.C.: Department of Health, Education and Welfare, 1972.

Powers, Edwin, and Helen Witmer. *An Experiment in the Prevention of Juvenile Delinquency: The Cambridge-Somerville Youth Study*. New York: Columbia University Press, 1951.

Prescott, Peter. *The Child Savers: Juvenile Justice Observed*. New York: Knopf, 1981.

Robison, James, and Gerald Smith. "The Effectiveness of Correctional Programs," *Crime and Delinquency* 17 (January 1971): 67–80.

Ross, Robert, and Paul Gendreau (eds.). *Effective Correctional Treatment*. Toronto: Butterworths, 1980.

Rothman, David J. *Conscience and Convenience: The Asylum and Its Alternatives in Progressive America*. Boston: Little, Brown, 1980.

Sampson, Robert J. "Community Structure and Crime: Testing Social-Disorganization Theory." *American Journal of Sociology* 94 (January 1989); 774–802.

Sarnecki, Jerzy. "Delinquency Networks in Sweden." *Journal of Quantitative Criminology* 6 (March 1990): 31–50.

Scarpitti, Frank R., and Richard M. Stephenson. "Juvenile Court Dispositions: Factors in the Decision-Making Process." *Crime and Delinquency* 17 (April 1971): 142–51.

Schlossman, Steven. *Studies in the History of Early 20th Century Delinquency Prevention*. Santa Monica, Calif.: Rand, 1983.

Schlossman, Steven, and Michael Sedlack. *The Chicago Area Project Revisited*. Santa Monica, Calif.: Rand, 1983.

Schneider, Anne L. *Deterrence and Juvenile Crime: Results from a National Policy Experiment*. New York: Springer-Verlag, 1990.

Schur, Edwin M. *Radical Non-Intervention: Rethinking the Delinquency Problem*. Englewood Cliffs, N.J.: Prentice-Hall, 1973.

Schwartz, Ira M. *(In) Justice for Juveniles: Rethinking the Best Interests of the Child*. Lexington, Mass.: Lexington Books, 1989.

Scull, Andrew T. *Decarceration: Community Treatment and the Deviant*. Englewood Cliffs, N.J.: Prentice-Hall, 1977.

Shaw, Clifford R. *The Jack-Roller: A Delinquent Boy's Own Story*. Chicago: The University of Chicago Press, 1930.

Shaw, Clifford R., and Henry D. McKay. *Juvenile Delinquency and Urban Areas*. Chicago: The University of Chicago Press, 1942.

———. *Juvenile Delinquency and Urban Areas*, rev. ed. Chicago: The University of Chicago Press, 1969.

Shaw, Clifford R., Henry D. McKay, and James F. McDonald. *Brothers in Crime*. Chicago: The University of Chicago Press, 1938.

Shaw, Clifford R., and Maurice E. Moore. *The Natural History of a Delinquent Career*. Chicago: The University of Chicago Press, 1931.

Shaw, Clifford R., Frederick M. Zorbaugh, Henry D. McKay, and Leonard S. Cottrell. *Delinquency Areas: A Study of the Geographic Distribution of School Truants, Juvenile Delinquents, and Adult Offenders in Chicago*. Chicago: The University of Chicago Press, 1929.

Shichar, David, and Clemens Bartollas. "Private and Public Juvenile

Placements: Is There a Difference?" *Crime and Delinquency* 36 (April 1990): 286-99.

Short, James F., Jr., and F. Ivan Nye. "Extent of Unrecorded Delinquency, Some Tentative Conclusions." *Journal of Criminal Law, Criminology and Police Science* 49 (November–December 1958): 296-302.

Slayton, Robert A. *Back of the Yards: The Making of a Local Democracy.* Chicago: The University of Chicago Press, 1986.

Smith, Beverly. "Female Admissions and Paroles of the Western House of Refuge During the 1880s: An Historical Example of Community Corrections." *Journal of Research in Crime and Delinquency* 26 (February 1989): 36-66.

Smith, Douglas, and Raymond Paternoster. "Formal Processing and Future Delinquency: Deviance Amplification as Selection Artifact." *Law and Society Review* 24 (December 1990): 1109-31.

Smith, Robert. *A Quiet Revolution: Probation Subsidy.* Washington, D.C.: U.S. Government Printing Office, 1972.

Snyder, Howard, Terrance A. Finnegan, Ellen H. Nimick, Melissa H. Sickmund, Dennis P. Sullivan, and Nancy Tierney. *Juvenile Court Statistics 1987.* Pittsburgh, PA.: National Center for Juvenile Justice, 1990.

Sorrentino, Anthony. *How To Organize the Neighborhood for Delinquency Prevention.* New York: Human Sciences Press, 1979.

———. *Organizing Against Crime.* New York: Human Sciences Press, 1977.

Southside Community Committee. *Bright Shadows in Bronzetown.* Chicago: Southside Community Committee, 1949.

Stratton, John R., and Robert M. Terry (eds.). *Prevention of Delinquency: Problems and Programs.* New York: Macmillan, 1969.

Sutton, John R. "The Political Economy of Madness: The Expansion of Asylum in Progressive America." *American Sociological Review* 56 (October 1991): 665-78.

Sykes, Gresham M. *The Society of Captives: A Study of a Maximum Security Prison.* Princeton, N.J.: Princeton University Press, 1958.

Tannenbaum, Frank. *Crime and the Community.* New York: Columbia University Press, 1938.

Tappan, Paul. "Treatment Without Trial." *Social Forces* 24 (March 1946): 306-11.

Toby, Jackson. "An Evaluation of Early Identification and Intensive Treatment Programs for Predelinquents." *Social Problems* 13 (Fall 1965): 160-75.

Tracy, Paul E., Marvin E. Wolfgang, and Robert M. Figlio. *Delinquency Careers in Two Birth Cohorts.* New York: Plenum, 1990.

Travis, Thomas. *The Young Malefactor: A Study in Juvenile Delinquency Its Causes and Treatment.* New York: Thomas Y. Crowell, 1908.

Walker, Jerry P., Albert Cardarelli, and Dennis L. Billingsley. *The Theory and Practice of Delinquency Prevention in the United States: Review, Synthesis and Assessment.* Columbus, Ohio: Evaluation Division, Center for Vocational Education, The Ohio State University, 1976.

Warren, Marguerite Q. "The Case for Differential Treatment of Delinquents." *The Annals of the American Academy of Political and Social Science* 381 (January 1969): 47–59.

Weiss, Carol. *Evaluation Research: Methods of Assessing Program Effectiveness.* Englewood Cliffs, N.J.: Prentice-Hall, 1972.

Weissman, Harold (ed.). *Community Development in the Mobilization for Youth Experience.* New York: Association Press, 1969.

Whelen, Ralph. "An Experiment in Predicting Delinquency." *Journal of Criminal Law, Criminology and Police Science* 45 (September–October 1954): 432–41.

Whitehead, John T., and Steven P. Lab. "A Meta-Analysis of Juvenile Correctional Treatment." *Journal of Research in Crime and Delinquency* 26 (August 1989): 276–95.

Wilson, James Q. *Thinking About Crime*, rev. ed. New York: Vintage Books, 1985.

Witmer, Helen, and Edith Tufts. *The Effectiveness of Delinquency Prevention Programs.* Washington, D.C.: U.S. Government Printing Office, 1954.

Wolfgang, Marvin E., Robert M. Figlio, and Thorsten Sellin. *Delinquency in a Birth Cohort.* Chicago: The University of Chicago Press, 1972.

Wolfgang, Marvin E., Terrence P. Thornberry, and Robert M. Figlio. *From Boy to Man, From Delinquency to Crime.* Chicago: The University of Chicago Press, 1987.

Wright, William E., and Michael C. Dixon. "Community Prevention and Treatment of Delinquency." *Journal of Research in Crime and Delinquency* 14 (January 1978): 35–67.

Yarborough, James C. "Evaluation of JOLT as a Deterrence Program." Michigan Department of Corrections, Lansing, Mich., July 18, 1979.

INDEX